Texas

OFF THE BEATEN PATH™

JUNE NAYLOR RODRIGUEZ

A Voyager Book

The Globe Pequot Press

Old Saybrook, Connecticut

Copyright © 1994 by June Naylor Rodriguez

All rights reserved. No part of this book may be reproduced or transmitted in any form by any means, electronic or mechanical, including photocopying and recording, or by any information storage and retrieval system, except as may be expressly permitted by the 1976 Copyright Act or by the publisher. Requests for permission should be made in writing to The Globe Pequot Press, P.O. Box 833, Old Saybrook, Connecticut 06475.

Off the Beaten Path is a trademark of The Globe Pequot Press, Inc.

Illustrations by Carole Drong
Cover map copyright © DeLorme Mapping

Library of Congress Cataloging-in-Publication Data
Rodriguez, June Naylor
    Texas : Off the beaten path / by June Naylor Rodriguez
        p. cm. — "A Voyager book."
    Includes index.
    ISBN 1-56440-483-8
    1. Texas—Guidebooks. I. Title.
F384.3.R63   1994
917.6404'63—dc20

94-12357
CIP

Manufactured in the United States of America
First Edition/Fifth Printing

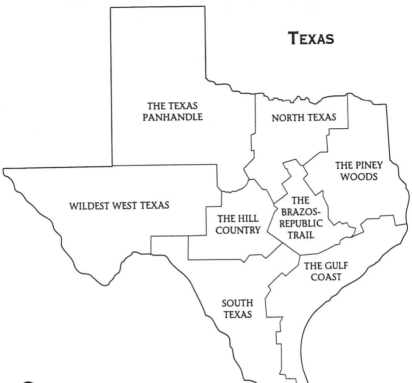

CONTENTS

For my parents—
I am grateful for your love and your
abundant Texan legacies.

INTRODUCTION

John Steinbeck wrote in *Travels with Charley*, "Texas is a state of mind. Texas is an obsession. Above all, Texas is a nation in every sense of the word."

Sam Houston—first president of the Republic of Texas and hero in the defeat of Santa Anna—would have loved Steinbeck.

But for all its staunch independence, Texas is one big welcome mat. Folks coming to call from elsewhere are often taken aback when greeted on the street by total strangers with a "Hidy," "Howdy," or "Hey." There's no catch—Texans are just greeters by nature.

Let's go ahead and dispel some myths: Texas is flat if you don't count those ninety-one mountains that reach over a mile into the sky; Texas is dry if you ignore 3.07 million acres of inland water made up of streams, rivers, lakes, springs, creeks, and 624 miles of Gulf of Mexico shoreline; and Texas has no trees if you overlook those 23 million acres of woodlands.

Texas is proud of its state flower, an odd, stalky gypsy called the bluebonnet. It arrives overnight in spring, thickly coating fields and highway shoulders in a spectacle of deep blue that would have given Renoir a lump in his throat. The bluebonnet first pops up in the Rio Grande Valley and the Big Bend in February, launching a six-month pilgrimage that eventually tints the high Panhandle plains. The bluebonnet's colorful pals every spring are the bright orange Indian paintbrush and the pink primrose.

Mesquite, the Texas tree that looks to be fragile in its slenderness, is actually a hearty survivor that thrives on the harshest land. It multiplies easily, makes a great flavoring for barbecue fires, produces a delightful blossom honey, and provides shade and food for cows and deer. On top of all that, its gnarled, thorny countenance completes the perfect ranch portrait.

Texas's farm-to-market roads serve not only today's farmers, but also those wanderers who just want to absorb the gentle, uncluttered environs. The first such road opened in 1941, and now there are more than 3,000, making up 41,000 highway miles of the state's total of 73,000. The shortest, FM 2413 in Robertson, is 528 feet. Two of the prettiest farm-to-market vistas are in the Piney Woods of East Texas and the Trans-Pecos wilds of West Texas.

When eating in Texas, be aware that Mexican meets southern, Cajun greets soul, and, somehow, dissimilarities welcome one another. From such mingling, southwestern cuisine rides a crest of fame, and country cooking soars higher than ever on all palates.

Trust places with signs that say IF YOU LEAVE HERE HUNGRY IT'S YOUR OWN FAULT, and put your faith in waitresses who are concerned you haven't been eating right and insist you need that piece of pie to keep up your strength. Also, if it sounds absurd, it's probably good; if it sounds French, it probably isn't Texan.

For fried alligator tail, a tender delicacy, look around East Texas lake joints, which also serve up lightly fried catfish with green tomato relish and jalapeño hushpuppies. Barbecue, a critical Texas staple, is best from the old places in Central Texas's Taylor, Lockhart, and Luling. If you can find barbecued pork or beef ribs, brisket, goat, shrimp, or sausage, eat it up.

How about buffalo? It's a tasty treat, lower in fat and cholesterol than beef and a wonderful way to eat Wellington, burgers, and steaks. No bull. The best wurst turns up in thickly German towns such as New Braunfels and Fredericksburg, while kolache heaven is spread out over the Czech communities of West and Caldwell.

A word about chicken-fried steak: Sounds weird, but this could be the national food of Texas; go for it only if it's fork-cutting tender and its breading is homemade and light. And whence came chili? San Antonio or Fort Worth? Both claim it. Beef or venison, spicy or mild, beans or no, there's plenty of it for the sampling at cook-offs all year long. Just don't confuse it with chile, which can be a fire-hot stew if eaten on one of Texas's two Indian reservations, or a velvety green or creamy red pepper sauce if found in one of South Texas's Hispanic-infused towns. Now, you'll get plenty of argument from fajita lovers, but the best Mexican eats are breakfast goods—migas, empanadas—found in cafes and bakeries.

For fruits of the Texas earth, look to Weatherford and Stonewall for peaches, Pecos for cantaloupes, and the Rio Grande Valley for citrus. For the nectar of Texas gods, we have nineteen vineyards and wineries, among them international award winners Llano Estacado Winery in Lubbock and Fall Creek Vineyards in Tow.

As Bubbas will tell you, this is one recreation-crazed state. In water action alone, there's rafting, canoeing, and kayaking on Hill Country rivers and the Rio Grande, while sailing and windsurfing are Corpus Christi favorites, surfers flock to Galveston, catamaran rentals are booming business on South Padre Island, and fishing charters and tournaments subsidize the Port Aransas economy.

Texans are always looking for an excuse to have fun. There are festivals celebrating black-eyed peas, mosquitoes, flowers, berries, hushpuppies, rattlesnakes, bluegrass music, fall foliage, and fire ants. Cowboys have a Christmas ball, American Indians have a championship powwow, and Scottish clans gather in kilts.

When exploring the sprawling state, it's usually helpful to do so by region. Eight easily defined areas—each with its own personality and shape—will keep you busy, to say nothing of intrigued.

In North Texas, all Dallas and Fort Worth have in common are a shared river, 27 miles of freeway, and the nation's second-busiest airport. Which is just the beauty of the area—in about a half hour, you can be someplace drastically different. Dallas is larger, more dashing and aggressive. It glitters and bustles and has a lifestyle ridden with haute cuisine and couture. Fort Worth defines Texas succinctly: business people wear boots and make deals over barbecue, and cowboy-hatted police officers ride horses on their downtown beats. Dallas's revolving Reunion Tower, the Cowboys and Mavericks, internationally flavored dining, and incomparable shopping bring Fort Worth folks over for visits. Conversely, Fort Worth's restored Stockyards and world-renowned art museums, the Caravan of Dreams and its acclaimed jazz stage, and the family-style Mexican food at Joe T. Garcia's bring Dallasites over in hordes.

East Texas's Piney Woods is something of an extension of the Old South, with several of the Republic of Texas's birthmarks. San Augustine and Nacogdoches are vintage towns packed with earliest history, while Jefferson appeals with its old riverboat town and antiques shop charm. Marshall, a stop on stagecoach and Victorian train lines, has restored mansions and bed-and-breakfasts in lovingly refurbished homes. Train buffs delight in traveling between Rusk and Palestine on the Texas State Railroad's steam locomotives. Tyler grows a third of America's commercial roses, and Canton brings up to 50,000 people each month to its century-old First Monday Trade Days. Four national forests jam the region, and the Big Thicket National Preserve is home to a precious virgin forest where twenty kinds of wild orchids and carnivorous plants and 300 varieties of birds coexist in an impenetrable natural fortress.

Some of Texas's deepest heritage is found in the humid, lush environs of the Texas Gulf Coast. Sam Houston's ravaged army rid the Republic of Santa Anna's Mexican troops on a field named San Jacinto, where now stands a breathtaking, 570-foot commemorative monument against the backdrop of Texas's largest city. Houston is an oil city, home to the NASA-Johnson Space Center, the Astrodome, and a sizeable selection of theaters, museums, and shops.

A short drive east, Galveston is the uppermost of Texas's significant beach communities. Once known as the Wall Street of the Southwest, the island-city boasts one of the nation's largest collections of restored Victorian buildings. The Strand, the 1894 Grand Opera House, Ashton Villa, and the *Elissa,* a square-rigged tall ship, highlight a long list of attractions. Padre Island is a long, thin finger of sand protecting the Texas coast from Corpus Christi to the Rio Grande. Most of the island's 113-mile stretch is national seashore, populated by 350 species of birds, sand dunes, and sea oats. The King Ranch—largest privately owned ranch in the world—sits inland from the windsurfing, sailing city of Corpus Christi. South Padre Island is a resort town glistening with new high-rise hotels and sleek condos, boutiques, and sun-bleached houses. Teens jam the beaches in spring, families ride the waves in summer, and anglers work the bay and beach year round.

Brownsville is the state's southernmost point and one entrance to Mexico. Slightly west, the communities of McAllen, Weslaco, and Mission are the heart of Texas's huge citrus industry and the home of Winter Texans, snowbirds from the Midwest. San Antonio, the most common gateway to South Texas, fairly reverberates with the passion of Texas's European origins and the tenacious Hispanic culture still enjoying growth. Some explorers make their way down to Langtry, home to the revered Judge Roy Bean, whose justice was once the only law west of the Pecos. In this southwestern corner, find the world's Spinach Capital; the state's oldest winery; the dramatic set of the epic film *The Alamo*; and an opalesque lake shared by two friendly countries.

If the spiritual heart of Texas is to be embraced, it will happen in the Hill Country. Spring-fed rivers course beneath limestone cliffs, through rolling hills dotted with live oak and wildflowers. It is a region for escape, for reflection, for rejuvenation. Small towns in the Hill Country embrace a serenity not quite duplicated elsewhere. Fredericksburg and New Braunfels gleam with their German heritage, displayed in the shops, historic lodgings, and plentiful wurst and bier. Kerrville is home to the Y.O. Ranch, and Burnet claims the Vanishing Texas River Cruise.

At the heart of Texas, figuratively and literally, is Austin, the state capital and an integral part of the Brazos-Republic Trail. This is an easy city to enjoy, one favored for its music and nightlife, where pleasures unfold from lakes and wooded hills, cultural centers at the University of Texas, and the National Wildflower Research Center. To the east are more small towns forming the core of the old republic.

John Wayne should have been required by law to make all his Westerns in the Texas Panhandle. The genuine, traditional Texan style is so thick here you could cut it with a knife. In the High Plains a great treasure is the shockingly beautiful and huge Palo Duro Canyon. An exciting musical drama plays under the stars there in summer, and real working cowboys take folks out to the canyon's edge for a Cowboy Morning Breakfast.

Texas's western heritage is defined and illustrated with great care at the Panhandle Plains Museum in Canyon and at the Ranching Heritage Center in Lubbock. Another Lubbock asset— wines produced from its sandy but rich land—is offered for sampling at three award-winning vineyards.

West Texas is a vast area distinguished by attractions as diverse as ancient Indians and pioneer forts, mountains, and unexplained moving lights—this is a region that could take years to truly explore. El Paso is a reservoir of Indian, Hispanic, and Anglo influences characterizing the city's architecture, art, food, shopping, and pastimes.

Due east from El Paso, Guadalupe Mountains National Park contains a wealth of scenery, from McKittrick Canyon and its blazing fall foliage to Guadalupe Peak, Texas's highest point at 8,749 feet above sea level. Fort Davis lies between the Guadalupe Mountains and the Big Bend's Chihuahuan Desert. Home to Fort Davis National Historic Site with its restored cavalry fort, Fort Davis sits beside the Davis Mountains State Park and its romantic Indian Lodge, and it claims Prude Ranch, a place with restorative qualities; McDonald Observatory, with fascinating "Star Parties"; and miles of cool, clean mountain air and vistas gained by a 74-mile mountain loop road.

The Big Bend is the site of a rugged, 800,000-acre national park, encompassing a wild stretch of the Rio Grande beloved by geologists, naturalists, and outdoorsy types who want to spend a day, week, or month camping and rafting in jagged canyons.

After driving around a spell, you'll notice bumper stickers with the image of the Texas flag emblazoned by the word "Native" or "Naturalized." Texans, whether born or transplanted here, like to advertise their Lone Star State status.

Such boasts shouldn't detract from the amiable intent—it's simply a friendly state, as the official motto proclaims. It won't take you long to find out for yourself.

The prices and rates listed in this guidebook were confirmed at press time. We recommend, however, that you call establishments before traveling to obtain current information.

THE BRAZOS-REPUBLIC TRAIL

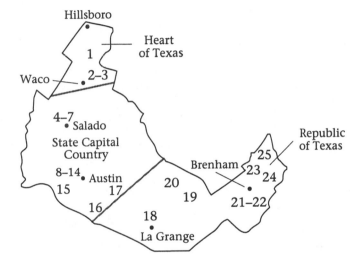

1. Kolache bakeries
2. Texas Ranger Hall of Fame and Museum
3. Dr Pepper Museum
4. Stagecoach Inn
5. The Central Texas Area Museum
6. Inn at Salado
7. Sir Wigglesworth
8. The LBJ Library and Museum
9. French Legation Museum
10. The Elisabet Ney Museum
11. Barton Springs Pool
12. Harry Ransom Humanities Research Center
13. National Wildflower Research Center
14. O. Henry Museum
15. Hamilton Pool
16. Kreuz Market
17. Bastrop State Park
18. La Grange
19. Round Top
20. Ledbetter Bed & Breakfast
21. Blue Bell Ice Cream
22. Monastery of Saint Clare
23. Independence
24. Browning Plantation
25. Star of Texas Museum

THE BRAZOS-REPUBLIC TRAIL

A train whistle blows steadily, and soon loudly, through the fragile darkness. Just before dawn, a rooster begins its intonation, and moos soon follow. Days begin early in the country, breaking clean and fresh—the sky, grass, and picket fences seem unusually pure along Central Texas's Brazos and Colorado rivers, through a region spreading just to the east of the Balcones Escarpment and the state's fabled Hill Country. German, Scottish, and Czech immigrants made their way to new homes through this rolling corridor, toughing out a life that could become hazardous when conflicts with Mexicans and Native Indians arose. Here, dairy and cotton farmers and horse ranchers carved lives with their families and friends, thanks in part to their own determined spirit and that of the Texas Rangers.

It was through this part of the frontier once called Tejas by the Mexicans and Indians that pioneers crafted a Republic, a sovereign nation that gave rise eventually to the Lone Star State. Today's explorers find great and lasting remnants of that period in peaceful towns that make wonderful discoveries on the way to someplace else, and in a fine capital city whose enduring beauty and character make it a popular place for people who love art, history, rhythm and blues, comfort food, lakeside scenery, and even bats—yes, the nation's largest urban bat colony lives under the Congress Avenue bridge spanning the Colorado River in Austin.

HEART OF TEXAS

Hillsboro, resting at the center of Hill County, is a town of 7,000, established as a trade center and county seat in 1853. People who've passed through most remember the **Hill County Courthouse**, built in 1890 to replace the original log cabin structure. The flamboyant, cream-colored design on the town square mixes styles to include classical revival, Italianate, and French Second Empire. A vintage *Saturday Evening Post* story called the courthouse "a monstrosity," while *Harper's* countered with a description declaring the ornate structure "like an outstanding cathedral." Tragically, the courthouse was destroyed by fire on New Year's Day, 1993; however, the town and some of its powerful children—such as country singer Willie Nelson—rallied quickly to raise funds to restore the masterpiece to its original glory. Work was underway at once, and architects expect the restoration to be completed in 1996. Call the chamber of commerce for details, (817) 582–9197.

People also come to Hillsboro for a much more modern pursuit–finding deals at **Southwest Outlet Center** at 104 Interstate 35 Northeast, (817) 582–9205. The fifty-plus stores here include Nike, Liz Claiborne, and Guess?, among other big names, all offering discounts from 20 to 75 percent off retail prices. The outlet center is open Monday through Saturday, 10:00 A.M. until 9:00 P.M., and Sunday, noon until 6:00 P.M.

Fifteen miles south on Interstate 35 West—at the apex of the lines forming McLennan County, the tiny town of West on Interstate 35 at Farm Road 2114 is a town of 2,500 residents rich in Czechoslovakian heritage. Folks in North and Central Texas know where West, Texas, is, but most people think we mean West Texas.

First and foremost, West is famous for Czech food, especially kolaches—thick fruit-filled pastries—and homemade sausage. Travelers en route from Dallas or Fort Worth south to Austin and San Antonio invariably stop off in West to fill orders from friends back home who want plenty of kolaches. Consequently, the half dozen or so ✦**kolache bakeries** on Main and Oak streets always have pan upon pan ready to box, as well as frozen packages to go.

The Village Bakery at 108 East Oak Street, (817) 826–5151, is one of the town's original Czech bakeries, opened in 1951. Kolache fruit varieties include peach, apricot, blueberry, prune, apple, and several others, as well as sausage, or klobasniki, kolaches, by far the most filling. The bakery sells coffee, juices, and soft drinks, and a few tables inside serve those patrons who can't wait any longer to get that kolache fix.

Around the corner, past a few good antiques shops, **Sulak's**, at 208 North Main Street, (817) 826–7991, is a longtime favorite of Central Texans and travelers alike. Opened in 1923, the Czech diner serves breakfast, lunch, and dinner Tuesday through Friday, and lunch and dinner Saturday. Best efforts are steaks, sausages, stews, bakery items, and Tex-Mex plates.

If you happen upon West on Labor Day weekend, join in the celebration at **Westfest**, one of Texas's favorite parties. Held at

Texas Ranger Hall of Fame

the West Fair and Rodeo Grounds at Main Street and Farm Road 1858, (817) 826–5058, the Saturday-Sunday affair features authentic Czech costume contests, folk dancing—including polkas and waltzes—and the music of a nuclear-polka group, Brave Combo. Count on plenty of kolaches, sausages, and other comfort food.

Driving another 17 miles south on Interstate 35, **Waco**, a city of 103,500 straddling the historic Brazos River, is a place destined to be noted in history books as one with a diverse heritage. Although Waco remains reminiscent of its cotton-cattle-corn heyday, few people will ever forget that the city was once prominent in international headlines for being the site of the tragic Branch Davidian episode in 1993.

Long populated by the Hueco Indians, from which the establishment took its name, Waco saw its first white explorers when a group of De Soto's men came through in 1542. Real civilization came when the Texas Rangers established a fort here in 1837, however. The town won the nickname "Six-Shooter Junction" later, when the Chisholm Trail was brought through the frontier post, but things have calmed down considerably, as the city is best known now for Baylor University and the Heart O' Texas Fair and Rodeo, held in early October.

Travelers enamored with wild west history will love the ✦ **Texas Ranger Hall of Fame and Museum** (Fort Fisher Park, exit 335B off Interstate 35, 817–750–5986). Inside there's a replica of that 1837 Texas Ranger fort, as well as dioramas and displays detailing the history of the Rangers since Stephen F. Austin founded them in 1823. A firearms collection, Native American artifacts, and western art are exhibited here, headquarters for today's Company F of the Texas Rangers. Camping and picnic sites are available in the thirty-seven-acre park. Open 9:00 A.M. until 5:00 P.M. daily. Admission is $3.50 for adults and $1.50 for children six to twelve.

Waco's newest attraction is the campy ✦ **Dr Pepper Museum** (300 South Fifth Street, 817–757–1024), housed in the original bottling plant for Dr Pepper, a favorite Texas soda pop. The fountain drink was originally mixed at the Old Corner Drug Store here in the 1880s, when R. S. Lazenby, a Waco beverage chemist and drug store customer, took interest in the new soda. After working with the formula for two years, he sold it commercially, and the formula is virtually unchanged. The original 1906 bottling plant–museum is on the National Register of Historic Places and features a restored period soda fountain and much Dr Pepper memorabilia, as well as audio-visual enhancement. It's open Monday through Saturday, 10:00 A.M. until 4:00 P.M., and Sunday, noon until 4:00 P.M. Admission is $2.00 for adults and $1.00 for children six to eighteen.

Another 55 miles south on Interstate 35, Salado (suh-LAY-doe) is a bucolic, creek-side stop in Bell County. Although only 1,500 residents call Salado home, it's a well-known jumping-off point for travelers en route to Austin. It was founded on a tract of land along the Chisholm Trail, originally in a grant by the state of Coahuila, Mexico, in 1830.

Scottish colonizer Sterling C. Robertson brought settlers to the area in the 1850s, and it fast became a thriving settlement with the opening of one grist mill inside the town limits and seven others in a 9-mile area. After the railroad bypassed Salado near the end of the century, however, forty-year-old Salado College closed, and the town nearly disappeared. Today there are nineteen state and eighteen national historic markers in town.

The town was named for Central Texas's Salado Creek, one of five creeks so named in Texas, and this creek was the state's first designated natural landmark. The lovely waterway is fed by springs that are the northernmost of the huge Edwards Aquifer, surfacing here on the Balcones Fault. Within a few minutes' walk along the creek, it's easy to see why the town has become a retreat for artists, writers, historians, and craftspeople.

Some important folks have passed this way—General Robert E. Lee, General George Custer, and General Sam Houston all stayed at an inn now called the ◆Stagecoach Inn, in a shady grove just east of the interstate on Main Street near Royal Street. In fact, it was on the inn's front gallery that Sam Houston made one of his impassioned speeches, urging Texans not to secede from the Union.

The Stagecoach was the town's reason for surviving when times were toughest, and it's still a destination for travelers. The motel is a modern structure, but the restaurant is legendary, serving bounteous lunches for $7.50 and $8.50 and enormous dinners for $12.95–$13.95; specialties include baked ham, fried chicken, roast lamb, orange roughy, and filet mignon. Lunch is served from 11:00 A.M. to 4:00 P.M., and dinner is from 5:00 P.M. until 10:00 P.M. Call (817) 947–5111.

◆The Central Texas Area Museum on Main Street, facing the Stagecoach Inn, is open during the **Gathering of the Scottish Clans,** held annually in early November, and by appointment. The building holding the museum is well over a century old, and exhibits inside detail the history of Central Texas. There's also the Wee Scot Shop inside, selling items of Scotland such as kilts and tartans. For information, call (817) 947–5232.

After lunch or a look through the museum, wander a few yards north to the creek and follow the bank just a bit to the right. There you'll find **Sirena,** a bronze mermaid, sitting in a tiny inlet. She is lonely and sad, eternally trying to remove a hook from her fin. The creek's grassy bank continues east and is traced by a road winding through **Pace Park,** a willow-shaded place to take a picnic and relax with a book.

Tops of the bed-and-breakfast stops in town is the ◆**Inn at Salado,** Main Street at Pace Park Road, (817) 947–8200. There are seven guest rooms, including three suites, all with private baths. Prices begin at about $75 for two. The lovely old home was built in

1873 and is wonderfully aged. Rooms are named for people important to Salado's past, such as General Custer. Antique furnishings are prominent, and books and games are abundant. Breakfast typically showcases something home baked and sensational.

One of the best dining stops along the interstate corridor is found within one of the town's pioneer mansions, **Tyler House.** Built in 1857 by a founder of Salado College, the large, imposing home rises high over Main Street and is equally impressive inside, with a wealth of fine antiques. The elegant restaurant has a warm piano bar with a fireplace, perfect for a cognac after a gourmet dinner and before sweet dreams. Lunch is served Tuesday through Saturday, 11:00 A.M. until 3:00 P.M., and dinner is offered Friday and Saturday from 6:00 P.M. until 10:00 P.M. Reservations are suggested, (817) 947–5157.

Among some thirty good antiques, art, gift, and clothing boutiques is standout ◆ **Sir Wigglesworth,** along Main Street at Rock Creek Drive. This delightful, whimsical cottage holds vintage glassware and china; mantle, garden, and lawn knickknacks; primitive furnishings; and fine English pieces. The store is open daily; call (817) 947–8846 for details.

STATE CAPITAL COUNTRY

Just 50 miles south of Salado lies Austin, the capital city, seat of Travis County, and haven for people who love to kick back. But the sun worshippers seen today around Barton Springs, the eternally cool spring-fed pool in Zilker Park, were not the first to find this a great place to hang around. Spaniards decided it was the best place to build a mission in 1730, and that was after American Indians had been established here for centuries.

The 1800s saw the creation of the fledgling settlement named Waterloo, and new Republic of Texas president Mirabeau B. Lamar liked the place so much he moved the seat of government here. A few ego struggles moved the capital back and forth from the Houston area until 1844, and the town was eventually named for the Father of Texas, Stephen F. Austin.

Since 1882, students of higher learning have found the **University of Texas**—with an enrollment today of fifty thousand—and the Austin environs a place to stay beyond the traditional four years, thanks to numerous graduate programs and jobs in state government. Indeed, with hilly scenery, an easygoing lifestyle, a wealth of homegrown music, and abundant Tex-Mex eats, Austin is easy to love and hard to leave.

◆ **The LBJ Library and Museum** at 2313 Red River Street, which is part of the university, is fascinating even for those who were not fans of the late President Lyndon B. Johnson. Great detail is used in chronicling his career, and personal items are quite interesting: There are early home photos, a fourth-grade report card showing excellent grades but a C in deportment, and a letter sent to his grandmother from his time at Southwest Texas State Teachers College, in which he expresses his deep desire to not be regarded as a black sheep. There are engagement photos of LBJ and Claudia "Lady Bird" Taylor, and there's an intriguing letter on Lady Bird Taylor's letterhead indicating her fear that Lyndon was thinking of a life in politics. The museum is open daily, 9:00 A.M. until 5:00 P.M. Call (512) 482-5136 for details.

Just east of the interstate, the ◆ **French Legation Museum,** 802 San Marcos Street, was regarded as ostentatious when built in 1841 for the French ambassador to the Republic of Texas. Today the French provincial cottage of Bastrop pine and French fitments seems modest, but it suited the arrogant Comte Alphonse Dubois de Saligny, if just for a short time. It was learned that the irritable chargé d'affaires held a fraudulent title, and that was after he'd shown great disdain for his Native American visitors and Austin neighbors. He spent most of his time in New Orleans, which he found much more enjoyable, and historians estimate he actually spent eight weeks at most in the Austin home.

Today the Daughters of the Republic of Texas operate the house-museum, situated behind grand iron gates atop a little hill and furnished with nineteenth-century antiques, a few of Saligny's belongings, and authentic items from a French Creole kitchen, such as copper pots and pewter tools. It's open Tuesday through Sunday, 1:00 P.M. until 5:00 P.M. Admission is $2.50 for adults and $1.00 for children. For details, call (512) 472–8180.

A few blocks to the southeast, **Cisco's** at 1151 East Sixth Street is a true Austin institution, especially at breakfast. The Mexican bakery and cafe has small-town friendliness for regulars and newcomers alike, and the eye-opening dishes to know are huevos rancheros and huevos migas, two sassy egg dishes. If you like something a bit heavier, order a basket of picadillos, homemade rolls stuffed with spicy beef. Lunches include traditional Mexican plates and chicken-fried steak; for a sweet, check out the bakery case in front. Note that Cisco's is a happy madhouse when the UT Longhorns have a home football game. It's open daily from 7:00 A.M. until 2:30 P.M.; call (512) 478–2420.

In the northwest quadrant of the city, ✦ **The Elisabet Ney Museum** at 304 East Forty-fourth Street at Avenue H awaits in one of the country's four existing studios of nineteenth-century sculptors. German immigrant Ney, a staunchly independent artist, came to the United States in 1873 and built this studio in 1892, naming it Formosa (meaning beautiful) after her studio in Europe. Some of her work is displayed here, while other pieces grace the Smithsonian National Museum of Art, various European palaces, and the Texas statehouse. Formosa was transformed to a museum by her friends and fans soon after her death in 1907. It's been restored but retains the rustic nature Ney loved. Art classes and audio-visual presentations are held here throughout the year. Visit the museum between 10:00 A.M. and 5:00 P.M. Wednesday through Saturday, and between noon and 5:00 P.M. Sunday. Call (512) 458–2255 for information.

If you need to be refreshed, head west of downtown to 400-acre **Zilker Park,** at 2220 Barton Springs Road, home to the renowned ✦ **Barton Springs Pool.** The thousand-foot-long, rock-walled swimming hole—fed by Barton Springs, the fourth-largest natural springs in the state—is an oasis, always a chilly 68 degrees. In warm weather, the grassy, shady lawns sloping down to the pool are covered by lounging or Frisbee-tossing sun lovers. Beyond the pool, you'll find the city's Botanical Garden Center, the Austin Nature Center, a miniature train, and 8 miles of hiking and biking trails. The park grounds are open daily from 7:00 A.M. until 10:00 P.M. The pool is open daily from 8:00 A.M. until 10:00 P.M., March 15 through October 15; admission is $2.25 for adults, 50 cents for children. Call (512) 476–9044 for pool information and (512) 477–7273 for park information.

Right in the center of town on the UT campus, the ✦ **Harry Ransom Humanities Research Center** at Twenty-first and Guadalupe streets has a remarkable collection of treasures. Visitors may view one of the nation's five complete copies of the Gutenberg Bible, as well as the world's first photograph—shot in 1826 by Joseph Niepce—in the fascinating Photography Collection, which contains more than five million prints and negatives.

The literary collection includes autographed editions by Dylan Thomas and E. M. Forster, among several; and the Hoblitzelle Theatre Arts Collection exhibits items from Harry Houdini's personal correspondence to some Burl Ives folk recordings. The center is open Monday through Friday from 9:00 A.M. until 5:00 P.M. Call (512) 471–8944.

In walking distance of the campus, **The McCallum House** is a wonderful 1907 home at 613 West Thirty-second Street made over into a most comfortable bed and breakfast. Etched glass doors, gables, porches, and wicker furniture make this a place where people want to stay a while, as do the breakfasts of egg-and-cheese casseroles, homemade coffee cakes, quiches, and muffins. All five rooms have a private bath, and the garden apartment offers a bedroom, a separate sitting room with daybed, and a fully equipped kitchen. Lodging starts at $60; call (512) 451–6744 for details.

Head northeast of downtown to find a bounty of Texas's natural beauty at the ◆**National Wildflower Research Center,** at 2600 Farm Road 973 North (512–929–3600). Lady Bird Johnson generously established the center in 1982, donating money and a sixty-acre tract of land. She continues as a dedicated champion of the beautification of America via horticulture and remains an active booster of this project. The center is considered an authority on conservation and reproduction of native plants and supports a nationwide educational program for various state highway departments interested in landscaping and beautification.

Individuals who want to visit the center are welcome to learn about various species of wildflowers, shrubs, trees, and varied native plants. Seminars, workshops, and classes are scheduled throughout the year, and an annual Wildflower Days Festival is held one April weekend. The bountiful gift shop sells seeds, as well as wildflower-emblazoned items such as calendars, note cards, T-shirts, and posters. The center is open Monday through Friday from 9:00 A.M. until 4:00 P.M. Donations of $2.00 per vehicle are appreciated; for details call (512) 929–3600.

Right downtown, the ◆**O. Henry Museum** at 409 East Fifth Street occupies the quaint Victorian home briefly lived in by the master of short stories and surprise endings. His real name was William Sydney Porter, and he published an extremely short-lived publication called the *Rolling Stone* from his Austin residence in the

1890s. The museum contains some of Porter's personal effects, including a yellowing original of his *Rolling Stone,* and various period pieces. Writing classes for adults and children are held here from time to time, and each spring brings the O. Henry Pun-Off, a good time for all. The home is open Wednesday through Sunday from noon until 5:00 P.M. Call (512) 472-1903 for more information.

Is it time yet to cool off again? If so, drive west from town on Texas Highway 71 about 16 miles to Farm Road 3238 and go south for 13 miles till you see ◈ **Hamilton Pool,** a Travis County park on Hamilton Pool Road. A swimming hole has been deemed the use of this stunning collapsed grotto since even old-timers can remember. There are 60-foot waterfalls cascading into the limestone-walled, jade-green pool. County conservation authorities limit use to the first one hundred carloads into the park, so it's wise to go early or call ahead to see if there's room. You can picnic and hike there and book a guided nature tour. Open daily from 9:00 A.M. until 6:00 P.M.; admission is $5.00 per vehicle, and visitors over sixty-two enter free. For details, call (512) 264-2740.

For some of the finest barbecue ever, head back east to town and follow U.S. Highway 290 across Interstate 35 about 5 miles, then turn south on U.S. Highway 183, traveling 30 miles to the burg of **Lockhart,** seat of Caldwell County and home to just over 9,000 residents. ◈ **Kreuz** (pronounced krytes) **Market,** a veritable institution at 208 South Commerce Street on the courthouse square, is a cultural and gastronomical experience that will be long remembered.

Lines are long before the noon lunch hour, and steady streams of people file through the searing-hot, smoky pit room where your barbecue is cut to order by weight. They'll pile your request for smoked brisket, pork brisket, pork chops, or sausage onto brown butcher paper, along with a stack of white bread, which you then take over to a counter in the lunch room to get "the fixins," such as sliced onion, tomato, cheese, avocados, jalapeños, and pickles. If you ask for barbecue sauce, be forewarned that you may insult the proprietors—the meat is so tender and flavorful none is needed. There are, however, bottles of hot pepper sauce on the tables for fire-eaters. Lunch is usually $4.00-$7.00, plus cheap beer or soda pops. Kreuz's is open Monday through Friday, 7:00 A.M. until 6:00 P.M., and Saturday, 7:00 A.M. until 6:30 P.M. Call (512) 398-2361 for details.

If it's a typically pretty day, get that barbecue to go. Head east 26 miles on Farm Road 20 to Texas Highway 71 and follow 71 east 8 miles to **Bastrop,** where you can have a quiet picnic at ⚜**Bastrop State Park.** There, in 3,500 acres of rolling land studded with the mysterious "Lost Pines," is a tranquil and rich nature sanctuary along Lake Bastrop to be enjoyed for more than a mere day. Fishing, camping, hiking, golf, and nature study are big draws at the park, as are rustic but comfortable cabins. Find the park just a mile east of Texas Highway 71's junction with Texas Highway 21. Call (512) 321–2101.

The town of Bastrop is the Bastrop County seat and home to about 6,000 residents. The **Bastrop County Historical Museum** at 702 Main Street occupies the distinctive Cornelson-Fehr House, a Texas Historic Landmark and an 1850 structure resting on the site of a much older Spanish fort. Among miscellaneous and interesting manuscripts, pioneer collections, and Native American artifacts are silver spoons that are said to have been crafted from coins taken from Santa Anna at the Battle of San Jacinto. The museum is open Saturday from 9:30 A.M. until 5:00 P.M. and Sunday from 1:00 P.M. until 5:00 P.M.; admission is just 50 cents. Call (512) 321–6177 for information.

THE REPUBLIC OF TEXAS

To explore deep into Texas's past, begin your journey by driving east on Texas Highway 71, stopping just 32 miles down the road at the hamlet on the mighty Colorado River called ⚜**La Grange.** Seat of Fayette County and home to 4,000 residents, the establishment dates to 1831, when the road passing through was simply a buffalo trail. Historical markers abound—at the old railroad depot, the old county jail, the 1890s courthouse, the vintage Episcopal church—and the local historical route called Texas Pioneer Trail courses through town.

Of particular interest is **Kreische Brewery State Historical Site and Monument Hill,** 3 miles south of the town center on Spur 92. Vestiges of a stone brewery and home erected by stonemason Heinreich L. Kreische, a German immigrant who arrived in 1840, mark the first commercial brewery in Texas and one that produced more than 700 barrels a year in its prime. Tours of the brewery and ruins are conducted on Saturday and

Sunday at 2:00 P.M. and 3:30 P.M. only, and are included in the admission to Monument Hill, also part of the state park.

The latter is a resting place of the Battle of Salado martyrs and victims of the tragic Black Bean Episode of the Mier Expedition, all during the Mexican War. The dramatic monument is a 48-foot creation of stone, bronze, and polychrome. There's a visitor center, as well as an interpretive trail, nature trail, picnic sites, and playground. The monument park is open daily from 8:00 A.M. until 5:00 P.M. Admission is 50 cents for adults, 25 cents for children. For more details, call (409) 968–5658.

The countryside is bound to make you yearn for home cooking, so look no farther than **Bon Ton Restaurant** at 890 East Travis Street in La Grange. It may not look like much from the outside, but customers have counted for years on its wonderful fried chicken, sumptuous pies, and sweet cream butter. Bon Ton's is open for breakfast, lunch, and dinner; call (409) 968–5863 for information.

If it's spring, endless **vistas of bluebonnets,** orange-and-yellow Indian paintbrushes, and pink primroses will be your vivid companions as you continue northeast on Texas Highway 159 just 15 miles to ✦**Round Top.** This wide spot in the Fayette County road seems small, with fewer than one hundred residents, but it packs a cultural punch. The miniature town was once called Jones Post Office back in 1835, but its new name came from the Round Top Academy, which operated here from 1854 to 1867, with tuition costing $10 per semester.

Today, on what passes for a town square, there's **Klump Grocery,** a homey German grocery open since 1910, serving cold beer and barbecued pork ribs, beef, roast, sausage, chicken, and trimmings on Saturday and Sunday. Come on Saturday morning and find fresh breads and coffeecakes. Open daily; call (409) 249–5696.

Bordering the square's east side, **Henkel Square** is an impressive, growing collection of homes and buildings dating from 1820 until 1870. Furnishings and artistic decor are examples of the period's Anglo and German influences. The collection is administered by the Texas Pioneer Arts Foundation. Open daily from noon until 5:00 P.M., there's a $3.00 admission for adults and $2.00 for children. Call (409) 249–3308 for more information.

Five blocks north, on Texas Highway 237, **Festival Hill** is the site of the International Festival-Institute. A concert weekend is scheduled monthly, and summer is devoted to popular performances by institute students with visiting orchestras and string quartets. Festival Hill is occupied by a marvelous array of restored period buildings. For a schedule, call (409) 249-2139.

It's only a 4-mile drive northeast of Round Top on Farm Roads 1457 and 2714 to the **Winedale Historical Center,** a picture seemingly realized from *An American Gothic.* Perfectly restored farms, ranch houses, plantation homes, log cabins, smokehouses, and barns represent more of the Anglo and German heritage prevalent in Texas. The center is an extension of the University of Texas, and it's open for weekday tours by appointment and all day on Saturday and Sunday.

Winedale's many events throughout the year include a summer Shakespeare Festival, Oktoberfest, Christmas open house, and spring craft exhibition. Some events cost $2.00 admission, but others are free. Call for complete information and appointments, (409) 278-3530.

An especially pleasant detour to make from Round Top is the one northwest 10 miles to ✦**Ledbetter Bed & Breakfast,** Farm Road 1291 at U.S. Highway 290 (409-249-3066). The farm spread is a great place to go for a family reunion or to meet fellow wanderers, as the B&B has fourteen rooms, eight with private baths and six with shared baths. A kitchenette is available, but you may not want to cook, as the hosts provide a huge country breakfast buffet every morning. There's an indoor heated pool, volleyball court, trails for walking and cycling, plus a big living area, where the jukebox is loaded with golden oldies.

From Round Top, drive north on Texas Highway 237 about 8 miles to U.S. Highway 290 and turn east on Highway 290, continuing 16 miles to **Brenham.** Yum—you've reached the home of "the little creamery," ✦**Blue Bell Ice Cream,** just 2 miles southeast on Loop Farm Road 577. *Time* magazine called it the best ice cream in the world, a small-town giant that now produces some twenty million gallons per year. Free tours and samples are given to visitors, who are also treated to a film and a look at production from an observation deck. Call for the seasonal tour schedule, (409) 836-7977.

Brenham, seat of Washington County—birthplace of the Republic of Texas—and home to 12,000 residents and plenty of antiques shops, is known also for sweetness of an altogether different nature. Head 8 miles north of town on Farm Road 50 to

14

Antique Rose Emporium, once strictly a wholesaler of antique rose varieties and now a beautiful nursery spread open to the public. You can buy rose bushes on site, or pick up a hefty catalog for mail orders. Open Monday through Saturday, 9:00 A.M. until 6:00 P.M., and Sunday, 11:00 A.M. until 6:00 P.M. Call (409) 836–5548 for details.

For yet another rare scene, take Texas Highway 105 northeast from Brenham 9 miles to the ◆**Monastery of Saint Clare,** where resident cloistered nuns breed, train, and sell gentle miniature horses. The ninety-eight-acre ranch is run by the sisters of the Order of Saint Clare, founded in the thirteenth century by a follower of Saint Francis of Assisi, now known as top breeders of the tiny horses. The ranch unfolds along fertile slopes, shaded by ancient, spreading oaks. The horses are scaled-down duplicates of their full-size cousins, appaloosas, pintos, and Arabians, but these are a playful, endearing variety. A gift shop and ceramics studio is also on view. Visitors may come between 2:00 P.M. and 4:00 P.M. daily or by appointment. Admission is $3.00 for adults and $1.00 for children. Call (409) 836–9652.

Nueces Canyon Ranch, just west of Brenham on U.S. Highway 290, is a working, eighty-acre horse ranch that accommodates visitors. If you choose, you can stay in a private, three-bedroom guesthouse alongside a trickling brook. There's horseback riding, volleyball, and horseshoe pitching. Breakfast is included, and it's hearty—eggs, hash browns, sausage, kolaches, and fruit. Overnight stays cost $75 to $95; call Bed & Breakfast Texas Style for reservations, (214) 298–8586.

A moving picture of Texas's past is seen in ◆**Independence,** just an 11-mile drive north of Brenham on Farm Road 50. The Washington County settlement of 150 was founded in 1824 by one of Stephen F. Austin's original 300 families. A town square was designed for the Washington County seat, but Brenham won the hotly contested vote by just two.

Old Baylor Park, a half mile west on flower-peppered Farm Road 390, holds the ruins of Old Baylor University and the restored home of John P. Coles, the founding settler. Also on Farm Road 390, you'll find the **Sam Houston Homesite,** noted by a granite marker. A few yards away, there's **Mrs. Sam Houston's Home**—one of the earliest surviving examples of Greek-revival architecture. Mrs. Houston bought it for herself and her eight children after her husband died in 1863. Sam Houston, Jr., other Texas pioneers, and veterans of wars from the American Revolution to World War II are buried in the town cemetery.

It's but another 10 miles east on U.S. Highway 290 from Brenham to **Chappell Hill,** a charming Washington County township of 300 established in 1847. Set amid rolling pastures of horse farms, wildflowers, and twisting post oak trees, Chappell Hill boasts a bevy of historic structures, the most remarkable being the ✦**Browning Plantation,** on Farm Road 1155 just south of town. Included on the National Register of Historic Places, the mansion dates to the 1850s and is a restoration masterpiece.

Fortunately for travelers, the Browning Plantation is also a bed-and-breakfast inn, where guests are spoiled with fine furnishings, scenery, 220 acres of natural trails, lake fishing, a swimming pool, and lavish breakfasts. Expect to pay between $85 and $110 for lodging; call (409) 836–6144 for reservations.

Another splendid B&B option in Chappell Hill is the **Mulberry House**, south of town off Farm Road 1155 and Farm Road 2447. The country house and renovated barn offer lodgings, all with private baths and phones. Good antique pieces are used throughout, and croquet is the game of choice in back. Breakfast lovers are in luck, as the hosts prepare extravagant spreads of casseroles and other baked dishes and myriad baked goodies. Rooms are $75 to $100; call (409) 830–1311 for reservations.

The inns make for a quiet place to stay after a trip to nearby **Washington-on-the-Brazos,** the legendary town where in 1836 the Texas Declaration of Independence was signed and where the constitution of the new Republic of Texas was drafted, also in 1836. From 1842 until 1846, Washington was also the capital of the Republic, and the town prospered as a commercial center for the cotton-rich Brazos Valley.

Today that heritage is memorialized at the ✦**Star of Texas Museum at Washington-on-the-Brazos State Park,** on Farm Road 1155, 18 miles north of Chappell Hill. The museum is indeed star shaped, and its exhibits offer interpretation of Texas as a separate and exclusive nation as well as its journey to statehood. Seasonal exhibitions, audio-visual presentations, and demonstrations of early nineteenth-century life are often scheduled. The museum is open daily March through August, from

10:00 A.M. until 5:00 P.M., and Wednesday to Sunday September through February, from 10:00 A.M. until 5:00 P.M. Call (409) 878–2461 for details.

The state historical park contains a portion of the historic town site; a reconstruction of Independence Hall; the home of Anson Jones, Texas's last president; an outdoor amphitheater; and a pecan grove doubling as a picturesque picnic area. Hours vary for the different sites, and special events are held on the Sunday closest to March 2, Texas's independence day. For information, call (409) 878–2214.

THE GULF COAST

Beaumont

Land of
Spindletop

Houston •

3
1–2
4–5
6–7

8–10

9   11–12

13

14–15

The Romantic
Seaside

24   19

17

16

The Coastal
Plains

18   21

The Coastal
Bend

Port Aransas

25   23

20
Corpus Christi

22

The Big
Beach

26   27

South Padre

5. Pompeiian Villa
6. Sabine Pass Battleground
   State Historical Park
7. Sea Rim State Park
8. Sam Houston Park
9. Taylor-Stevenson Ranch
10. San Jacinto Battleground
    State Historical Park
11. Space Center Houston
12. Armand Bayou Nature Center
13. Attwater Prairie Chicken
    National Wildlife Refuge
14. The Strand
15. Galveston Island State Park
16. Matagorda Island State Park
17. Goose Island State Park
18. Fulton Mansion State
    Historical Structure
19. Aransas National
    Wildlife Refuge
20. Mustang Island State Park
21. San Jose Island
22. Padre Island National
    Seashore
23. The Lighthouse
24. Goliad
25. King Ranch
26. Port Isabel Lighthouse
    State Historic Park
27. Turtle Lady

1. Spindletop–Gladys
   City Boomtown
2. Texas Energy Museum
3. The Big Thicket
   National Preserve
4. La Maison des Acadienne and
   Dutch Windmill Museum

THE GULF COAST

The lengthy, shimmering curve of seashore known as the Gulf Coast of Texas has long been a place of fascination for visitors. The Spaniards arrived in 1528, when Cabeza de Vaca shipwrecked just off Galveston Island; he was followed by conquistadors looking for fabled treasures in cities of gold, and although none were discovered, the Spanish priests established missions as was necessary for colonization.

The French came, too, led by the explorer La Salle, who landed in 1685 at Indianola, which became a thriving port— German colonists came through here in the 1840s—but it's now only a ghostly stretch of sand. French buccaneer Jean Lafitte enjoyed a lucrative stay at Galveston Island from 1817 until 1821, when the U.S. government ran him off for making moves on an American ship.

Significant milestones in American history came to pass on this shoreline: Texas's first oil well, the gusher Spindletop, blew in 1901 at Beaumont; NASA astronauts found a new home address in Houston's Lyndon B. Johnson Space Center in the early 1960s; and rock-and-roll legend Janis Joplin was raised in Port Arthur—if not for her, we might never have learned a great hum-along song, *Me and Bobby McGee*, written for her by fellow Texan Kris Kristofferson, who hails from the Gulf Coast town of Corpus Christi.

The 624 miles of coastline you find on Texas's Gulf offer everything from a Mardi Gras to symphony concerts, deep-sea fishing to whooping-crane watching, weekends whiled away in Victorian mansions to gambling the night away aboard a Mexico-bound cruise ship. You may never want to go home.

THE LAND OF SPINDLETOP

As the state's rich forests unwind en route to the gulf, the land turns to that which has seen massive bursts of industry yet still languishes in woodsy radiance. **Beaumont,** a city of 114,500 connected to the gulf by the Neches River, is a pulse point of this section, begun in 1837 as a lumber center that literally exploded onto the energy map in 1901 when the world's first gusher, Spindletop, erupted here. The little settlement of a few hundred suddenly grew to a city of 30,000—literally overnight—

and became the birthplace of oil companies such as Exxon, Texaco, and Mobil.

To see just what Beaumont looked like at its moment of glory, pay a visit to ◆Spindletop–Gladys City Boomtown (University Drive at U.S. Highway 69, 409–835–0823). The whole place has been re-created, down to the post office, oil derricks made of wood, blacksmith shop, saloon, surveyor's office, photo studio, and so on. Here, too, is the 58-foot granite monument honoring Anthony F. Lucas's landmark well that blew in at 10:00 A.M. on January 10, 1901. The boomtown is open Tuesday through Sunday, 1:00 P.M. until 5:00 P.M. Admission is $2.00 for adults, $1.00 for children.

A modern look at the complex petroleum industry is found at the ◆Texas Energy Museum (600 Main Street, 409–833–5100), touted by the Smithsonian Institution as being one of the world's finest. A remarkable parade of exhibits includes multimedia displays that simulate rig functions, and robotics. Visit the museum Tuesday through Saturday, 9:00 A.M. until 5:00 P.M., and Sunday, 1:00 P.M. until 5:00 P.M. Admission is $2.00 for adults, $1.00 for children.

Beaumont's other claim to fame is being home to Babe Didrikson Zaharias (1914–56), undoubtedly the world's greatest female athlete, some say the most gifted of all American athletes. The **Babe Didrikson Zaharias Museum** (1750 Interstate 10 East, 409–833–4622) offers tourists a chance to learn more about the woman who was the three-time basketball All-American, double Olympic gold medal winner in track, and world-class golfer. A wealth of documents, awards, medals, and such chronicle her illustrious career and life. The museum is home also to a good visitor center, offering travelers a variety of information on the area. The museums and center are open daily from 9:00 A.M. until 5:00 P.M.

As you'll find throughout the state, early industrialists built extraordinary, lasting structures that we're fortunate enough to enjoy today. Beaumont is no exception, offering sensational vintage architecture. One such place is the **McFaddin-Ward House** (1906 McFaddin Avenue, 409–832–2134). The 1906 Beaux-Arts home is filled with the finery of its day and is open for touring Tuesday through Saturday, 10:00 A.M. until 3:00 P.M., and Sunday, 1:00 P.M. until 3:00 P.M. Admission is $3.00.

Visitors with an eye for history will also enjoy the nearby **Tyrrell Historical Library** (695 Pearl Street, 409–833–2759).

Listed on the National Register of Historic Places, the fine 1903 Romanesque-Gothic building, formerly a Baptist church, is a treasure chest of Texas history books, genealogical research materials, and art. It's open Tuesday through Thursday and Saturday, 9:00 A.M. until 6:00 P.M.

You'll not find a better Cajun dinner than that at **Sartin's**, at 6725 Eastex Freeway, (409) 892–6771. The seafood's super fresh—and frequently spicy—and the surroundings make you feel as though you're at a friend's cozy dining table. The restaurant is open for lunch and dinner daily.

In just a few minutes you can be out in the country enjoying an offbeat tour or two. It's a quick drive to **Plum Nearly Ranch** (409–722–2637 or 722–1192), a working Arabian horse ranch, offering tours by reservation. Or, you could take in a tour at the **Alligator Island Gator Farm** (409–794–1995). A bit more on the tame side, drive east on Interstate 10 about 25 miles to the town of Orange, where you can tour and taste the vintages of **Piney Woods Country Wines** (3408 Willow Drive, 409–883–5408). The winery is open Monday through Saturday, 9:00 A.M. until 5:30 P.M., and Sunday, 12:00 noon until 5:30 P.M.

But if it's simply another fix of pure nature you need, drive north to the city limits, where the nation's biological crossroads—known best as ◆ **The Big Thicket National Preserve**—awaits. Spreading across seven counties, it's the only national preserve and the only place in the United States where eight ecosystems coexist. Established in 1974, the Big Thicket National Preserve is the focal point of a tranquil, woodsy region with deep heritage and plenty of recreational opportunities. Once an ancient, 3½-million-acre wild forest, it's now an inverted L-shaped, 84,000-acre ecological miracle struggling against the wrecking forces of human nature. The Big Thicket is a refuge for nature supporters who enjoy fishing, hiking, canoeing, and wildlife and wildflower watching. It's also a lab for naturalists and other scientists. The preserve is open daily, but hours vary by section and activity. For details, contact the headquarters at (409) 839–2689 or the visitor center, 30 miles north of Beaumont via U.S. Highway 69 and Farm Road 420, (409) 246–2337.

It's but a 17-mile drive south of Beaumont via U.S. Highway 96 to the waterside town of **Port Arthur**. Originally called Aurora in 1840, the town on the shore of coastal Sabine Lake, on the

Louisiana state line, changed its name to honor the financier responsible for bringing the railroad to town. Is it possible then, if he coaches teams to more Super Bowl titles, that Port Arthur would change its name to Jimmy Johnson City for its more famous son? That's more likely to happen than Port Arthur changing its name for its infamous daughter Janis Joplin— although her memory is honored each year in January with a birthday celebration of concerts and she's the focus of a new exhibit on rock-and-roll stars at the **Museum of the Gulf Coast,** 317 Stillwell Road, (409) 983–4921, ext. 337.

The oil boom brought prosperity to this town, which has served as one of the state's melting pots. French, Dutch, and early American heritage can be seen in Port Arthur's architecture and museums. A place with a particularly eclectic flair is ◆ **La Maison des Acadienne and Dutch Windmill Museum** (just north of town in Nederland, 409–722–0279), where the combined mix of exhibits includes a park dedicated to the memory of country singing star Tex Ritter; a 40-foot reproduction of a Dutch windmill; and a replica house of the French who were forced out of Nova Scotia by the British more than 200 years ago and wound up in Louisiana and Texas. From March until September, the museum is open Tuesday through Sunday, 1:00 P.M. until 5:00 P.M.; after early September, it's open Thursday through Sunday, 1:00 P.M. until 5:00 P.M.

In marked contrast, there's the ◆ **Pompeiian Villa** (1953 Lakeshore Drive, 409–983–7977), a 1900 mansion nicknamed the Billion Dollar House for the owner who acquired the home in exchange for 10 percent in the newly formed Texas Company— which later became Texaco; the man's stock would be worth a billion dollars today. Look inside for its magnificent antiques. Tour hours are Monday through Friday, 9:00 A.M. until 4:00 P.M. and by appointment. Admission is $2.00.

Another cultural twist is found at **Queen of Vietnam Church** (801 Ninth Avenue, 409–983–7676), where a *Hoa-Binh*— or shrine—was erected by Vietnamese Catholics grateful to the city that was a welcoming new home after their escape from Vietnam. Within the dedicated Area of Peace, there are exceptional gardens, a giant statue of the Virgin Mary, and at Christmas, biblical scenes decorated with 700,000 lights. The church and grounds are always open.

History lessons are fascinating at ◆**Sabine Pass Battle-ground State Historical Park** (south of town 14 miles via Texas Highway 87 at Sabine Pass, 409–971–2451). The park is dedicated to the Confederate forces under Colonel Dick Dowling, who managed a victory against staggering odds and much more powerful Union forces in an 1863 battle. In addition to a statue of Dowling, there are picnic areas and a boat ramp. The park is open daily, 8:00 A.M. until 10:00 P.M.

While windsurfers and sailors are drawn to **Sabine Lake**, it's the camping, picnicking, nature study, and shell-collecting opportunities that make ◆**Sea Rim State Park** a popular place. The state's only marshland park—spread over 15,109 acres—is 14 miles west of Sabine Pass on Texas Highway 87. Interestingly, the highway splits the park into two separate parts, the southern being the Beach Unit, with stretches of sandy beach and a biologically unique spot where the salt tidal marsh-lands join the gulf; the northern section is the Marshlands Unit, where canoe trails, observation platforms, and blinds are found. Bug repellant is a plus here, as mosquitoes can be vicious. Look for notices about airboat rides. For information, call the park at (409) 972–2559.

While you're in the neighborhood—or even if you're not—make every effort to have lunch or dinner at **Channel Inn** (on Texas Highway 87 at the entrance to Sabine Pass, 409-971-2400). The no-frills place, an outgrowth of a commercial fishing business, simply serves up an astoundingly delicious platter of barbecued crabs—piles and piles of the wonderful things. Platters are offered of frog legs, catfish, stuffed crab, fried shrimp, and oysters in season.

A trip to the nation's fourth-largest city, **Houston,** about 90 miles west of Port Arthur, can seem daunting; the key is to approach it simply, by focusing on a handful of special places. Even though the entire metropolis sprawls across 500 square miles and is home to two million people, it is the city's individ-ual elements that make it an intriguing whole.

Named, of course, for Sam Houston, the first president of the Republic of Texas, the town was founded in 1836, the year of the Republic's birth. A city that boomed with the development of both the oil and the space exploration industries, Houston has a surprising number of historical and natural attractions.

Sam Houston Park

The first of these, appropriately, is ❖**Sam Houston Park** (1100 Bagby Street, 713–655–1912), a twenty-acre spread immediately west of downtown Houston containing an array of the city's first buildings, dating from 1823 to 1905. There's a small church, a gazebo, and an early commercial building. On site there's the Museum of Texas History, with changing exhibits, and next door, the Long Row, a reconstructed office building, has a tearoom and gift store. Tours are offered Monday through Saturday, 10:00 A.M. until 3:00 P.M., and Sunday, 1:00 P.M. until 4:00 P.M. Admission is $4.00 for adults, $2.00 for children.

Historic in its own way, the **Astrodome** (8400 Kirby Drive, 713–799–9595) was touted as the Eighth Wonder of the World at its 1965 opening. A forerunner to the domed stadiums that are now common, the Astrodome not only hosts the pro-football Oilers and pro-baseball Astros but also welcomes tour visitors to inspect the skyboxes and press area and see a slide show detailing the stadium's amazing construction. Tours are offered daily at 11:00 A.M., 1:00 P.M., and 3:00 P.M., except when events are scheduled. Admission is $4.00 for adults, $3.00 for children.

For a Texas experience with a conscientious spin on it, visit the ◆**Taylor-Stevenson Ranch** (11822 Almeda Road, 713–433–4441), where the roles of African Americans, Hispanics, Native Americans, and women in western heritage are emphasized. That's the icing on top of the cake: a day spent riding horses, going on a hayride or nature walk, and feeding ranch animals. Call for reservations.

Now, you can't have a true visit to such a prestigious Texan city without diving in headfirst to a real Lone Star meal, and the best in town is at **Goode Co. Barbecue** (5109 Kirby Street, 713–522–2530, and 8911 Katy Freeway, 713–464–1901). The mesquite-smoked ribs, brisket, chicken, and sausage links are outrageously succulent and richly flavored, and you'll rave over the homemade sauce, freshly baked bread, and other excellent fixins, such as potato salad and beans. You'll be back for more someday.

A visit to the site where Texas finally won its long, tragically difficult fight for independence from Mexico means driving 22 miles east from the city center to La Porte, where ◆**San Jacinto Battleground State Historical Park** (3800 Park Road 1836, 713–479–2421) is situated. Sam Houston and his army defeated the forces under Santa Anna in an eighteen-minute battle here in 1836, and markers on the battlefield detail positions and tactics of both armies. Rising from the park is the magnificent 570-foot **San Jacinto Monument,** honoring all who fought for Texas independence and particularly those at this site. The observation floor allows a view of the Houston Ship Channel and permanent mooring slip for the **battleship *Texas*,** the sole surviving dreadnought dating to before World War I. The **San Jacinto Museum of History** has exhibits covering 400 years of area history, as well as a new theater showing **"Texas Forever!"** a multimedia presentation chronicling the events pertaining to the Texas Revolution and Battle of San Jacinto. You'll also find a gift boutique, picnic grounds, and concession stand in the park. It's open daily from 9:00 A.M. until 6:00 P.M. Admission is charged only to the observation tower, $2.00 for adults and 50 cents for children, and to the show, $3.50 for adults and $2.00 for children.

To gain deep, new appreciation for NASA and its work, pay a visit to ◆**Space Center Houston** (1601 NASA Road 1, 713–244–2100), situated 20 miles south of downtown Houston at Johnson Space Center. The sensational new attraction is essentially

NASA's visitor center, but the effect is marvelous. Upon arrival, visitors are briefed via continuous NASA update videos and first-hand greetings by Johnson Space Center engineers, scientists, and astronauts. There's a Space Shuttle Mock-Up with flight deck and sleeping quarters to examine; Mission Status Center, where you can see space flight and training activities; The Feel of Space, an interactive area where visitors can use computer simulation to land the shuttle or launch a satellite; two theater presentations—including one IMAX show; and a guided tram tour going behind the scenes at Johnson Space Center. Go early, as this is one pop-ular place—visitors in 1993 alone were expected to number at least two million. It's open daily from 9:00 A.M. until 7:00 P.M.; admission is $9.00 for adults and $5.50 for children.

From here, it's a quick trip to ❖**Armand Bayou Nature Center** (8500 Bay Area Boulevard, 713–474–2551), an unusual 1,900-acre wildlife preserve encompassing forest, bayou, prairie, and marshland ecosystems. Choose one of several trails to hike or join up with a natural history or boating tour. A recreated farm-house recalls Victorian days and is designed to illustrate human-and-nature connections. Visit Wednesday from 9:00 A.M. until dusk; Thursday and Friday, 9:00 A.M. until 4:00 P.M.; Saturday from dawn until 4:00 P.M.; or Sunday from 12:00 noon until dusk. Call for tour times.

If this nature excursion leaves you inspired, you'll want to make time for an even greater communion with wildlife and the outdoors: This involves a journey west of Houston to the area of Eagle Lake, about an hour's drive west on Interstate 10, then southwest on Farm Road 3013 to Colorado County, near the river of the same name. First you'll find the ❖**Attwater Prairie Chicken National Wildlife Refuge** (Farm Road 3013, 409–234–3021). If you make your visit to the 8,000-acre reserve for the odd and endangered species between late February and early May, listen for the male's resounding mating call and watch the mates' ritualistic dance. It's open daily from dawn until dusk.

Just 7 miles down Farm Road 3013, you'll find U.S. Highway 90 and the town of **Eagle Lake**—population 3,550—home to **Wildseed Farms,** (409) 234–7353. The nation's largest work-ing wildflower farm not only harvests the flowers for seed but also offers spring tours during the height of wildflower beauty. Forty-minute narrated wagon rides carry visitors through extraordinary fields, and walking trails are opened to the public. The farm's Country Store sells seeds for more than seventy varieties of wildflowers, as well as gifts. Tour admission is $4.00 for adults and $1.00 for children. For more information, contact the Prairie Edge Museum tour headquarters at 408 East Main Street, (409) 234–2780.

THE ROMANTIC SEASIDE

The utterly Victorian island-city known as **Galveston,** population 72,000, is a one-hour drive from Houston via Interstate 45. Plan to spend a few days here, because you'll be reluctant to leave.

Galvestonians lived lavishly in the mid-nineteenth century: In 1858 alone they bought 23 grand pianos, almost $2,500 dollars worth of silverplate, more than 3,600 gallons of French wine, and nearly 800 gallons of brandy.

Galveston was the largest city in Texas, the second wealthiest city in the nation, and the busiest port in the Southwest. Cotton was king, ships called from around the world to the deep natural harbor, and deals were made by the hundreds on ◆ **the Strand**, the waterfront banking center dubbed "the Wall Street of the Southwest" and today's tourism magnet.

The opulent era of the island-city was characterized by full-scale mansions built by the local gentry; even an average family was housed quite comfortably in a pretty frame house, profuse with gingerbread trim. These are generally viewed on walking and driving tours in the **Silk Stocking and East End Historical Districts**. Several homes are showcased annually during the first two weekends of May during the **Historic Homes Tour.** Brochures from the Galveston Visitors Center (2016 Strand, 409–765–7834) have maps illustrating these neighborhoods.

An abrupt and terrifying end to the glamour came upon the dawn of the twentieth century: On September 8, 1900, a devastating hurricane claimed 6,000 lives and most of the city's structures, leaving Galveston in a deathly stillness. The event still ranks as the worst natural disaster in U.S. history.

In reconstruction, a 4½-mile seawall was built, and for seven years, silt was pumped onto the land to raise the city's grading. The resilience of Galveston and its people was remarkable. Yet business moved in the meantime 50 miles north to Houston, and commerce on the Strand dwindled while countless stately Victorian homes lapsed into sickly states of disrepair. The Galveston Historic Foundation gathered its energy just in time, and wonderful vestiges of a golden era were saved from the wrecking ball in the 1970s.

Ashton Villa, a red brick Italianate mansion at 2328 Broadway, was a primary salvage from threats of demolition in 1971. Built in 1859, the exceptional, antique-filled, three-story estate is open for tours daily; an excellent multimedia presentation on the hurricane and the rebuilt city is shown in Ashton Villa's carriage house. For tour information, call (409) 762–3933; admission is $3.50 for adults, $3.00 for children.

The greatest of Galveston's historic structures, the **Bishop's Palace** (1402 Broadway, 409–762–2475), has a prestigious reputation among architectural experts, who compare its ornate design to the Biltmore House in Asheville, North Carolina. Crafted from Texas granite, limestone, and red sandstone, the Bishop's Palace is the only Texas creation included on the list of one hundred outstanding buildings in the United States by the American Institute of Architects. Completed in 1893, its great pitched roofs, cupolas, gables, and cast-iron balustrades bear the mark of famed architect Nicholas J. Clayton. It's open for tours Monday through Saturday, 10:00 A.M. until 5:00 P.M., and Sunday, 12:00 noon until 5:00 P.M., from Memorial Day through Labor Day, and closed Tuesdays the remainder of the year. Admission is $3.50 for adults and $2.00 for children.

The spit-'n'-polish process continues on the Strand. This National Historic Landmark district, containing one of the nation's larger collections of restored Victorian buildings, is once again a vibrant and colorful mercantile center fixed within the old wharfside business zone. Great revelry invades during early spring for a massive **Mardi Gras** and again in December for a veddy British **Dickens on the Strand** celebration.

In the nineteenth-century banking buildings and cotton ˅warehouses along the Strand is a trove of shopping and entertainment. Among the myriad stores are little galleries and boutiques such as Crabtree & Evelyn and Room With a View. Among wonderful antiques repositories are Somewhere in Time and the Antiques Mall.

Centerpiece for the Texas Seaport Museum is the *Elissa,* Texas's tall ship and another National Historic Landmark. The

1877 iron barque, built in Scotland, provides an exciting look at Galveston's seafaring past. The ship and adjacent museum, with superb exhibits and a dramatic film, are open daily, 10:00 A.M. until 5:00 P.M., at Pier 21, near the Strand at the foot of Twenty-second Street. For information, call (409) 763–1877.

Three blocks from the Strand, the **Grand 1894 Opera House** is a distinctive, lavishly decorated theater whose stage has been graced by dignitaries from Anna Pavlova and John Philip Sousa to Hal Holbrook and Ray Charles. Recently restored to the tune of $7 million, the Grand, at 2020 Post Office, continues to offer a full schedule of renowned entertainers. Self-guided tours are available Monday through Saturday, 9:00 A.M. until 5:00 P.M., and Sunday, 12:00 noon until 5:00 P.M. For information, call (409) 765–1894 or (800) 821–1894.

Either tour Galveston Bay aboard a giant paddlewheeler, the *Colonel*, or take the cheery **Galveston Island Trolley** from the Strand down to Seawall Boulevard for diversions of the beach variety. Gulf-front activities range from leisurely touring on rented bikes or pedal-powered surreys to the incomparable thrill of bungie-jumping. The *Colonel* docks at Pier 22 at Twenty-second Street, (409) 763–4666, and makes two cruises daily from April through Labor Day and weekend cruises only from September through March; dinner-and-jazz cruises and moonlight cruises are offered seasonally. Call for hours and prices. The trolley costs $1.00 for adults and 50 cents for children and seniors; for a schedule, contact the Galveston Island Convention & Visitors Bureau, 2106 Seawall Boulevard, (409) 763–4311.

The island has 32 miles of beaches to explore, with **Stewart Beach** and **R. A. Apffel Park** among busy city areas with concessions, and ✦**Galveston Island State Park,** Farm Road 3005 near 13 Mile Road, (409) 737–1222, where people go for bird watching, nature walks, and camping. Admission fees are charged at some beaches, and entry to the state park is $2.00 per vehicle. Be watchful on the sand at all beaches for tar deposits, generated by offshore oil rigs, and jelly fish, two sure vacation dampers.

At **Moody Gardens** (on Hope Boulevard, adjacent to the airport, 409–744–1745) the **Rainforest Pyramid** is the newest in a series of eight spectacular facets comprising the 140-acre multimillion-dollar project for education, recreation, and therapy. This super greenhouse is a growing copy of the world's primary tropical forests, and an IMAX theater with 3-D presentations is on site. Hours and admission vary, so please call first.

Old-fashioned rest and relaxation are obtainable in Galveston's several historic hostelries. The **Hotel Galvez,** a Spanish-style stucco mansion built in 1911, faces the gulf at 2024 Seawall Boulevard (409–765–7721). The sophisticated **Tremont House,** built in 1872 and located a block off the Strand at 2300 Ship's Mechanic Row (800–874–2300 or 409–763–0300), has impressive appointments. Charming and genteel bed and breakfast lodgings are numerous; for information, contact the convention and visitors bureau (409–763–4311), or try Bed and Breakfast Reservations (800–628–4644 or 409–762–1668).

Dining has become a favorite reason to make escapes to Galveston. **Gaido's** (3828 Seawall Boulevard, 409–762–9625), founded in 1911, remains a place for divine fried blue crabs, five kinds of baked oysters, and homemade pepper cheese bread. It serves lunch and dinner daily. **Christie's Beachcomber** (Stewart Beach, 409–762–8648), serving lunch and dinner Monday through Saturday, is the best place to find fresh Texas seafood right on the beach.

THE COASTAL BEND

The tricky aspects of following Texas's jagged coastline southward are fully realized on wildly meandering drives from Galveston Island down to the Coastal Bend. Travelers making just this journey will pass through Brazoria, Matagorda, and Calhoun counties, skirting the coast's series of inward jutting bays, driving 200 miles southwest on Texas Highway 35.

The first likely detour from this path is just past Lavaca Bay, where you can make a trip to the perfectly solitary beaches of ◆**Matagorda Island State Park,** accessed via Texas Highway 316, Farm Road 1289, and Texas Highway 185—and then a passenger ferry from Port O'Connor. Sounds complicated, perhaps, but the diversion is well worth the trouble: The barrier island, which reaches almost 38 miles southwest beside the mainland, is an undeveloped wildland owned by the U.S. Department of the Interior and managed by the state parks department. Some 36,000 of the 45,000 acres are a wildlife management area; the remainder is a public park with 80 miles of immaculate beaches, bike and hike paths, and shoreline areas for bird watching, shell collecting, swimming, fishing, and picnicking. Be sure to bring your own water and food, as no concessions whatsoever are here.

The passenger ferry operates between the dock at Sixteenth and Maple streets in Port O'Connor and the island three times daily on Saturday, Sunday, and holidays. Once on the island, you'll take a shuttle bus on a quick ride to the island's sandy gulf shore. The ferry ride costs $8.00 for adults and $4.00 for children; the shuttle is $2.00 for adults and $1.00 for children; reservations should be made by calling (512) 983-2215.

A pair of slightly simpler detours en route south are found together just shy of the LBJ Causeway, the portion of Texas Highway 35 spanning **Copano Bay**. At the tiny community of Lamar—it's too small even to be listed on the state highway map—you'll find Park Road 13, which leads to ◆**Goose Island State Park** (512-729-2858), a 314-acre recreation area covering a little peninsula and an assortment of islands in the waters where Aransas, Copano, and St. Charles bays meet. You can fish from a 1,620-foot lighted pier, bird watch, take nature and wildlife walks, swim, and camp, and you'll have a chance to see a historical Karankawa Indian meeting site, **The Big Tree of Lamar.** This coastal live oak is possibly 2,000 years old and measures more than 35 feet around, 44 feet tall, and 89 feet at its crown span.

When you decide to head on down to the Corpus Christi area, you'll stay on Texas Highway 35, cross the LBJ Causeway, and find yourself at the other end in the adjoining towns of **Rockport** and **Fulton.** Rockport, the Aransas County seat and home to a seaside art colony of about 4,700, is a quiet community fostering its cultural growth in places like the **Rockport Art Center** (at the point, Rockport Harbor, 512-729-5519), which occupies the restored nineteenth-century Bruhl-O'Connor home. Studios, classrooms, and four galleries are inside; the center is open Tuesday through Saturday, 10:00 A.M. until 5:00 P.M., and Sunday, 2:00 P.M. until 5:00 P.M.

Also at Rockport Harbor, the **Texas Maritime Museum** (1202 Navigation Circle, 512-729-1271) showcases the state's seafaring heritage from the arrival of early Spanish explorers and Texas's battle for independence to the development of a dozen deep-water business ports and offshore oil exploration. Exhibits include ship-wreck relics nearly 450 years old, portraits of every ship that sailed in the Texas Navy, and a new collection of watercolors of Texas lighthouses. The museum is open Wednesday through Saturday, 10:00 A.M. until 4:00 P.M., and Sunday, 1:00 P.M. until 4:00 P.M. Admission is $2.50 for adults, $1.00 for children.

Barely 5 miles away in Fulton—also on Texas Highway 35 and not far from the exotic-looking windswept leaning trees, twisted by constant winds—is the ✛**Fulton Mansion State Historical Structure** (Fulton Beach Road at Henderson Street, 512-729-0386). A four-story showpiece dating to 1876, the innovative home was uniquely outfitted with central air and hot and cold running water at its beginning. A French Second Empire design surrounds the thirty-room mansion, which was restored by the state parks department. Visitors are asked to wear soft-soled shoes to protect the floors, and you're advised to call ahead in summer to find out if touring lines are long. The home is open Wednesday through Sunday, 9:00 A.M. until 12:00 noon and 1:00 P.M. until 4:00 P.M.; adult tickets are $3.00, and children's tickets are $1.50.

Rockport and Fulton most often host nature enthusiasts visiting ✛**Aransas National Wildlife Refuge** between November and March, prime months for viewing the rare whooping cranes, which numbered only fourteen in 1941. The United States and Canada have joined together in a sensational effort for almost fifty years to save these remarkable migratory birds, who journey annually from Canada in October and November to spend winter in these nesting grounds. The 55,000-acre asylum, home now to some 140 whooping cranes, is operated by the U.S. Fish and Wildlife Service for protection and management of around 300 species of birds, including Canada geese, sandhill cranes, and pintail and baldpate ducks, as well as white-tailed deer, javelina, and raccoon. You can view the birds from an observation point or from one of several boat tours along the intracoastal canal from Rockport.

Information on the refuge, situated 37 miles north of Rockport and reached by car via Texas Highway 35, Farm Road 774, and Farm Road 2040, is available by calling the visitor center at (512) 286-3559; the refuge is open daily from dawn until dusk, and the visitor center is open daily from 8:00 A.M. until 4:30 P.M. Boat tours departing Rockport cost about $20 to $25 per person; for a list of skippers, contact the Rockport-Fulton Chamber of Commerce at (512) 729–9952, (800) 242–0071, or (800) 826–6441.

Fourteen miles southeast of Rockport via Texas Highway 35, Port Aransas can be reached via **free ferry**—which departs from a huge dock in Aransas Pass—operated twenty-four hours daily by the state highway department. For decades the little beach community fondly called Port A, at the northern tip of Mustang Island, has been a vacation spot where families spend days or weeks deep-sea fishing and body surfing in the gulf and shell collecting on the hot sand. While it was once known as a lazy town, better access spurred the growth of multistory condos, beachwear boutiques, and nightspots.

Now as then, however, Port A, population 2,200, is a place meant for dawdling—if not feasting on fresh shrimp and crab, taking long walks on the shore, horseback riding, or jet-skiing. Children and grownups get a kick out of clinging to the rail and watching for porpoise acrobatics during the five-minute ferry trip to the island. The other island access is at the southern end, where a highway connects Corpus Christi on the mainland to Mustang and to Padre Island, adjacent to the south.

At either end of the ferry run are several brightly painted shacks selling fresh seafood. These bear come-on banners: BEST LITTLE SHRIMP HOUSE IN TEXAS and MAKE A COW HAPPY—EAT SHRIMP. Here people buy five pounds of shrimp for as low as $15.00 for bargain suppers in their rented cottages or for icing down in a take-home cooler, or for fish bait. For more information on the ferry or shrimp shacks, call the chamber of commerce, (512) 749–5919 or (800) 452–6278.

Mustang Island was one of Texas's barrier islands frequented by Jean Lafitte and his buccaneer buddies in the 1820s. Now and then, island romantics, perhaps with the help of a little grog, set out in search of a legendary Spanish dagger that is said to mark the spot of a buried pirate treasure. The most common booty, however, is a wealth of sand dollars and varied seashells found just after high tide on the light brown sand. The island's 18 miles of beach are cleaned daily, and the tar deposits are significantly fewer than those at Galveston. Cars are no longer allowed free rein of the beaches as they were until the 1980s, but are limited to a narrow path alongside the dunes.

Crowds are naturally drawn to ✦**Mustang Island State Park** (on Texas 361, 512–749–5246), almost 3,500 acres decorated with sand dunes, sea oats, and morning glory. The park, just 14 miles south of the town of Port A, has 5 miles of gulf-front beach, and it offers camping, picnicking under arbors, a nature trail, a fish-cleaning station, and showers. The park is open daily from 8:00 A.M. until 10:00 P.M. for day use and at all times for campers. Admission is $2.00 per day per vehicle. For a more private, open expanse of white sands, hop the Jetty Boat at Woody's Boat Basin for a fifteen-minute ride to ✦**San Jose Island** (Woody's Boat Basin at Cotter Street, 512–749–5252)—or as the locals call it, St. Jo. The uninhabited beach reserve is known for excellent shelling, and it's an ideal place to take a picnic, fresh water, and some fishing gear for a real getaway. The passenger-only ferry operates from 6:30 A.M. until 6:00 P.M.; fares are $8.00 for adults and $4.50 for children.

Mostly, though, people come to Port A to see what they can find in the water. The town calls itself the place "where they bite every day," and fishing for redfish, speckled trout, flounder, and drum is free in the surf from the south jetty and the Station Street Pier. Group fishing aboard party boats such as the *Island Queen* gives anglers a chance to reel in bigger game fish for just $20 per person, which includes rod, reel, and tackle. Private charters, which can cost in the hundreds, go in search of tarpon, sailfish, marlin, kingfish, mackerel, bonito, red snapper, amberjack, barracuda, yellow-fin tuna, wahoo, and shark. For charter companies, ask at the chamber of commerce, 512–749–5919 or 800–452–6278.

People who just want to look at sea life can go to the **University of Texas Marine Science Center** (Cotter Street, opposite Port Aransas Park, 512–749–6711). The research facility has seven habitat aquariums, as well as impressive shell displays. It's open from 8:00 A.M. until 5:00 P.M. daily during summer months and Monday through Friday only from September through May.

Because travelers want to simply stay and stay once they've arrived in Port A, comfortable condos have become plentiful without being congestive—and most are reasonably priced. Some of the high-rises are a bit south of town, while many of the two-story complexes are close to the commercial area, and everything's on the beach. Generally, condos are individually owned and well maintained and have large pools, tennis courts, cable

TV, and landscaped boardwalks reaching across the dunes to the beach. For something a little on the funky side, check out the **Tarpon Inn** (200 East Cotter Street, 512–749–5555), now in its fourth incarnation. Originally built in 1886 by a boat pilot and lighthouse keeper who used surplus lumber from nearby Civil War barracks, the inn burned down and then its replacement was destroyed in a hurricane. Today's version is a renovation of the 1920 structure, and it remains popular with anglers. A list of noted guests includes Franklin D. Roosevelt, and the inn is included on the National Register of Historic Places. Beulah's is the inn's restaurant, serving fresh seafood, Gulf oysters, and Texas beef.

The **Crazy Cajun restaurant** on Alister Street Square offers a Louisiana-style shrimp and crawfish boil: hot fresh shrimp, crawfish, stone crab claws, new potatoes, corn on the cob, and smoked sausage. The gumbo and sourdough bread are good, too. It's open for dinner only, Tuesday through Friday, and lunch and dinner Saturday and Sunday; closed Monday; call (512) 749–5069.

Just across Corpus Christi Bay, which laps at Mustang Island's western shore, is the same-name city with almost 300,000 residents. The Nueces County seat, **Corpus Christi** is reached on a half-hour drive inland from Mustang Island and is the most common arrival spot for travelers flying to Texas's Coastal Bend area.

Corpus is thought to have first hosted a European in 1519, when explorer Alonzo de Pineda made a visit. Today the city is separated from the Gulf by a lengthy **seawall,** which was designed by sculptor Gutzon Borglum of Mount Rushmore fame. Just a few years ago eight gazebolike *miradors*—Spanish for "lookouts"—were added to the seawall; the brilliant white miradors, capped by pointed, barrel-tile roofs and complemented by Victorian-style street lamps, function as both resting spots and wedding sites.

Corpus is a magnet for sailing and windsurfing fans, as well as a new breed of tourists interested in ecology. **The Dolphin Connection,** a small business run by a husband-wife team conducting dolphin research, illustrates the ecotourism premise that things educational can be fun, with dolphin-feeding tours departing twice every morning. Guides provide dolphin data throughout the expedition, which begins with a five-minute trip into the bay's shrimping zone. As soon as a tour boat arrives, nearly a dozen dolphins appear, flipping and jumping and practically begging for attention. During the next hour, the Judge, Mary, Whistler, Fritz, June Bug, and several other family members pop up out of the water, much to everyone's amusement, and the audience of ten tourists gets to know the entertainers, feeding long, stringy ribbon fish to the dolphins, petting their necks, and calling them by name. The dolphins respond, showing their pleasure by changing their undersides from dull gray to a distinctive pink. The tours are seasonal, and information is available from the Corpus Christi Convention & Visitors Bureau, 1201 North Shoreline Drive, (512) 882–5603 or (800) 766–2322.

The Dolphin Connection dock is just a two-minute drive from the sleek **Texas State Aquarium** (Corpus Christi Beach at the Harbor Bridge, 800–477–GULF or 512–881–1300), a wonderfully unique place, opened in 1991. The $31.5 million Gulf of Mexico Exhibit, the first of four planned phases, manages to entertain both adults and children while providing a sea of knowledge. Besides 350,000-gallon salt water tanks full of ocean life, the bayside aquarium has displays requiring observers' participation and a water-bird rehabilitation area. The cool dark blue and gray interiors are perfect for escaping summer heat, and the spaciousness of what appear to be tanks without walls imparts a soothing, otherworldly climate. Crowds are frequently gathered around the hurricane video screen, which gives the viewer an exciting opportunity to play Corpus Christi's mayor in the event of an oncoming hurricane. The Islands of Steel exhibit features a portion of a mammoth offshore oil rig, which is a substitute feeding station for fish in an area where no reefs or rocks exist. Nurse and bull sharks, giant turtles, and enormous groupers swim amid the rig's barnacle-encrusted legs. A quick elevator ride leads to an observation deck masted with huge blue sails that give the white building a shiplike appearance from a distance. This 50-foot-high vantage point affords panoramic views of Corpus Christi Bay and the ship channel not found elsewhere in the city. The aquarium is open Monday through Saturday, 10:00 A.M. until 6:00 P.M., and Sunday, 12:00 noon until 6:00 P.M. Admission is $6.50 for adults; $4.50 for seniors, active military personnel, and students; and $3.50 for children.

Since 1992, when the World War II aircraft carrier **USS Lexington** opened as a museum in the port near the aquarium, naval history has been observed as never before on the Texas coast. Only the fourth carrier to make such a conversion, the *Lexington*—nicknamed the *Lady Lex*—was commissioned in 1943, participated in all major Pacific battles from Tarawa to Tokyo, collected eleven battle stars, and was the first to enter Tokyo Bay in September 1945. Among sixteen decks to explore are the cavernous hangar area, where immense elevators carried fighters and attack planes from the landing deck for maintenance, and the landing deck, where volunteer guides—mostly retired naval officers—show center lines and arrest and catapult areas, and explain the complications that go into running a small oceantop landing strip where planes land as often as every 30 seconds. The *USS Lexington* is open Monday through Saturday, 9:00 A.M. until 5:00 P.M., and Sunday, 11:00 A.M. until 5:00 P.M. Adult tickets are $7.00; children are $3.75; and seniors and active-duty military are $5.00. For more information, call (512) 888–4873.

The soaring white Harbor Bridge stretches south over the busy port to the **Bayfront Arts and Sciences Park** (north end of Shoreline Boulevard) and downtown. At Bayfront, kids get a kick out of summer melodramas at **Harbor Playhouse** (512–882–3356) and at the "Shipwreck!" exhibit, which illustrates Corpus Christi's sixteenth-century heritage, at the **Corpus Christi Museum** (512–883–2862); the museum is open Tuesday through Saturday, 10:00 A.M. until 5:00 P.M., and Sunday, 1:00 P.M. until 5:00 P.M., and a small admission is charged. Across the centerpiece Water Garden—a sunken ring of 150 jet fountains—lies the widely noted **Art Museum of South Texas** (512–884–3844). The austere white building is its own masterpiece, while the interior is acclaimed for both its huge picture window looking over the water and its traveling exhibits, which have included such varied works as those of Remington and Warhol. Open Tuesday through Friday, 10:00 A.M. until 5:00 P.M., and Saturday and Sunday, 12:00 noon until 5:00 P.M., the museum also charges a small admission.

Heritage Park (512–883–0639), still within the Bayfront complex, provides an opportunity to look at various historic homes all conveniently situated on one block. The structures are among the best of old Corpus Christi, dating back to 1851. Among them are elaborate designs, such as the Colonial revival–Victorian Lichtenstein House and the ornate Queen Anne Sidbury House, as well as simpler cottages. The homes have been painstakingly restored and are open for tours. Stop in the Merriman-Bobys House—the second-oldest house in the city—home now to Olde Tyme Deli, for a BLT, a bowl of chili, a piece of apple pie, or a lemonade.

Thrusting seaward from the huge wall is the **city marina**, bustling within the shadows of tall downtown buildings. Watery diversions found in the marina vary from sailboat and windsurf rentals to fishing excursions. People arrive in droves in the afternoon to make cheap buys from fishermen of live shrimp (small and large mixed, $4.50 per pound) and blue crabs ($3.50 per dozen). The marina is home, too, to the reproduction paddlewheeler *Flagship*, which makes daily morning, afternoon, and evening sightseeing cruises. The triple-decked white ship plies water from the bay to the port and back, with interesting detailed narration of the city, past and present. In the port, huge tankers from distant places around the world—Moravia is just one spotted on a recent trip—are passed. Nighttime cruises often offer live jazz music. Cruise times and prices vary according to the season; for details call (512) 643–7128 or (512) 884–1693.

At the south end of town, Corpus Christi Bay meets Laguna Madre at the JFK Causeway, the connection to ◆ **Padre Island National Seashore.** The legendary narrow island extends 113 miles southward nearly to Mexico and is the longest of all barrier islands on the Texas coast. No commercial development is allowed on the 80-mile mid-island stretch, but National Park Service rangers provide information on camping and four-wheel-driving areas. Beachcombing and shell collecting are the national seashore's primary attractions, but federal law forbids taking flint points, coins, or anything that might be considered historical. Daily programs offered in summer by National Park Service rangers at **Malaquite Beach** include a 1:00 P.M. walk and study of the sea's natural flotsam and jetsam, and a 2:00 P.M. in-water look at marine animals in Laguna Madre. Rangers also conduct fireside talks at dusk on Friday and Saturday on a variety of island topics. For information, call the National Park Service's Padre Island office on the mainland at (512) 937–2621. At Malaquite Beach, the ranger office number is (512) 949–8068.

Memories of fantastic fresh fish will linger if you dine downtown at **Water Street Seafood Company** (309 North Water Street, 512–882–8684), open daily for lunch and dinner. The food is every bit as good but the view is better at ◆ **The Lighthouse**

(444 North Shoreline Boulevard at the Lawrence Street T-Head, 512–883–3982), which has an ideal location looking out over the marina. U-peel-em shrimp, fried oyster sandwiches, grilled fresh shrimp, and steaks are served at lunch and dinner daily.

THE COASTAL PLAINS

An excursion from Corpus that won't easily be forgotten is the one to ✛ **Goliad,** a deeply historic spot northwest about 78 miles via U.S. Highway 181, U.S. Highway 77, and U.S. Highway 183. There you'll find the most fought-over and exemplary Spanish fort in Texas and the state's true birthplace. A metal plaque outside the heavy chapel doors at **Presidio La Bahía** seems to glow with the poignancy of the words it bears:

> Here fell the men in martyred death to gain the freedom and independence of Texas; and here for centuries to come generations of men will gather in reverence and appreciation of La Bahia's glorious past.

The rough-hewn building dates to 1749 and is the nation's only completely restored inland fort. Among several important roles the presidio played is one from the Republic of Texas, one wrought with utter tragedy: The stillness of the tiny chapel here continues to emanate the desolation of Palm Sunday morning, 1836, when Colonel James Walker Fannin and 352 Texas volunteers were held captive there before being marched out and shot under orders of Mexican dictator Santa Anna. The death toll was twice that of the Alamo's.

The first flag of Texas independence, emblazoned with a bloody arm wielding a saber, is still flown here in remembrance of La Bahía's stature as the place where independence was first planned and where the Declaration of Texas Independence was signed December 20, 1835. A museum in soldiers' quarters and officers' barracks details nine levels of civilization uncovered in artifacts, as well as artifacts from the revolution. Behind the presidio you'll find the Fannin Monument and Grave. The presidio, on U.S. Highway 183 about 2 miles south of Goliad, is open daily from 9:00 A.M. until 4:45 P.M. Admission is $2.00 for adults, 50 cents for children; call (512) 645–3752 for more information.

Across the San Antonio River from La Bahía rises the white-walled majesty of **Mission Espíritu Santo de Zúñiga,** once

Mission Espiritu Santo de Zuñiga

New Spain's finest outpost north of the Rio Grande. The mission is now contained within **Goliad State Historical Park,** also on U.S. Highway 183, just a quarter mile south of modern Goliad. Espiritu Santo functioned as a mission for 110 years and was the home of Texas's first large cattle ranch. Within the old mission building is a superb if small museum detailing Spain's attempt to colonize the New World.

The surrounding 2,200-acre park has wonderfully scenic shaded picnic and camping areas, interpretive nature trails, and river fishing. Across the highway, a junior-Olympic swimming pool is operated by the city of Goliad. Park admission is $3.00 per vehicle; for information, call (512) 645–3405.

The **Goliad town square** surrounds a grand limestone courthouse, built in 1894, and an enormous live oak known as the

Hanging Tree. Court was held here during the mid-nineteenth century, and the guilty were hanged, as many as five men at a time. Wonderful old Victorian and Texas pioneer buildings line the square. Nearby, at Franklin and Market streets, **Fannin Park Plaza** contains a cannon from the revolution and a memorial to Fannin and his men. In June the town square is the site of the **Goliad Longhorn Stampede,** a festival celebrating the "Fastest Parade in History," which occurred in a 1976 Bicentennial party when a reenactment of a big cattle drive got out of hand and the one hundred longhorn steers created the last stampede in an incorporated city. For information on the town square and the annual stampede party, call the Goliad County Chamber of Commerce, (512) 645–3563.

It's only an hour's drive back to the beach, but you can find a restful sleepover in Goliad at the **Dial House** (306 West Oak Street, 512–645–3366). Lovely gardens surround an old family place, wherein wait five guest rooms, including a bridal suite. Breakfasts are bountiful, and the hostess is known for her crepes, pastries, and sweets.

From Goliad, it's an easy, 95-mile path south via U.S. Highway 183 and U.S. Highway 77 to **Kingsville,** home of still more pure Lone Star heritage. Former riverboat captain Richard King established the legendary ◆ **King Ranch** in 1853 in the southeast Texas coastal plains by purchasing 75,000 acres of a Spanish land grant for $300, originally naming it the Santa Gertrudis Ranch for the rare creek running through it. That the ranch succeeded in such an uninhabited place and time is as profound as the modern accomplishments that would come in the next dozen decades.

Ranch workers and King's family fought off armed attacks by Mexican bandits on at least two dozen occasions; the towers from which guards kept watch remain the most notable design element on the ranch's oldest structure, a big white commissary built in the 1850s. Visitors straggled through the area without much regularity, but King and his wife, Henrietta, took in overnighters. One guest is said to have been Jesse James, who gave a gray stallion to King after the captain admired it; today, ranch lore holds that all gray stallions are descendants of James's horse.

King brought longhorn cattle to Texas from Mexico, luring entire Mexican villages to come along and work the livestock for room and board. The offspring of these *kiñeos,* or king's men, work today with King's own kin.

By the early twentieth century, 1.175 million acres with departmentalized operations formed an empire that would be known worldwide as innovative in the cattle and horse industries. Today, the spread measures 825,000 acres and reaches over Nueces, Kenedy, Kleberg, and Willacy counties. Its fences, if placed in a straight line, would reach from the plains near Corpus Christi to Boston. The ranch is larger than the state of Rhode Island and home to 50,000 head of cattle, 1,000 head of horses, and 300 artesian wells reaching 600 feet into the earth.

Tours aboard minibuses take travelers through the brushy landscape, and guides point out the romantically named vegetation that characterizes this challenging corner of the world. The anaqua, or sandpaper tree, often grows up to 50 feet high, guides explain, and the sprawling, low-lying lantana brightens the terrain with a rainbow of colored flowers. In addition to live oak, persimmon, yucca, hackberry, and prickly pear, you'll find fragrant purple sage at home on the King Ranch range. Mesquite, that most defiant of Texas trees, gave the Kings plenty of problems, so a massive root-digging plow was invented expressly to clear mesquite from the King Ranch. One of the hostile, fanged machines is displayed with other model equipment near a cattle pen.

During the 12-mile tour, travelers can see where Santa Gertrudis cattle—the first beef breed developed in the United States—are worked, as well as the horse areas, famous for having contributed to American quarter-horse development.

A much photographed building is the 1909 livery stable, a classic blend of western and Victorian influences. The only real disappointment is not being able to see the fabulous main house. It's open to tour groups of twenty or more—if there's no official ranch business being conducted at the time by any of the one hundred King descendants. Birding tours are becoming more popular here. The scissortail flycatcher, whose males sport beautiful orange breasts, is one of 350 species living on the ranch. Basic bus tours are $6.00, and packages with tours of the ranch and town with camphouse meals are $18–$25. For details, contact the King Ranch, (512) 592–8055 or (800) 282–KING.

The adjacent town of Kingsville was created in 1903 when King's widow, Henrietta, deeded 853 acres of the ranch for a town to be built. An interesting stop after ranch exploration, it's home to the **Connor Museum.** Situated on the campus of Texas A&I University, the Connor has a unique collection once belonging to Graves Peeler, a rustler and hunter whose assemblage of horns, arrowheads, game trophies, spurs, and such is strange and almost creepy, but a collection that's worth a stop. Also at the Connor, "The Living Mosaic" is a polished educational TV production illustrating the Texas coastal plain, its natural resources and history. The photography of plant and animal life, especially wildflowers, is nothing but stunning. Open Tuesday through Saturday, 9:00 A.M. until 5:00 P.M.; call (512) 595–2819 for more information.

At the **King Ranch Museum** (405 North Sixth Street, 512–595–1881), larger-than-life Toni Frissell photos of daily work and life scenes from the King Ranch in the 1940s are riveting. Historic ranch items of note at the museum include a saddle collection, impressive even to people who see no need ever to go near a horse.

The **Running W Saddle Shop** (Sixth at Kleberg streets, 512–595–5761 or 800–282–KING) is the place to spend big dollars in a short time, although it takes a few hours to really see the spectacular inventory. A very sophisticated boutique, its pale hardwood floors and rough wood walls are adorned with artfully composed displays and beautiful Indian saddle blankets and rugs. Custom-made goods include leather backpacks, "gunpowder" shoulder or belt bags, antler candlesticks, Running W collector's china, a gift crate of mesquite, cactus and jalapeño jellies, and jewelry, including sterling silver cufflinks bearing the King Ranch's Running W brand against prickly pear cactus.

THE BIG BEACH

From Kingsville, it's a little more than a two-hour shot straight south to Texas's most famous spread of sand. To reach **South Padre Island,** just follow U.S. Highway 77 down to Los Fresnos, then turn east on Texas Highway 100, which ends at the state's southernmost beachfront.

The only reason to pause even for a moment before hitting the beach is to stock up on supplies in **Port Isabel.** Certainly there are legions of stores on the island, but you'll save money by shopping for groceries and fresh-caught fish in the placid little fishing village.

While you're at it, take note that the smallest state park in Texas is right here—the ◆ **Port Isabel Lighthouse State Historic Park** (Texas Highway 100 and Tarvana Street at the Causeway, 210–943–1172). It's the only lighthouse on the coast open to the public, casting its light 16 miles out on the gulf from its erection in 1853 until it was closed in 1905. Those in shape can scale the winding seventy-plus steps to the top to gain a view of Port Isabel, the Causeway, South Padre Island, and on to the Gulf of Mexico.

If the condos and beach houses at the beach don't float your boat, try Port Isabel's **Yacht Club Hotel** (700 Yturria, 2 blocks north from Texas Highway 100, 210–943–1301). The two-story hotel has been restored to its 1920s look; it offers a restaurant and bar, outdoor pool, and free continental breakfast.

Note that after a few days at the beach, you may be back here in Port Isabel in order to spend a day or night on the sea aboard *Le Mistral* (1250 Port Road, 210–943–SHIP or 800–334–9489), a 450-passenger cruise ship making briefs trips to the Mexican coast and back. The strongest attraction is Las Vegas–style gaming, which commences once the ship is in international waters. There's everything in the way of entertainment, from music and dancing to games and contests—or you can simply lie on the deck and catch some rays. Buffet meals are included in some packages, which begin at about $40 per person. Cruises last six hours and are made during the day on Wednesday and Sunday, and in the evenings on Thursday, Friday, and Saturday. There's a $2.00 parking fee at the Port Isabel dock.

Can't wait to get to the waves? Then head east, crossing the great blue Laguna Madre Bay on the **Queen Isabella Causeway,** Texas's longest bridge, stretching just over 2½ miles. The center span rises 73 feet above the mean high tide, allowing ships heading to sea to pass below; its strength will withstand threefold hurricane-force winds.

The lower end of long, skinny Padre Island gained its name, South Padre, when the Mansfield Cut—about 35 miles north of this developed tip—was created by state engineers in 1964, severing the island in two. Padre Island National Seashore (profiled in the Corpus Christi section) is north, and this mega resort area is south.

From a scattering of simple beachy bungalows in the 1960s grew a city of high-rise hotels and condominiums in the 1980s known for its powerful tourism magnetism. Along with the resort lodgings are shopping centers, tennis clubs, restaurants, and bars comprising the single busiest place in the lower half of the United States during Spring Break—lasting from mid-March until early April—when some 100,000 students from across the country and Canada come to party.

Things are a bit more sane during other periods of celebration, including the big **Windsurfing Blowout** in May; the **Windjammer Regatta** in June; the **Texas International Fishing Tournament** in late July; and **Christmas by the Seas** and **Island of Lights Festival** throughout December.

While plenty of people come to South Padre Island simply to play in the waves and build sandcastles, or ride horseback and play miniature golf, others find reward in visiting the ❖ **Turtle Lady**, the nickname given to Ila Loetscher, eighty-odd-year-old rehabilitator of endangered sea turtles. The entertaining, tiny woman puts on a cornball show in order to raise money to save from extinction Kemp's ridley sea turtles and seven other endangered species of marine turtles. Not only is she interesting for the data she shares and live turtles she works with, but she also has some fascinating stories to tell about her days as one of the first female pilots in the nation. The Turtle Lady's programs are held at 5805 Gulf Boulevard, 9:00 A.M., Tuesday and Saturday, May through August; and 10:00 A.M., Tuesday and Saturday, September through April. A $2.00 donation is requested for Sea Turtle, Inc. For more information, call (210) 761-2544.

At mealtime, your options are numerous. **Blackbeard's,** at 103 East Saturn Street, (210) 761-2962, is known for outstanding blackened shrimp fajitas, other seafood, and steaks at lunch and dinner. Across the main road and overlooking the Laguna Madre, **Louie's Backyard,** at 2305 Laguna Boulevard, (210) 761-6406, has a delightful seafood and prime rib buffet every evening. In addition, there are restaurants specializing in Mexican, Chinese, Italian, and vegetarian fare. And, of course, you'll find plenty of fast-food places, too.

There are hundreds of options along the beach and along the bay in the way of condos, beach houses, luxury hotels, and bargain motels, and the number of rental agencies seems to grow daily. For a complete lodging listing, call the South Padre Island Convention & Visitors Bureau, (800) 343-2368.

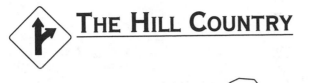

THE HILL COUNTRY

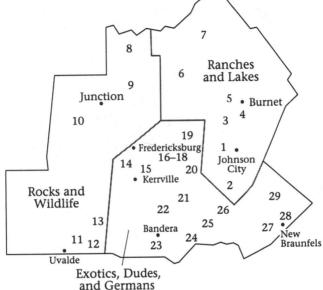

1. The Lyndon B. Johnson National Historic Park
2. Christ of the Hills Monastery
3. Horseshoe Bay Country Club and Resort
4. Longhorn Caverns State Park
5. Vanishing Texas River Cruise
6. Llano
7. Colorado Bend State Park
8. World Championship Barbecue Goat Cook-Off
9. Fort Mason Officers Quarters
10. South Llano River State Park
11. Garner State Park
12. Utopia
13. Lost Maples State Natural Area
14. Y.O. Ranch
15. Cowboy Artists of America Museum
16. Admiral Nimitz State Historical Park
17. Hill Top Cafe
18. Enchanted Rock State Park
19. Willow City Loop
20. Luckenbach
21. Hygieostatic Bat Roost
22. Camp Verde
23. Dixie Dude Ranch
24. PoPo Family Restaurant
25. Cave Without a Name
26. Guadalupe River State Park
27. Gruene Historic District
28. Aquarena Springs
29. Wimberley

THE HILL COUNTRY

Visualize two-lane roads, twisting and climbing, leading to an antique borough here, a pioneer settlement there. Imagine hills, soft and scrubby, green valleys, limestone cliffs. Conjure up ranches and communities of German heritage, wineries and fields of wildflowers, sparkling rivers lined with cypress and oak.

Ah, the Hill Country realized. To some, it's the state's greatest natural resource. No big cities, no bustle. Just cafes with country cooking, water for fishing and innertubing, and old places with time-worn comfort.

Raised by the Edwards Plateau, the hilly region extends west from Interstate 35, which follows the edge of the Balcones Fault. You can find this land of escape below U.S. 190 and above U.S. 90. Wander alone or take the whole family. But don't venture too far west of U.S. 83, where the hills—and the Hill Country—taper off. Just go armed with plenty of film.

Spring—when Texas is blanketed in glorious wildflowers—is by far the most popular time to wander through the Hill Country. Experts at the National Wildflower Research Center in Austin are deluged with calls every year in early March, when travelers are begging for information as to when the bluebonnets, the state flower, will sprout their colorful hats.

These experts manage to patiently explain time and time again that everything depends on whether or not fall and winter rains reached the wildflower seeds after germination, whether or not sunshine followed, and whether or not Mother Nature decides to cooperate. In other words, blooming is just too hard to predict.

While there's no guarantee for abundant *Lupinus texensis* (the bluebonnet's proper name), you'll usually find plenty of opportunities to pose children amid the colored country fields for an Easter portrait. What the country's wildflower authorities will promise is that they'll pass along to you whatever bluebonnet and other flower information they have. Call the center's hotline, generally available from March 20 through May 30, at (512) 370–0000, ext. 9500. A five-minute recording, updated weekly, will offer the best highway routes in Texas for wildflower watching.

As the deeply blue carpet spreads northward from South Texas, we cross our fingers in hopes that the sapphire blooms—mixed in with the palette of Mexican hat, Indian paintbrush, black-eyed

Susans, primroses, and hundreds of others—will make a timely appearance in the Hill Country for a scattering of festivals. The Hill Country's upper reaches, called the Highland Lakes for the 150-mile, sparkly string of seven lakes formed by the Colorado River, are particularly vibrant for two weeks in spring when the Highland Lakes communities throw out floral welcome mats during the annual Bluebonnet Arts & Crafts Trail.

Here, it's easy to spend a day or a weekend at a medley of arts and crafts fairs, featuring works by more than five hundred artists in all, as well as related musical events, street parties, cook-offs, and fishing tournaments. Waterside pastimes—golf, tennis, and hiking among them—are handy, too, on cliff-lined lakes that offer more total shoreline than even the whole Texas coast. Stay the night at a lakefront resort, waterfront cabin, or bed-and-breakfast inn. Just pick your pace and do the self-guided tour, aided by a free Bluebonnet Trail brochure and map. Call the Highland Lakes bluebonnet hotline at (512) 793–2803 between 9:00 A.M. and 5:00 P.M. daily, from mid-March through the end of April.

Before you begin touring, you may want to note on your map the Hill Country's best lanes for spring wildflowers and year-round scenery. They include U.S. 281 from Lampasas south to San Antonio; Texas 16 from Llano south to Medina; U.S. 290 from Austin to west of Fredericksburg; Texas 71 from Austin northwest to Llano; Texas 29 from Burnet west to Llano; and Texas 46 from New Braunfels to just east of Bandera.

RANCHES AND LAKES

There's no better place to begin the Hill Country tour than in **Johnson City,** found about 50 miles west of Austin at the junction of U.S. 290 and U.S. 281. The seat of Blanco County, the town of only 932 residents and its nearby neighbor, **Stonewall** (just across the Gillespie County line, 16 miles west on U.S. 290), lay in relative obscurity a hundred peaceful years before one of the most colorful men in political history became president suddenly in 1963. Lyndon Baines Johnson was profoundly attached to his roots and made his family ranch in Stonewall, just 14 miles west of his Johnson City birthplace, the Texas White House.

◆ **The Lyndon B. Johnson National Historic Park,** with units on U.S. 281 in both Johnson City and Stonewall, and adjacent

Lyndon B. Johnson State Park do a fine job of detailing the heavy heritage of this bigger-than-life figure and his land. The national park visitor center has a multimedia program on the illustrious LBJ and Johnson City history, as well as a gift shop. There's also the president's boyhood home, a humble 1886 frame house where LBJ's parents moved in 1914; it's been restored and furnished to 1920s style.

The park's ranch unit spreads along the serene **Pedernales River** and is where LBJ retired (some say as a lonely and fractured man). National Park Service buses take groups through the grounds, to view the ranchhouse, cattle, family cemetery where LBJ is buried, and a reconstruction of the president's birthplace. A living historical farm, small church cemetery, two furnished, pioneer dogtrot-style houses, swimming pool, and tennis court are spread about the parks, but it's riverside picnic areas shaded by ancient live oaks that provide unparalleled peace. From here you can look across the water at cattle grazing on the Johnson Ranch and at the white ranch house where Lady Bird Johnson still spends time.

For details on the state park, contact park headquarters at (210) 644-2252 or 644-2241. For national park information, call (210) 868-7128.

Overnight stays in Johnson City are coziest at **Carolyne's Cottage** (103 Avenue D, 210-868-4548 or 868-4374), a bed and breakfast nestled in a native-stone house outfitted with English and Texas antiques and lace curtains. Breakfast goodies are stocked in the refrigerator.

Pedernales Falls State Park, about 10 miles east of Johnson City via Farm Road 2766, (210) 868-7304, is a stunning spread of nearly 5,000 acres of former ranch land with 6 miles of spectacular riverfront for tubing, swimming, fishing, hiking, and camping. The park is open daily and charges a small admission.

Another detour for naturalists is to **Westcave Preserve,** a thirty-acre nature reserve northeast of Johnson City, near the Pedernales River. A Lower Colorado River Authority property, Westcave is first seen as upland savannah, replete with wildflower meadows, before it descends to a verdant canyon formed hundreds of centuries ago when a huge limestone cave collapsed. As you hike along, you'll find an amazing development, as a spring-fed creek meanders a while before sharply turning into a 40-foot waterfall spilling into a radiantly green pool. Sensational bird watching and wildflower spotting can be had in the preserve. Tours are given Saturday and Sunday at 10:00 A.M., 12:00 noon, 2:00 P.M., and 4:00 P.M., weather permitting. No admission is charged but contributions are welcome. You can reach Westcave by driving north on U.S. 281 from Johnson City about 12 miles, turning east on Ranch Road 962, and continuing another 12 miles. For information, call (210) 825–3442.

From Johnson City, it's also easy to make a side trip to **Blanco,** south just 14 miles on U.S. 281. A bucolic burg of the first order, this is the place to go to spend idle hours on the Blanco River banks. Named the Blanco County seat upon organization in 1858, the town of 1,200 lies about 45 miles north of San Antonio.

The town's pride is the old **Blanco County courthouse**, a Second Empire design built in 1886 but then abandoned when the county seat moved to Johnson City in 1890. Now undergoing an impressive restoration effort, it is open to the public. For tour information, contact the Blanco Chamber of Commerce at (210) 833–5101.

Throughout the town, century-old limestone buildings are a testament to the German colony that settled in the river valley, and some of the best historic buildings line the **courthouse square**. Businesses here now include Lindeman's Grocery, a general store in business since 1870; a covey of antiques shops with some funky collectibles; a tiny library; and a handful of cafes.

Of more peculiar interest is the Weeping Icon, a Virgin Mary shrine at the ✦**Christ of the Hills Monastery.** She's said to have been found crying tears of myrrh by one of the monks less than ten years ago, and pilgrims come for services and to be annointed "with the tears of the Mother of God." Women are asked to wear dresses or long skirts, and all visitors are asked to speak softly. The monastery is about 5 miles west of town via Ranch Roads 102 and 103; call (210) 833–5363 for more information.

My Little Guest House is a cozy cottage facing the Blanco River, with breakfast fixings provided; on the river across from the park, (210) 833–5264. **Pecan St. Bakery and Cafe,** 306 Pecan Street, (210) 833–5737, is full of healthful lunches; offerings include bean soups, chicken salad, and a variety of muffins.

After your Blanco diversion, it's time to journey from Johnson City north on U.S. Highway 281 to the **Highland Lakes.** You'll

51

first reach **Lake Marble Falls** in Burnet County, about 25 miles north of Johnson City. Overlooking the lake is a town of the same name, at U.S. 281's junction with Ranch Road 1431, one of the Hill Country's most scenic highways. **Marble Falls,** with 4,000 residents, is home to **Granite Mountain,** situated just west on Ranch Road 1431, an 860-foot-tall dome of rusty-red granite sprawling across 186 acres. It's this rock source from which the spectacular state capitol in Austin was built over a century ago. You can see it from the highway, but the quarry isn't open to the public.

A good reason to stop in Marble Falls is to eat at the **Bluebonnet Cafe** (211 U.S. Highway 281, 210–693–2344), a delightful country diner serving Texas and southern specialties, such as chicken and dumplings, cobbler, catfish, chicken-fried steak, steaks, and all-day breakfasts. It's open for breakfast, lunch, and dinner daily.

During the spring bluebonnet season, the **Highland Arts Guild,** at 318 Main Street in this tiny but historic downtown, exhibits original paintings, sculpture, and crafts. For details, contact the Marble Falls Chamber of Commerce, (210) 693–4449.

The best scenic drives from Marble Falls can easily fill a morning or afternoon. Try heading northwest on Texas Highway 71 for a 32-mile jaunt to Texas Highway 16; or go west on Ranch Road 1431, which unwinds 18 miles through the tiny towns of **Granite Shoals** and **Kingsland** before its intersection with Texas Highway 29. This latter route follows the lakes trail, as the Colorado River meanders past dams creating Lake LBJ and then Inks Lake and Lake Buchanan Dam.

If you reach Kingsland during bluebonnet weekends, handcrafted items are exhibited and sold at the **Kingsland House of Arts and Crafts,** on Ranch Road 1431.

Lake LBJ, immediately west of Lake Marble Falls, lies on the line shared by Burnet and Llano counties and is probably the best liked of the Highland Lakes in terms of recreation and scenery. The 6,300-acre impoundment of the Colorado River is shielded from winds by tree-cloaked bluffs and granite cliffs and is consequently a big lake for water-skiing, sailing, jet-skiing, and fishing.

Some travelers who make Lake LBJ their destination settle in at ✦**Horseshoe Bay Country Club and Resort** (Ranch Road 2147 just west of U.S. 281, 800–531–5105, 800–252–9363, or

210–598–2511). Guests stay in hotel-style rooms, condos, or townhouses and spend time playing golf on three eighteen-hole courses spread around the lake. There's also a beach, marina, indoor and outdoor tennis, and stables.

Your traveling path will likely take you from Marble Falls 12 miles north on U.S. Highway 281 to **Burnet** (pronounced BURN-it), seat of Burnet County and home to 3,423 residents. Frontier Fort Croghan was established here in 1849, and the town grew up around it. Today, Burnet—known as one of the most interesting geologic spots in the world—is a magnet for rockhounds, as well as professional and amateur geologists.

◆**Longhorn Caverns State Park** (south on U.S. 281 5 miles to Park Road 4, 512–756–6976) is a remarkable, 11-mile underground maze of caves and passages a million years in the making. What's odd about this cavern is that it was the site of big speak-easy parties during Prohibition. Guided tours are scheduled frequently, and the snack bar and souvenir shop are better than some. Tour hours vary; admission is $6.00 for adults and $4.00 for children.

Newest to Burnet is the arrival of the **Hill Country Flyer,** a restored seventy-five-year-old steam locomotive making trips on Saturday and Sunday throughout the spring and summer. The train departs Cedar Park, about 20 miles northwest of Austin, at 10:00 A.M., arriving in Burnet at noon. Passengers shop and lunch until boarding for the two-hour return trip to Austin at 2:30 P.M. Tickets are about $25 for adults, $10 for children, or $40 for first class for all ages. For details and a complete schedule, call (512) 477–8468.

Burnet's Bluebonnet Trail offerings include a show from the **Burnet Creative Arts,** which includes original work by creators of ceramics, china paintings, oils, jewelry, stained glass, woodwork, weavings, and porcelain dolls. You'll find the show on Texas Highway 29 at the Catholic Educational Building. Call the Burnet Chamber of Commerce for details, (512) 756–4297.

Head west from Burnet to find wildlife adventure aboard the ◆**Vanishing Texas River Cruise.** To reach the dock, follow Texas 29 west just 4 miles from Burnet, then turn north on Ranch Road 2341 and watch for signs to the lakeside. At all times of the year, you'll see a variety of wildlife, plus waterfalls, cliffs, and primitive river, with the guidance of naturalists. From

Vanishing Texas River Cruise

November until March, emphasis is on the American bald eagles in their wintering grounds along the lake. Trips are usually two and a half hours. Sunset dinner cruises are offered May through October, and morning trips are offered year round. Tickets range from $8.95 for children and $12.95–$21.95 for adults. Reservations are required; call (512) 756–6986.

After the cruise, continue on Texas 29 west to **Inks Lake State Park,** just an 8-mile reach from Burnet, (512) 793–2223. This 1,200-acre spread—one of the smaller but prettier lakes in Texas—is perfect for anybody who wants beautiful surroundings in which to read, sketch, or write postcards, and it affords camping, picnicking, fishing, and hiking. The park is open daily and charges a small admission.

Just 5 miles west of Inks Lake via Texas Highway 29, across the line into Llano County, is the town of **Buchanan Dam** (pronounced buck-ANN'n), sitting on the lovely Lake Buchanan. Only 1,100 people call it home, but it's a busy place in mild weather and spring flower time. The 2-mile-long dam is a work of arches and is likely the largest multi-arch dam in the nation. Built in the 1930s, it holds the Colorado River and forms the highest and largest of the Highland Lakes. One of the better places to view the lake and dam is at the Lake Buchanan Chamber of Commerce office, on Texas Highway 29 in the observation building at the dam, (512) 793–2803.

From the town and lake, it's an easy, 14-mile side trip up to the town of Tow, on the lake's northwestern shore, to visit **Fall Creek Vineyards** (west on Texas 29, north on Texas 261, north on Ranch Road 2241; 915–379–5361 or 512–476–4477). One of the more successful wineries in the state, Fall Creek offers an impressive visitor center, guided tours, tasting room, and gift shop. Admission is free, but hours vary.

From Buchanan Dam, the Hill Country tour continues 17 miles west again on Texas Highway 29 to ◗**Llano,** seat of Llano County. Nearly 3,000 folks find Llano a comfortable place to live, and it's largely due to an undisturbed array of historic buildings. You'll want to explore the town one afternoon—it's easy to see on foot—to have a look at places such as the **Llano County Courthouse** (Main and Ford streets), built in 1892; **Acme Dry Goods** (109 West Main Street), dating to the same time; the **Southern Hotel** (201 West Main Street), built in 1881 and housing a century-old hardware business; and the **Old Llano County Jail** (Oatman Street, northeast of the courthouse), today occupied by a museum. All details are available from the Llano Chamber of Commerce, (915) 247–5354.

The town is extremely popular with deer hunters in late fall and with rockhounds year round. As the county is on the 1½-billion-acre **Llano Uplift,** described as a geological phenomenon, the ground is riddled with sensational finds of amethyst, azurite, dolomite, galena, garnet, quartz, serpentine, gold, and llanite, a brown granite with blue crystals and pink feldspar unique to this area.

People have been known to drive quite a way to eat Llano's barbecue. **Cooper's,** just west of Texas 16 on Texas 29 (705 West Young Street, 915–247–3003), produces outstanding smoked ribs, brisket, pork, chicken, sausage, and cabrito (baby goat), with a fine pot of beans and savory barbecue sauce. It's open for lunch and dinner daily.

A delightful place to overnight in Llano is the **Badu House**, a two-story bed-and-breakfast inn (601 Bessemer Street, 915–247–4304). A converted bank, the building dates to the town's iron boom in 1891 and is included on the National Register of Historic Places. Antiques are used throughout the inn, and the downstairs bar is covered by the world's largest piece of polished llanite, discovered by N. J. Badu, who transformed the bank into a home years ago.

The wildflower period in spring signals a show and sale of paintings, sculpture, drawings, weavings, pottery, and more at **Llano Fine Arts Guild Gallery** (503 Bessemer Avenue, 915–247–5354).

Llano is the best place to strike out for a side trip to ◆ **Colorado Bend State Park.** Reach it by driving north on Texas 16 for 16 miles, then, inside San Saba County, turn east on Ranch Road 501 for 15 miles. A relatively new park, it's not yet well known and is sometimes a private Eden for travelers. Beautiful scenery unwinds along the banks of the Colorado River, where primitive camping sites, hiking trails, and picnicking areas are scattered. Anglers say the fishing is unsurpassed, and occasional tours aboard the Vanishing Texas River Cruise make stops at the park. The park is open daily and charges a small admission. For information, call (915) 628–3240.

ROCKS AND WILDLIFE

From Llano, point your car northwest on Texas Highway 71 to **Brady.** It's a 54-mile drive to the seat of McCulloch County, home to 7,000 residents, and the town closest to the geographic center of Texas—hence the nickname, the Heart of Texas.

Any Texan who holds Lone Star foods near and dear to the heart can tell you Brady is the site of the ◆ **World Championship Barbecue Goat Cook-Off,** held annually on the Friday and Saturday before Labor Day. Don't laugh—the competition draws over one hundred teams from around the United States and from abroad. The weekend brings plenty of entertainment and unique contests, all held at Richards Park on Commerce Street, just west of downtown. Admission is free; for details call (915) 597–3491.

For a look into the past, check out the **Heart of Texas Historical Museum** (High and Main streets, 915–597–3491), a converted old jail (1910–74) that rises three stories into the sky and resembles a castle. You'll see exhibits on area history and the background of the jail cells and gallows. Open Saturday through Monday, 1:00 P.M. until 5:00 P.M.; admission is free.

In case you miss the cook-off and want to sample some barbecued goat before heading out of town, stop in at **Charlie's Barbecue and Steakhouse** (U.S. Highway 87 at the railroad tracks, 915–597–0603). Besides goat, there's tender beef brisket and mammoth steaks. Open for lunch and dinner daily.

Anyone who finds romance in history—and has a soft spot for animals—will want to stop in **Mason,** south of Brady 28 miles via U.S. Highway 377. The seat of Mason County—home to just two thousand—took its name from Fort Mason, built in the early 1850s as one in a chain of army posts established to protect against Indian attacks between the Red River and the Rio Grande.

Mason was unusual among Texas towns in that it endured an internal war in the 1870s when cattle rustlings and prejudices between German and Anglo settlers stirred up angry emotions; the upshot is that more than ten men were killed in ambushes and lynchings before the Texas Rangers were summoned to reestablish peace in the community.

You can explore the fort and town history at ◆ **Fort Mason Officers Quarters** (Rainey and Post Hill streets, 915–347–5758). Among the illustrious soldiers who were once stationed at the fort were George Armstrong Custer, Albert Sidney Johnston, and Robert E. Lee. Today's fort is a reconstruction on the original foundation, and a miniature of the fort is among the exhibits. The museum is open daily, but it's best to call ahead for hours.

If you read the book or saw the film *Old Yeller*, you probably never stopped crying long enough to wonder where its author, Fred Gipson, was from; Mason, it turns out, was his hometown. Gipson and other local notables are detailed in the local library, found at Post Hill and Schmidt streets.

Rather unexpectedly you'll come upon the **Reynolds-Seaquist Home** (400 Broad Street, 915–347–5413), a sensational three-story, Queen Anne Victorian mansion. Remarkable are its twenty-two rooms, fifteen fireplaces, beautiful wooden staircase constructed without nails, galleries wrapping around two stories on the exterior, and third-floor ballroom. The house was started in 1891, then renovated in 1919 by a Swede who made his fortune in boots. Tours are scheduled by appointment, and at least four people are required for a tour; admission is $5.00 per person.

There's no shortage of down-home, country stays in the Mason area: There's **Bridges House Bed & Breakfast** (108 Olmos Street, 915–347–6440 or 800–776–3519), an 1884 home in a historic area with porches and lovely antiques; **Hasse House** (east from town square 6 miles on Texas Highway 29, 915–347–6463), a spacious place on a 300-acre working ranch; and **Martin Guest Ranch** (south 9 miles on Farm Road 1723, 915–347–6852), a 5,000-acre ranch on the Llano River with modern cabins, big lodge, game room, hiking, fishing, swimming, and innertubing.

Finally, rockhounds will be thrilled at the area's fantastic variety of minerals and rocks located in the geologic outcroppings. Specifically, blue topaz, the state gem—a rarity in North America—is found here. The public can hunt topaz at the **Seaquist Ranch** (915–347–5413) and the **Hofmann Ranch** (915–347–6415); both are situated just northwest of Mason, charge fees, and permit camping.

Continuing along the Hill Country trail, turn southwest on U.S. Highway 377 and go 39 miles through big deer-hunting country to **Junction,** the seat of Kimble County, home to about 2,600 people and more flowing streams than any other Texas county.

Most people citing Junction as a destination do so for its wildlife watching and other outdoorsy pursuits. ❸**South Llano River State Park** (4 miles south of town on U.S. 377, 915–446–3994) is just the right place for these, as animals often seen here include white-tailed deer, wood ducks, fox squirrels, rock squirrels, javelina, and the Rio Grande turkey. The turkey roost in bottomlands, and this site is closed to visitors from October through March. At the park, enjoy camping, hiking, picnicking, canoeing, and innertubing between wildlife sightings. The spring-fed river is simple pleasure itself.

Even more spectacular scenery is ahead, however. From Junction, take U.S. Highway 83 south, making a 57-mile journey to **Leakey** (LAY-kee), the Real County seat and a town of 400 tucked into an especially picturesque corner of the Edwards Plateau. About 12 miles shy of town, you'll be happy if you packed a picnic lunch, because there's a particularly good road-side park with superb scenery right there.

Although you won't see Comanches and Apaches living in the area around Leakey as did the Spanish explorers, you will find flocks of registered Angora goats, from which area ranchers harvest mohair. This, too, is a popular hunting ground for white-tailed deer, mourning dove, quail, wild turkey, and javelina.

Consider taking a day or two to revel in the surroundings, putting your feet up at a places such as **River Run Villas** (intersection of Farm Road 1120 and Farm Road 2748, 210–232–5695), offering condos, swimming pool, and access to the Rio Frio (Frio River to gringos); **Rio Frio Bed and Breakfast** (Farm Road 1120 and Farm Road 2748, 210–232–6633), with cabins and homes on the river; and **River Haven Cabins** (Farm Road 1120, 210–232–5400), with log cabins and fireplaces.

An appealing park in the area is ◆ **Garner State Park** on the Frio River, just inside Uvalde County, a 9-mile drive south of Leakey via U.S. Highway 83. Here, the fun in warm weather is all about settling into a big innertube and floating down the clear, cold Frio, surrounded by limestone shelves and shady cypress lining the way. Stone-and-timber cabins at the park offer a comfortable night's rest; call (210) 232–6132 for reservations. Other diversions include pedal boats, miniature golf, camping, hiking, fishing, and grocery facilities. (Note: Spring break crowds tend to be wild.) The park is open daily, and a small admission is charged.

If the park is full, check out **Neal's Vacation Lodges,** right on the Frio River near the park, (210) 232–6118; rustic cabins are available, and Neal's cafe serves country breakfast, lunch, and dinner.

From Garner State Park, your next destination is east on Farm Road 1050—one you'll always remember for climbing views of bluffs and valleys and blooming cactus—15 miles to ◆ **Utopia,** an appropriately named town if ever one existed. The farming-ranching hamlet—population just 360—in Uvalde County was established on Sabinal Creek in 1852 and is a second home to hunters and campers; spring wildflowers and fall foliage bring plenty of fans, too.

Sparkling spring water drinkers have likely heard of Utopia by now—the crystal liquid is bottled here and shipped around the world. Notice how at the post office, the general store, and the cafe, all those friendly people seem unusually happy? It must be the water.

Unbeatable country cooking is the pride at **Lost Maples Cafe** (in the middle of town on Ranch Market 187, 210–966–2221). Chat with the local game warden, park rangers, neighboring farmers, and outgoing staffers over Frisbee-sized pancakes or fresh-fresh chicken-fried steak, enormous baked potatoes, and barbecue.

People who want the restoration found in long, breathtaking drives come to the Leakey-Utopia area to see where the Frio, Nueces, and Sabinal rivers etched vividly shaded canyons, from which hills and mesas rise between 1,500 and 2,400 feet. The specific drives from Leakey that attract photographers, painters, and other artists of the soul are Farm Road 337 west to Camp Wood, past wooded rises and lonely, green valleys—colored purple in spring with mountain laurel; and Farm Road 337 east into Bandera County to **Vanderpool**, then north on Ranch Market 187.

◗ **Lost Maples State Natural Area** is on every Texas fall foliage fan's list as a must-see, but be assured the park is roaring with beauty in all seasons. These bigtooth maples are said to be lost because they're far from any other stands of their kind, which are scattered over the western United States and northern Mexico. The brilliant orange, red, and gold peak is usually in early November, and crowds tend to be staggering.

There are more than 90 plant families in the park, represented by more than 350 species. Bird population is healthy, as well, with the golden-cheeked warbler among uncommon finds. Camping and hiking are the park's other big draws, and reservations are a good idea; call (210) 966–3413. The park is open daily, and admission is $3.00 per vehicle on weekdays, $4.00 on weekends.

The town of Vanderpool, population twenty, is 4 miles south of the park on Ranch Market 187. You'll find accommodations here, including **Foxfire Cabins** (1 mile south of the park facing the Sabinal River, 210–966–2200), offering log cabins; **Las Campanas Guest Ranch** (3 miles from the park, 210–966–3431), a resort with wildlife photo tours; **Mountain View Ranch** (3 miles north of town on Ranch Market 187, 210–966–6136), a bed and breakfast and country house; and **Tubbs Heritage House** (Old Utopia Road, 210–966–3510).

The Texas Longhorn

EXOTICS, DUDES, AND GERMANS

From Vanderpool, journey north on Farm Road 187 for 19 miles to Texas Highway 39, then eastward on Texas 39 26 miles, through the town of **Ingram** to the intersection of Texas Highway 27; take this highway just another 7 miles east into **Kerrville,** the seat of Kerr County, largest city in the Hill Country and home to more than 17,000 people.

Easily the spiritual center of the Hill Country, Kerrville straddles the peaceful **Guadalupe River** and captures all that Texans treasure about this agreeable region—clean air, clear water, limestone bluffs, and pure repose. Kerrville owes its success to developer Charles Schreiner, who became a Texas Ranger at age sixteen and later served as a captain in the Civil War, and whose grandson brought the Texas longhorn breed back from the brink of extinction.

An enduring foundation of the area, Schreiner's ◆ **Y.O. Ranch,** 26 miles west on Interstate 10 and Texas Highway 41, is a top working ranch and a top attraction in the state. Forty thousand acres remain of Schreiner's 550,000 acquired in 1880, and a Longhorn Trail Drive is still held annually one weekend in early May. There are herds and herds of longhorn, sheep, and goats, plus free-ranging animals from around the globe; this is considered North America's largest collection of exotic wildlife.

In all, there are some ten thousand of fifty-five species, including wildebeest, oryx, addax, Japanese sika, aoudad, black buck antelope, ostrich, giraffe, zebra, and Watusi cattle, to name a few. The owner-family's conservation efforts are visible in the ranch's programs for children. Most day-trippers come for a tour and chuckwagon lunch, while springtime brings photo safaris and an annual cattle drive. Summer afternoons are whiled away in a pretty swimming pool, and horseback rides can be arranged. Century-old log cabins and a former ranch home accommodate thirty-five overnight guests. For details and reservations, call the ranch at (210) 640–3222.

You may spend a day seeing the Y.O.'s animals, but you won't want to miss a weekend in town, where culture and cowboys prevail. Kerrville's a bastion of artistic diversity, with folk music and folk art festivals in May, and then there's the **World Mohair Extravaganza in January,** billed by organizers as the World Series of Goat Shearing. Along with shorn goats at the Hill Country Youth Exhibit Center, you can find a trade show offering a variety of fleeces and fabrics. Demonstrations include spinners and sheep dogs at work, while arts and crafts and a mohair fashion show are also on the bill. For details contact the chamber of commerce at (210) 896–1155.

Kerrville is also home to possibly the nation's only museum dedicated to the work of a single group of living artists. The ◆ **Cowboy Artists of America Museum** features the paintings and sculptures of about thirty members, some of whom are considered the country's foremost artists of Western American Realism. The building itself is wonderfully artful, incorporating light Mexican brick in *bóveda* domes that need no supporting forms or wiring. The museum charges $2.50 admission for adults, $1.00 for children, and is just south of downtown on Texas 173; call (210) 896–2553 for more information. The museum is open Monday through Saturday, 9:00 A.M. until 5:00 P.M., and Sunday, 1:00 P.M. until 5:00 P.M. It's closed Monday, September through May.

For a lovely sunset drive, head west from Kerrville on **Ranch Road 1340**, which winds its way through the scenic communitites of Ingram and Hunt. The ribbon of road twists and turns, repeatedly crossing the Guadalupe River, passing a scattering of summer cottages, boys' and girls' summer camps, and deer-hunting country. In the middle of one field, you'll see a Stonehenge replica, of all things.

There are three good places to find rest in Kerrville, starting with the **Inn of the Hills River Resort** (1001 Junction Highway, 210–895–5000), a spreading complex with motel rooms, suites, and condo-apartments. Four pools, pretty landscaping, games and activities for kids in summer, three restaurants, an exercise facility with sauna and whirlpool, bowling lanes, putting green, bike and boat rentals, fishing in a stocked lake, and lighted tennis courts make this a full-service resort.

The **Y.O. Ranch Hilton** (2033 Sidney Baker Boulevard, 210–257–4440) is a charming hotel accented with western design. The huge lobby is lighted with chandeliers crafted from branding irons and is dominated by a bronze of a mounted cowboy working to bring a longhorn back to the herd. Room furnishings continue the theme.

Lazy Hills Guest Ranch (west on Texas Highway 27, just past Ingram, 210–367–5600) offers horseback riding, tennis, swimming, fishing, hot tubbing, and family-style dining in a beautiful hilly setting.

Next stop after Kerrville is found north on Texas 16, 24 miles away in **Fredericksburg**, seat of Gillespie County. Texas's cache of German heritage is a miniature Bavarian treat with a proliferation of bed-and-breakfast lodgings, the backbone of Old World touring. In Fredericksburg guests have the state's largest selection of places to spend rest periods off the road in quaint historic homes and inns, much more appealing to some than sleeping in cookie-cutter hotels. Here you'll make new friends along the way, sharing a cup of tea, a glass of wine, or breakfast with hosts and fellow guests.

Fredericksburg's B&B abundance has fairly mushroomed in recent years, numbering around 110 today—a remarkable count for a town of around 7,000 people. Descriptions vary widely, from tiny, cute cottages to big Victorian homes and rambling ranch houses. Inside, owners have created atmosphere with decor that can be anything from country charm to sophisticated luxury. Rates include breakfast, of course, which may be of the lighter continental variety or an elaborate multicourse affair. For information, call the Fredericksburg Convention & Visitors Bureau, (210) 997–6523. Or, contact the three reservation services handling most of Fredericksburg's B&B business: Gastehaus Schmidt, (210) 997–5612; Bed and Breakfast of Fredericksburg, (210) 997–4712; and Be My Guest, (210) 997–8555.

Fredericksburg Inn on the Square is an imposing Victorian residence a block off Main Street, with three impressive bedrooms and a rear cottage. The Willow Suite on the home's first floor is beloved for its four-poster canopy bed, bare rock walls, and cellar sitting room. Four porches surrounding the house are laden with locally handcrafted willow furniture, and the yard is a visual feast of blooms. Make reservations directly by calling (210) 997–7083.

While in Fredericksburg, take time to explore history a bit. The town was the 1885 birthplace of Admiral Chester W. Nimitz, commander-in-chief of the Pacific fleet during World War II. A tribute to him is the ◆**Admiral Nimitz State Historical Park,** a collection of attractions at 340 East Main Street, including the restored Nimitz Steamboat Hotel, a renowned frontier inn that hosted U. S. Grant, Robert E. Lee, and Jesse James and now is home to the Museum of the Pacific War. Behind the building is the Garden of Peace, a gift from Japan, and across the street a history walk winds through an array of rare aircraft, tanks, and guns. The park is open daily, 8:00 A.M. until 5:00 P.M., and a small admission is charged; (210) 997–4379.

Shoppers will delight in Fredericksburg's **Main Street**, thick with boutiques and stores, selling everything from candles, books, quilts, and pewter mugs to straw hats, peach jelly, and primitive antiques. Ranch-style housewares, such as candlesticks shaped like cowboys, and kitchen accessories decorated with ranch brands are sold at Chisum, no. 138; headboards painted with Western designs are stocked at Homestead, no. 223; dried herbs and flowers, herbal bath gel and soaps, herbal teas, and edible flowers are sold at Fredericksburg Herb Farm's shop at no. 222; and artwork by Western artist G. Harvey is offered at the

Peach Tree, no. 148B. Along the way, bakeries and German beer gardens are welcome rest stops.

If you happen upon Fredericksburg just before the Christmas holidays, see if you're in time for **Kristkindl Markt,** an Old World–style affair staged at Market Square in the center of town. The Fredericksburg Shopkeepers Guild creates a Christmas village featuring music, German foods, handcrafted toys and gifts, art, and sweets. Admission is $4.00 for adults, $1.00 for children. For details, call the guild at (210) 997–8515.

Without question, the best food in the Hill Country is found at the ◆ **Hill Top Cafe,** 11 miles northwest of Fredericksburg via U.S. 87. Specialties include crawfish étouffée, frog legs, Greek salads, chicken-fried steak, and fresh fish with deluxe herb-and-spice treatments, as well as spectacular desserts; reservations are advised, (210) 997–8922. Open from 6:00 P.M., Wednesday through Saturday.

For schnitzel, bratwurst, burgers, and Tex-Mex, stay right in Fredericksburg and try the **Altdorf Biergarten and Restaurant,** 301 West Main Street, (210) 997–7774; open for lunch and dinner, Wednesday through Monday.

Side trips from Fredericksburg are abundant, and the first to consider is the jaunt to ◆ **Enchanted Rock State Park,** 18 miles north of town on Ranch Road 965. The park surrounds an otherworldly, huge, monolithic dome of pink granite, rising 600 feet into the sky—a challenge perfect for ambitious hikers. Climb it if you have stamina, good athletic shoes, and the foresight to have arrived early enough to find a parking space inside the park. The surprising vegetation up top is as impressive as the views, particularly in the first light of day. On summer nights, the huge rock creaks and moans as it cools down, an occurrence the Comanches understandably found to be of a powerfully spiritual nature. The park is open daily and charges a small admission. Details from (915) 247–3903.

If you tackle Enchanted Rock in the morning, leave the afternoon free to take what's possibly the most unusual scenic drive in Texas, the ◆ **Willow City Loop.** To begin this adventure, head north from town on Texas Highway 16 about 12 miles, then turn east on Farm Road 1323, and you'll go just 3 miles before picking up one of Texas's more fiercely beautiful roads at the town of Willow City. Watch for a little wooden sign indicating the

Willow City Loop and get ready for a sensory trip: Drive a ridge the first few of the 13 miles, then prepare to swoop down into Coal Creek Valley, also called the Devil's Kitchen, the Dungeon, and even Hell's Half-Acre. Centuries ago, heavenly bodies crashed into the ground here, leaving a massive depression filled with sleek meteoric rocks. The valley vistas of bluebonnets in spring go on forever, giving rise to Cedar Mountain, whose blooming yuccas crown the picture. Here, 8 miles into the drive, find Texas's sole serpentine quarry, where the stone with a luminous polish is mined for terrazzo floors. Oh, and watch for wandering cattle on the road.

Another diversion out of Fredericksburg is found at **Oberhellmann Vineyards** (Texas 16 north about 14 miles, 210-685-3297), one of several Hill Country vineyards. This winery scales the side of Bell Mountain and offers its products—including Chardonnays, Rieslings, and pinot noirs—for tasting on tour day, Saturday, Easter to Christmas.

The most famous detour of all is ◆**Luckenbach,** population twenty-five, reached by driving 6 miles east of town on U.S. 290, then turning south (right) on Ranch Road 1376; continue on this little road about 5 miles till you see signs. If you cross the creek, you've gone too far—maybe it's time to stop and ask directions, as signs to Luckenbach just don't last long, thanks to souvenir hunters.

"In Luckenbach, Texas, ain't nobody feelin' no pain," is how the Willie Nelson–Waylon Jennings song goes, and, honestly, everybody feels fine when they're in Luckenbach because it's mostly a state of mind. It isn't even a town, but a little pocket of peace where the population is really just the number of people sitting around drinking longnecks on the porch of the eternally unpainted general store, playing dominoes, or pitching horseshoes. Some Saturday nights you'll find the dance hall overflowing with folks two-steppin' to the likes of Gary P. Nunn, who stops in occasionally to entertain the idea of going "home with the armadillo" in his song "London Homesick Blues."

An 1850 German settlement, Luckenbach was unremarkable for more than a century, with the exception of Jacob Brodbeck, who—twenty-five years before the Wright Brothers—invented an airplane powered with coiled springs. He abandoned the project after a discouraging crash in 1865.

Luckenbach post office

Then in the 1970s humorist-writer and legendary Texas character Hondo Crouch invited like souls to share in Luckenbach's bucolic remoteness, laced with bluebonnets and pioneer flavor. This made it a place where "everybody's somebody," as prescribed by Waylon Jennings and Jerry Jeff Walker, whose song propelled the tiny spot in the road into fame.

The Hell-Hath-No-Fury-Like-A-Woman-Scorned Chili Society found a friend in Hondo, and Luckenbach's lazy pace would forever be radically altered one weekend each year. The group—formed when a woman was turned down as an entrant in a Texas chili cook-off—hosts its **Ladies' State Championship Chili Cook-Off** in Luckenbach annually on the first weekend in October.

You can find great T-shirts, postcards (stamped with a Luckenbach postmark), jewelry, snacks, beer, and plenty of conversation in the general store, and a barbecue stand next to the dance hall is open generally on weekends. For information, call the general store at (210) 997-3224.

From Fredericksburg, the tour continues south on U.S. Highway 87 to **Comfort,** a 23-mile drive. Barely inside the Kendall County line, the borough of almost 1,500 was settled in 1854 by free-thinking German intellectuals, some of whom later joined Union forces in the Civil War; you'll see the Treue Der Union Monument, a tribute to them, on High Street between Third and Fourth streets.

Comfort is also known for being batty: the ❖ **Hygieostatic Bat Roost,** 1½ miles east on Farm Road 473, was a 1918 experiment; seventy-five years later, the bats still use it. Sunset is the time to watch for them here and at the Old Railroad Tunnel, 14 miles north via Farm Road 473 and Old Highway 9, where several thousand bats live in a tunnel abandoned in 1942.

Take a stroll down **High Street**, particularly the 800 block, to have a close-up look at one of the state's more complete nineteenth-century business districts still intact. The Chamber of Commerce office, at Seventh and High streets, (210) 995–3131, has free, helpful guides. Of particular interest to shoppers is **Comfort Common** (818 High Street, 210–995–3030), a bevy of antiques and gift boutiques in the old Ingenhuett-Faust Hotel. Note that the Common doubles as a bed-and-breakfast inn.

Cozy sleepovers can be had, too, at **Gast Haus Lodge** (952 High Street, 210–995–2304), a historic little hostelry with a swimming pool and fishing behind the complex in Cypress Creek. The main building was a stage stop in Comfort's earliest days.

Do arrive in Comfort with an appetite, as the home cooking at **Cypress Creek Inn** (Texas Highway 27 at the Cypress Creek Bridge, 210–995–3977) aims to fill you up with chicken-fried steak, sausage, liver and onions, fried chicken, or meat loaf. And please leave room for dessert—the pies are super.

❖ **Camp Verde,** west of Comfort 17 miles via Texas 27 and then Ranch Road 480, is barely a wide spot in the road. The community has only forty residents but a Texas-sized heritage. At its heart is Camp Verde General Store, in continuous operation since 1857 (intersection of Texas 173 and Ranch Road 480, 210–634–7722). Inside, you'll find great souvenirs such as camel bells, T-shirts, gift baskets, Hill Country jams and jellies, wood carvings, books, and home decor items. Don't forget to ask about (and buy for yourself) the store's lucky pigs—the stories you'll hear are memorable. For a snack, pick up some homemade tamales, fried pies, jelly beans, or hard candies.

The camel theme you probably noticed in the store recalls a military experiment in 1856, in which Secretary of War Jefferson Davis established Camp Verde to house his new camel corps for the U.S. Army. He had camels and handlers shipped here to prove that camels would be a good means of communication and transportation through the arduous west to Fort Yuma, California. While there was some success, the fort was commandeered by Confederate forces in 1861, and the camels were allowed to die or wander away. All that remains is the store.

If you're ready to be a dude, head south on Texas 173, about 15 miles to **Bandera,** the Bandera County seat and home to a population of nearly 900, and growing fast. It claims the title "Cowboy Capital of the World" not just for its cattle-drive and ranching heritage but also for the record number of National Rodeo Champions who lived there or still do. And, what travelers most like to find, Bandera is home to seven terrific dude ranches.

Long before dudes began showing up, about forty Texas Rangers were ambushed by several hundred Comanches in Bandera in 1841. Peace eventually prevailed, and settlers arrived in 1852, finding the cypress-and-live-oak–laden banks of the Medina River a good place to put down roots. The primitive countryside about 45 miles west of San Antonio still holds that appeal, and vacationing cowboys and cowgirls have all the western-style fun they want.

The dude ranches each offer family lodging in bunkhouses or cabins, horseback and hay rides, trick-roping and snake-handling (!) demonstrations, rodeos, country-western dancing, chuckwagon meals on the trail, golfing, swimming, fishing, and innertubing on the river.

✦ **Dixie Dude Ranch** (9 miles south of town on Ranch Road 1077, 210–796–7771 or 800–375–9255) has been in the family for more than fifty years, and now the fourth generation is running the 800-acre spread. The place is nothing if not homey, and guests find themselves making friends from all over the globe during fried-chicken suppers, poolside cookouts, and Saturday-night barbecues. The ranch hands—especially good at matching riders with mounts—lead trail rides through a wild terrain, pointing out historic sites along the way.

Mayan Dude Ranch (1½ miles northwest of town via Main and Pecan streets, 210–796–3312) is more like summer camp; it's an all-year affair for a hundred or more guests of all ages. Days begin with cowboy-made breakfast on a trail beside the Medina River and usually continue in the saddle or in the Olympic-sized pool. Nights are never dull—each one brings a different theme and activity, such as a Mexican fiesta, a ghost-town trip and steak fry, or a cocktails-barbecue-and-ice-cream party. The **Flying L Ranch** (1½ miles south on Texas 173, 210–796–3001 or 800–292–5134) has golf and tennis facilities, along with horseback riding.

Nearby, **Bandera Hideaway** (5 miles north of town on Texas Highway 16, 210–396–3739) sits on the river and offers a main house and guest house; and **Bandera Homestead** (4 miles east of town on Texas 16, 210–796–3051) has condos, a pool, tennis, and river frontage. Also, **Hackberry Lodge** (2 blocks off Main Street, 210–796–7134) is an 1890 hotel with suites, kitchenettes, and fireplaces.

If you're on your own for meals, the **OST**—named for the Old Spanish Trail on which Bandera lies—(305 Main Street, 210–796–3836) will do you right with its chicken-fried steak, biscuits, and gravy; Mexican food; and grilled steaks.

Even people just passing through Bandera should take just thirty minutes or so to have a peek at one of the funkier collections ever assembled: The **Frontier Times Museum** (506 Thirteenth Street, 210–796–3864) exhibits more than 40,000 items, including bottles from Judge Roy Bean's saloon; 500 bells from around the world; antique firearms and saddles; and spear- and arrowheads.

Bandera Downs (2 miles east of town on Texas Highway 16, 210–796–7781) has parimutuel racing of thoroughbreds and quarter horses from early March through late October. The **Texas International Apple Festival** comes in midsummer; contact the Bandera Convention & Visitors Bureau, (800) 364–3833, for more information.

After living the ranch life, it may be time to search for more of that German Hill Country; you can do that by driving east on Texas Highway 46 23 miles from Bandera to **Boerne** (BURN-ee), seat of Kendall County, with a population of more than 4,200. The cerebral Germans who settled the town in 1851 named it for Ludwig Boerne, one of their fellow countrymen who was a political satirist, journalist, and refugee. You may run into day-trippers from San Antonio, just 30 miles southeast, while out browsing through the creaky old antiques shops—packed with great little finds—or at one of the pleasant restaurants in town. You can't go hungry in Boerne, that's certain. A favorite is ◆**Po Po Family Restaurant** (at Interstate 10, 7 miles west of Boerne, at the Welfare exit, 210–537–4194), in an old stone house and former dance hall decorated with an array of at least one thousand china plates on the wall, serving solid American and southern fare. It's open daily for lunch and dinner.

Also, consider **Cafe Ye Kendall Inn** (128 West Blanco Street, 210-249-2138), where steaks, seafood, and salads are good choices. It's in a two-story inn, dating to 1859, facing the town square (800–364–2138).

Spelunkers will be happy to know that two caves open to the public are nearby. The larger is **Cascade Caverns** (3 miles south on Interstate 10 to Cascade Caverns Road, 210–755–8080), fascinating for its 90-foot interior waterfall, crashing from an underground stream. Tours last forty-five minutes; a nice park with campsites, picnic areas, dance pavilion, swimming pool, snack bar, and bunkhouses is outside the cave. Admission is $6.95 for adults, $4.75 for children; open Wednesday through Monday, 9:00 A.M. until 5:00 P.M.

The smaller, far less commercial cave is simply known as ◆**Cave Without a Name** (Farm Road 474 east 6 miles to Kruetzberg Road, 5 miles along this road to the cave, 210–537–4212), so called because the 1939 contest held to give it a title was won by a local boy who declared the cave "too pretty to name." It isn't easy to find, as the directional signs are greatly faded, but it's worth the effort. The cave, 98 percent still active, is enormous—it takes from about an hour to ninety minutes to tour—and is filled with stalagmites and stalactites, soda straws, strips of bacon, gnomes, and all sorts of mushrooming formations. Call ahead for tour schedules, which change without much notice; admission is $5.00 for adults, $2.00 for children.

◆**Guadalupe River State Park** (Texas 46 and Park Road 31, 16 miles east of Boerne, 210–438–2656) occupies 1,900 acres where cypress, limestone bluffs, and natural rapids blend to make a place of beauty on the gracious Guadalupe River. Canoeing, fishing, hiking, camping, and nature study are all available. Open daily; admission is $3.00 per vehicle on weekdays, $5.00 weekends.

Just in case you haven't had enough of Texas's rich German heritage, more awaits in **New Braunfels**, a 43-mile drive east of

71

Boerne on Texas 46. The seat of Comal County, New Braunfels has more than 27,000 citizens and a history that was almost very romantic.

The story goes that the town was settled in 1845 by a German prince and 200 immigrants; the prince named his establishment for the town in Germany where his castle stood. He was to build a new castle for his fiancée, Princess Sophie, but she refused to come to this rough, unknown land, so he returned home to marry her and never saw Texas again. This and the remaining history of New Braunfels are told at the **Sophienburg Museum**—named for her anyway—at 401 West Coll Street, (210) 629–1572.

The newest addition to New Braunfels is the **Hummel Museum** (199 Main Plaza, 800–572–2626 or 210–625–2385), featuring the art of a German nun, M. I. Hummel. Hummels, as they're known, are the famous figurines of children who have a certain Alps-and-Black-Forest appeal. These and the Hummel plates are collector's items, and they're costly. Sister Hummel was the creator of more than 500 drawings prior to and throughout World War II; the New Braunfels collection, which for the moment contains 300-plus, is the world's largest Hummel exhibit. Usually the display contains about eighty drawings, and some extremely valuable illustrations will be visiting exhibits from time to time.

One of the state's lovelier places to rest is the **Prince Solms Inn** (295 East San Antonio Street, 210–625–9169), a luxury bed-and-breakfast hotel, filled with antiques and housing a fine restaurant, Wolfgang's Keller. The historic **Faust Hotel** (240 South Seguin Street, 210–625–7791) is restored and filled with antiques.

If you happen upon New Braunfels in the fall, plan to dance a polka and drink a stein or two to the oompah-pah in Wursthalle, as the town hosts well over a hundred thousand people each year at **Wurstfest**, an enormous German party held over the first two weekends in November. A generous schedule of events is always offered, as is food and drink. For details, call (210) 625–9167.

If you miss the celebration, there's always good German food ready at **Krause's Cafe** (148 South Castell Street, 210–625–7581), a 1938 establishment with the basics, plus chili, chicken, steaks, and sinful pies.

For anyone looking for a little watery excitement, head north a couple of miles to the restored town of **Gruene** (north on Interstate 35 to Farm Road 306, west about a mile and a half to Hunter Road, then follow the signs). There, on the Guadalupe River, several river outfitters (call 210–625–2385 for a list) offer trips lasting anywhere from three to five hours. If it's late spring or early summer, the river will probably run high and fast, so do as the instructors say and paddle like crazy through the little rapids. If it's late in summer and there hasn't been much rain, you're likely to have a slow trip. For a lonely, peaceful trip, tackle the river on a weekday, when high-spirited rafters and tubers won't be clogging the waters.

While in Gruene, plan to spend time poking around ❖ **Gruene Historic District**, a quaint 1870s cotton-gin town containing what is now the oldest dance hall in Texas; restored buildings housing antiques shops, clothing boutiques, woodwork, leather goods, and pottery shops; a winery tasting room; and good restaurants, starting with the **Gristmill** (1287 Gruene Road, 210–625–0684), purveyors of excellent fried catfish, grilled chicken, steaks, burgers, and frosty margaritas. Weekend nights, there's live music on the patio under the stars.

Next door to the Gristmill, **Gruene Mansion Inn** (1275 Gruene Road, 210–629–2641) is a gorgeous Victorian home overlooking the Guadalupe River and operating as a bed-and-breakfast inn.

From New Braunfels, head north on Interstate 35 just 16 miles to reach **San Marcos,** seat of Hays County and home to nearly 29,000 residents. The headwaters of the San Marcos River are here, where Indians are thought to have lived some 12,000 years ago, making this one of the oldest continuously inhabited places on the continent. Springs forming the river come from the Edwards Underground Reservoir, pushing up through the Balcones Escarpment limestone at a rate of at least a million gallons daily.

San Marcos is famous mostly for ❖ **Aquarena Springs** (in the middle of town at Interstate 35 exit 206, 512-396-8900), which sits on the shore of Spring Lake, which is fed by the same underwater springs that feed the San Marcos River. Here, attractions are Texas's only collection of glass-bottom boats; the Submarine Theater; a Mexican market in hillside gardens; mission ruins; a diving pig named Ralph; a skyride across the lake; Texana Village, containing the town's first log cabin; and a revamped, 1928 resort inn (210–396–8901 or 800–999–9767).

From San Marcos, you're in for a day in shopping heaven and a charming bed-and-breakfast night at ◆ **Wimberley,** a 15-mile drive west of San Marcos via Ranch Road 12. It's a small town—population 3,000—but its stature is large, indeed, among the enlightened.

Here's a mini–resort town that happens to rest between two of the prettiest little streams in Texas, the Cypress Creek and the Blanco River. It's a hub of shopping activity on weekends, when dozens of pottery studios, art galleries, antiques shops, and boutiques are open for business. The Blue Hole, on Cypress Creek, is one of the state's primo swimming holes, and most guests at resorts, ranches, and B&Bs spend a few lazy hours floating under the clouds.

In addition to little sandwich and ice cream shops on the square, there's good dining at **John Henry's** (on the square, 210–847–5467), with a deck in back overlooking the peaceful creek. Feast on mesquite-fired steaks, fajitas, fish, or chicken.

7A Ranch Resort (1 mile west on River Road from Ranch Road 12, 210–847–2517) has rustic cottages and lodges, river frontage, and a reconstructed pioneer village–amusement park. Wimberley also has a good stock of B&Bs; contact **Bed & Breakfast of Wimberley** (210–847–9666).

A good night's rest is needed to prepare you for a drive on the **Devil's Backbone**, the wildly twisting Ranch Road 32, reaching from Ranch Road 12 immediately south of Wimberley almost 25 miles toward Blanco. This, a dramatically nicknamed route, is easily a contender for the state's most scenic drive, cutting a winding path along a sharp ridge through the hills; be on the watch early or late in the day for white-tailed deer. It's spectacular at any time, but with spring wildflowers or autumn foliage, it's the ultimate.

SOUTH TEXAS

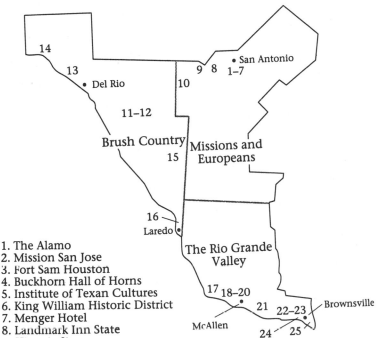

14

13

● Del Rio

9 8 1–7
● San Antonio

10

11–12

Brush Country

15

Missions and
Europeans

16

Laredo ●

1. The Alamo
2. Mission San Jose
3. Fort Sam Houston
4. Buckhorn Hall of Horns
5. Institute of Texan Cultures
6. King William Historic District
7. Menger Hotel
8. Landmark Inn State
    Historic Site
9. 777 Exotic Game Ranch
10. Garner Museum
11. Alamo Village
12. Seminole Indian Scout
    Cemetery
13. Amistad National
    Recreation Area
14. Langtry
15. Statue of Popeye the Sailor
16. La Posada Hotel
17. La Borde House
18. Bentsen–Rio Grande
    Valley State Park

The Rio Grande
Valley

17 18–20

McAllen

21

22–23

24   25

Brownsville

19. Santa Ana National
    Wildlife Refuge
20. Shrine of La Virgen de San
    Juan del Valle
21. Marine Military Academy and
    Texas Iwo Jima War Memorial
22. Palo Alto Battlefield
23. Palmitto Ranch Battlefield
24. Gladys Porter Zoo
25. Brazos Island State Park

SOUTH TEXAS

Resting beneath the Hill Country's lower reaches, San Antonio is undisputably the gateway to vast South Texas—often a lonely, wide open region. Long, unhurried drives impart views that must have been overwhelming to early settlers, so endless is the fiercely blue sky, the ferocious and scrubby land.

The Spaniards came to colonize the new land, doing so mightily in the San Antonio area with their missions, and other Europeans eventually followed. Fanning southward from the great Alamo City are settlements reflecting varied origins, from Alsatian to Polish and, of course, Hispanic.

Only a few communities in South Texas are heavily populated, but most towns have surprising depth of character. In between are protracted stretches of road, ranchland, and thickets of mesquite—a tough tree if ever one lived. For an hour or more you'll see nothing piercing the horizon other than clumps of cactus, fence posts, an occasional telephone pole, a very rare windmill, and that tenacious mesquite. For anyone who appreciates truly raw beauty, this might be heaven.

Along the Mexican border various small settlements still simmer with Texas's Old West heritage, and all are permeated by a binational spirit that flows alongside the Rio Grande as it continues quietly and at length to the Gulf of Mexico. It's easy to picture, right there in your mind's eye, pioneer ranchmen of a century ago surveying the border, hoping somehow to tame a hopelessly wild land.

MISSIONS AND EUROPEANS

Kaleidoscopic vistas of bluebonnets, Indian paintbrush, and other wildflowers frame U.S. Highway 281, Texas Highway 16, and Interstate 35 as you approach San Antonio in spring and summer, a subtle prelude to the year-round symphony of sights waiting in this cultural paradise. Get ready, because this vast storehouse of heritage and diversion knows how to entertain.

San Antonio, now the nation's tenth largest city, boasts a healthy German and Native American influence, but Hispanic culture dominates San Antonio. This Mexican-American accord will always be part of San Antonio, as the city was part of colonial or independent Mexico for nearly 150 years.

No written records tell us much of the area's early Native American period, but writings show that in the late 1690s resourceful Spaniards camped on the San Antonio River, then called Rio San Antonio de Padua. Six Spanish missions were established in the early 1700s, but only five were successful. The first was Mission San Antonio de Valero in 1718, best known later under its nickname, ◈ **The Alamo.**

The Alamo mission doubled as a fort, where Davy Crockett, Jim Bowie, and William B. Travis were among the patriots who gave their lives for the Texas Revolution. For thirteen days in late February and early March 1836, 187 men were surrounded and then crushed by the Mexican Army. The would-be liberators managed to deplete Santa Anna's forces considerably before falling, enabling the Texans to win the Battle of San Jacinto and the revolution.

Heavy doors bearing bullet holes still front the Alamo, which sits before one of four Spanish plazas downtown, all connected by winding streets. Some people are disappointed to find the landmark to be such a small place, but its size doesn't diminish its significance. The Alamo, at 300 Alamo Plaza downtown, is open Monday through Saturday, 9:00 A.M. until 5:30 P.M., and Sunday, 10:00 A.M. until 5:30 P.M.; (210) 225–1391.

Behind the Alamo, in the elaborate RiverCenter Mall, there's an **IMAX Theatre** presenting an excellent docudrama entitled *Alamo: The Price of Freedom* on a six-story-tall film screen. Historians double as actors in this production, telling a more factual story than the John Wayne movie version. For show schedule and ticket information, call (210) 225–4629; tickets are $5.95 for adults, $5.45 for seniors, $3.95 for children.

◈ **Mission San Jose** (6539 Mission San Jose Drive at Mission Road, 210–229–4770), founded two years after the Alamo, is the most interesting of the four still functioning as churches. The mission, noted for its rare and opulent hand-sculpted Rose Window, is home each Sunday to a lively mariachi mass at 12:00 noon. Today San Antonio is the only U.S. city with as many missions within its city limits, and the five erected here comprise the **San Antonio Mission National Historic Park** (2202 Roosevelt Avenue, 210–229–5701); missions are open daily from 9:00 A.M. until 6:00 P.M. in summer and 8:00 A.M. until 5:00 P.M. in winter.

Certainly San Antonio has always been a bastion of military history. ◈ **Fort Sam Houston** (North New Braunfels Avenue at Grayson Street, 210–221–1211) dates from 1876, making it the city's oldest fort. Continuing as a working army base, Fort Sam is engaging, with its Victorian officers' quarters and Quadrangle, where special events include period reenactments and dress parade drills. Two museums include one with military artifacts and one with medical exhibits. Call ahead for hours, which vary.

In the city's northwestern quadrant, Opryland's amusement wizards have opened a whimsical, unusual theme park called **Fiesta Texas** (17000 Interstate 10 West, 210–697–5000). The hundred-million-dollar venture focuses on the music and heritage of Hispanic, German, and western influences that shaped Texas. Along with dozens of nonstop musical shows are plenty of restaurants, boutiques, snack stands, and rides, including the world's tallest, fastest, and longest roller coaster, the Rattler. Be sure to stay until dark—that's when Fiesta Texas throws an absolutely sensational laser show against a canyon wall, masterfully weaving together Texas's history and music in unforgettable light and sound. Open daily Memorial Day through Labor Day, 10:00 A.M. until 10:00 P.M., and on weekends in spring and fall. Admission is $24 for adults and $16 for children, but special discounts are usually available.

The park's name probably was borrowed from the biggest of Texas's parties, **Fiesta San Antonio,** begun as a festival honoring visiting president Benjamin Harrison. Everyone had such a good time they didn't notice that the prez was a no-show, and the bash—now in its second century—is repeated annually. Fiesta, put on by some 50,000 residents, covers a ten-day period in the latter part of April and includes 150 events. Among the flashier are the Battle of Flowers Parade, the King's River Parade, Fiesta Night Parade, and A Night in Old San Antonio. There's also a king's coronation, Alamo pilgrimage, arts fair, and *charreada*, or Mexican rodeo. For information, call the Fiesta office at (210) 227–5191.

A rather bizarre cultural assemblage is that found at the ◈ **Buckhorn Hall of Horns,** situated in the Lone Star Brewery at 600 Lone Star Boulevard at St. Mary's Street (210–270–9467). Inside there's the historic Buckhorn Saloon, dating from 1881, where visitors can relax with complimentary beer and root beer. A rest is just what you'll need after touring Buckhorn's incredible gallery of animal horns and antlers, plus hundreds of fish, bird, and large mammal trophies, combining to deliver visual overload. There's also a remarkable collection of antique and custom-made firearms, plus a wax museum that chronicles Texas history in figures from Cabeza de Vaca to Teddy Roosevelt. And finally, there's the preserved San Antonio home of the writer O. Henry. Open daily from 9:30 A.M. to 5:00 P.M., the museum charges $3.50 admission for adults, $3.00 for seniors, and $1.50 for children ages 6-11.

HemisFair Park (Alamo Street, Interstate 37, Durango, and Market streets, 210–299–8610) is home to the 750-foot Tower of the Americas, the symbol built for the 1968 World's Fair. A glass elevator whisks you to the top in less than a minute, and the sky-high restaurant makes one revolution per hour. On the ground, there's a pleasant configuration of walkways, ponds, and waterfalls.

The park is home to the ✦ **Institute of Texan Cultures,** by far one of the nation's superior ethnic history museums. Exhibits focus on the people of twenty-six ethnic and cultural groups of Texas; the multimedia show and museum store are also superb. Open Tuesday through Sunday, 9:00 A.M. until 5:00 P.M.; call (210) 226–7651 for information.

For a dime, you can hop aboard a renovated, motorized trolley and ride from the Alamo–HemisFair Plaza area to **Market Square,** a re-created Mexican mercado (514 West Commerce Street, 210–299–8600). Time and money easily disappear among the bustle of mariachis, whir of margarita machines, and come-ons from vendors in hundreds of booths packed with arts, crafts, jewelry, and produce and other foods. While you're there, **Mi Tierra** (210–225–1262) is the place to find good Tex-Mex eats twenty-four hours daily—and the bakery case is where you'll satisfy that sweet tooth.

Just south of downtown, the ✦ **King William Historic District** (on and around King William Street) is a trove of wonderful mansions built by the city's German gentry. Walking and cycling this area on spring or fall days is a pleasure that will be long remembered, but you can have a look inside, too. The **Steves Homestead** (509 King William Street, 210–225–5924) is a century-old Gothic-revival mansion on the San Antonio River containing period antiques owned and maintained by the San Antonio Conservation Society; admission is $2.00 for adults, and the home is open daily from 10:00 A.M. until 12:00 noon and from 1:00 P.M. until 5:00 P.M.

The city is chock full of art galleries, clothing boutiques, gift shops, craft markets, and the like. Those accessible on foot are found on the flagstone banks lining the **River Walk,** or *Paseo del Rio*, sitting beneath street level downtown and following the river's twisting contours. Arbors of palms, olive trees, cottonwoods, cypress, and willows shade sidewalk cafes, and pots of flowers are set between doors to shops, galleries, boutiques, hotels, bistros, and watering holes. Beware that crowds on weekends can be crushing.

San Antonio's sightseeing and shopping are nothing if not exhausting, so it's probably time to check into the ◆**Menger Hotel,** outfitted recently with the new Alamo Plaza Spa, where an old-fashioned two-hour treatment includes steam bath, sauna, and herbal scrub. The Menger, next door to the Alamo, was a splendid hotel at its 1859 opening, and its claim to fame is that Teddy Roosevelt came to this wild and raucous city and this very hotel in 1898 to recruit his Rough Riders—or so the story goes. It's still a good hotel with choice rooms in the older section, and the bar has a friendly, comfortable feel. It's located at 204 Alamo Plaza, (210) 223–4361 or (800) 345–9285.

Keep in mind that the Alamo City grows ever more popular: Recent polls conducted by a national travel magazine show San Antonio ranking consistently in the top ten favorite U.S. destinations. Between ten and eleven million people visit annually, so don't think you can just show up and get a room in the central area without a reservation.

If **La Mansion del Rio** (112 College Street, 800–292–7300 or 210–225–2581) and the **St. Anthony** (300 East Travis Street, 800–338–1338 or 210–227–4392) are too pricey, try some of the historic places, such as the Menger. Other good historic choices are the **Fairmount Hotel** (401 South Alamo Street, 210–224–8800 or 800–642–3363) and **Plaza San Antonio** (555 South Alamo Street, 210–229–1000 or 800–421–1172). Bed-and-breakfast offerings include the **Ogé House** (pronounced oh-ZHAY) in the King William District, 800–242–2770 or 210–223–2353), an 1857 home with period antiques; most rooms include fireplaces—which may not be ideal in spring and summer but are nice touches, nonetheless.

New and elaborate for Texas is the **Hyatt Regency Hill Country Resort** (9800 Hyatt Resort Drive, 210–647–1234 or 800–233–1234), a hundred-million-dollar, 200-acre spread in San

Antonio's northwest corner, unique as Texas's first true resort. Designed in the spirit of a mega-ranch, the enormous facility exhibits woodwork and decor detail with pioneer day influences, and the structure consists of native limestone particularly prevalent in the Hill Country's German towns. What's to do there? Try golfing on an eighteen-hole course, tennis on lighted courts, tubing on a river winding through the property, working out and being pampered at an outdoor spa, and swimming in two pools. There are also programs for children and for teens. Travelers who appreciate nature will perhaps just want to wander through live oak–studded pastures, along bluffs over the creek and—of course—in meadows filled with wildflowers.

Complete information is offered by the San Antonio Convention & Visitors Bureau, (800) 447–3372; a handy visitors center is situated steps from the Alamo at 317 Alamo Plaza, (210) 299–8155, open daily from 8:30 A.M. until 5:00 P.M.

Head to **Castroville,** 20 miles west on U.S. 90, a town of just over 2,000 in Medina County. It became the "Little Alsace of Texas" after founder Henri Castro brought a band of Alsatian settlers with him from that region of France. It's the only Alsatian community in the country and has clung tightly to its heritage; it's a lucky visitor who comes across descendants of those settlers, especially those who can speak the original, unwritten dialect, which is more German than French.

For a look into Alsatian history, visit **Mount Gentilz Cemetery** (U.S. Highway 90 and Alsace Street), also called Cross Hill. Here, you'll have a far-reaching view of the Medina Valley, and you can see the burial spot of Amelia Castro, Henri's wife. Also, see **St. Louis Catholic Church** (U.S. Highway 90 and Angelo Street), built 1868–70 next to the colonists' original chapel, built 1846. The big, three-story building is the **Moye Center,** a convent erected in 1873 for the Sisters of Divine Providence.

Travelers will be pleased to find the Alsatian community's ◈ **Landmark Inn State Historic Site** (Florence and Florella streets, 210–538–2133), a hotel on the San Antonio–El Paso road when built in 1863; it's said that Robert E. Lee was among its guests. Now it's the only historic inn run by the state, which restored it to a 1940s look. A visitor center and an old gristmill are here, too.

Continue west from Castroville on U.S. Highway 90, traveling another 20 miles to **Hondo,** which became the seat of Medina County after the Southern Pacific Railroad bypassed Castroville in the 1880s. Today, it's a community of 6,000 known best for attractions of the four-legged kind.

At the ◈ **777 Exotic Game Ranch** (2½ miles west of town via U.S. 90, 210–675–1408), wildlife photography subjects include axis and fallow deer, Indian blackbuck antelope, aoudad sheep, and Alpine ibex. During fall and winter, visitors can hunt white-tailed deer, javelina, and wild turkey, and anglers can fish the lake stocked with lunker catfish and Florida bass. There's swimming, tennis, and skeet shooting, too, and lodging.

Much older and far more exotic, **dinosaur tracks** cast in stone are easily viewed in Hondo Creek's bed, almost 24 miles north of town via Farm Road 462. Scientists speculate these were made by 15-ton, 40-foot herbivores called trachodons.

Forty-two miles farther west on U.S. Highway 90, **Uvalde**, seat of the same-named county and home to 15,000 thousand residents, is known as the crossroads of two roads spanning the whole country—U.S. Highway 90 and U.S. Highway 83—and a fat little pocket of Old West and U.S. history.

In the 1880s, **J. K. King Fisher and Pat Garrett**—two unforgettable lawmen of their day—lived in Uvalde. Fisher was an outlaw who became a deputy, though some said he was both at the same time, and Garrett was the man who killed Billy the Kid in nearby New Mexico in 1881.

And Uvalde's John Nance Garner served as vice president of the United States from 1933 to 1941; his life is chronicled in detail at the ◈ **Garner Museum** (333 North Park Row, 210–278–5018). Garner went to Congress in 1903 during Teddy Roosevelt's administration, served as speaker of the house, and stayed in Washington, serving as the number two man under FDR. It's said that his signature Texan candidness earned him the nickname "Cactus Jack." The museum is housed in his former home, a beautiful building, and he was buried shortly before his ninety-ninth birthday at the west end of the City Cemetery (on U.S. Highway 90 West). The museum is open Monday through Saturday, 9:00 A.M. until 12:00 noon and 1:00 P.M. until 5:00 P.M. Admission is $1.00 for adults, 50 cents for children.

Take time to look at **Uvalde Grand Opera House** (104 West North Street at North Getty Street, 210–278–4184). A building befitting its name, this two-story creation seated 370 patrons and is now partially occupied by a museum. Open Monday through Friday, 9:00 A.M. until 4:00 P.M.

BRUSH COUNTRY

From Uvalde, proceed 40 miles west on U.S. Highway 90 to reach **Brackettville,** seat of Kinney County. Be assured that this is the epitome of isolation: There's only one other town in the county, which is more than twenty times the size of Rhode Island.

You'll see a familiar sight here, and maybe it will seem like a mirage: The Alamo right here in Brackettville's ◈ **Alamo Village** is the one in the 1959 John Wayne movie, not the one in San Antonio. That's because an entire set had to be built for the epic film—it's still one of the larger and more thorough sets ever built in this country—and this lonesome land provided ideal scenery. Adobe craftsmen from Mexico created the Alamo replica, which continues to overlook a complete frontier village straight out of the nineteenth century. Rounding out the village are a cantina and restaurant, stage depot, jail, bank, livery, and trading post. In summer there are musical shows and melodramas, often interrupted by Old West gunfights. To reach the village, drive 7 miles north from town on Ranch Road 674; admission is $6.00 for adults, $3.00 for children, and it's open daily, 9:00 A.M. until 5:00 P.M., except December 21–26. Call (210) 563–2580 for details.

On the town's eastern edge on U.S. 90, find **Fort Clark Springs**, a resort resting on old Fort Clark, one of the country's best preserved cavalry posts. Built in 1852 to protect western settlers against Indians and banditos, the fort is famous for having been the training ground for ninety years for several infantry units, including the Ninth and Tenth Infantry's black Buffalo Soldiers and almost all of the army cavalry units. Others stationed at Fort Clark included generals George S. Patton, Jr., and George C. Marshall. Historic buildings remain, some of which have been restored. The Old Guardhouse contains a small museum, and the resort offerings include a motel in old limestone barracks; two restaurants; a large, spring-fed pool; tennis courts and golf courses; and a fitness center. Call (800) 937–1590 or (210) 563–2493 for details.

At ◆**Seminole Indian Scout Cemetery,** 3 miles south of town on Farm Road 3348, you'll find the burial sites of several scouts hired by the army to help in campaigns against the warring Apaches. These Seminoles were descended from escaped Georgia slaves who intermarried with Florida Indians and moved west. Four of those buried here received the prestigious Congressional Medal of Honor, and some of the Seminole offspring still reside in Brackettville, working at ranching or farming.

From Brackettville, keep steady on U.S. Highway 90 another 32 miles to **Del Rio,** the seat of Val Verde County and nicknamed Queen of the Rio Grande. In this corner of dry, hot South Texas, Del Rio is a blessing, as it rests atop bubbling San Felipe Springs, the outlet of an underground river pouring forth ninety million gallons of crystal water daily. *That's* why you see so many ranches around—the irrigation opportunity is abundant for those prospering in sheep and Angora goat ranching nearby.

Another gaping surprise out here is **Lake Amistad,** home of ◆**Amistad National Recreation Area,** northwest of town 10 miles via U.S. 90. This 67,000-acre, vividly blue impoundment on the Rio Grande is a perfect example of the unity enjoyed today between Mexico and the United States, and particularly Texas. As the United States shares the river with Mexico, it also shares the dam creating the mesmerizing, binational lake, which stretches 75 miles upriver and offers 1,000 miles of shoreline. Fishing permits are offered by both countries, and there are dozens of other diversions, including camping, boat rentals, picnicking, and bow hunting. The dam is topped by a 6-mile road, offering access between the lake's two sides. For information, contact the National Park Service office on U.S. Highway 90 West, just at the Del Rio city limits, (210) 775–7491.

For true international flavor, plan a day a few yards away, crossing over the border into **Ciudad Acuna, Mexico,** Del Rio's Mexican twin—to miss such a treat is to neglect the legacy created between Texas and Mexico through generations. Along **Avenida Hidalgo** you'll find shops stocked with baskets, pottery, leather goods, silver jewelry, glassware, tiles, and other handcrafted items—and you can bet the prices are low even on items of very high quality. Don't hesitate to bargain with shopkeepers, many of whom speak English and accept American dollars, as it's an expected practice. Cafes and bakeries offer good snacks, too. You can drive across the border, but it's better not to hassle with the insurance necessities; just park on the U.S. side of the river and walk across the bridge. To reach it, follow Garfield Avenue, also called Spur 239, west about 3 miles to the river.

Another look into history is discovered at **Val Verde Winery** (100 Qualia Street, 210–775–9714), Texas's oldest winery, begun in 1883 by Italian immigrant Frank Qualia. It's still in the same family, whose members offer free tours of the vineyards, storage vats, aging room, and bottling processors. Among eight wines made here, one is the Lenoir, the first wine produced more than 110 years ago. Tasting and buying opportunities follow the tour. It's open Monday through Saturday from 9:00 A.M. until 5:00 P.M.

Set aside ample time for two outstanding side trips from Del Rio, which can be done on the same drive northwest of the city along U.S. Highway 90. The first stop is **Seminole Canyon State Historical Park,** 45 miles from Del Rio and about 9 miles past the village called Comstock. The rugged setting of desert and canyons showcases a collection of Indian paintings and pictographs thought to be more than 8,000 years old. Look in Fate Bell Shelter, just below the park's interpretive center, for the most brilliant pictographs. Discoveries of other human artifacts—possibly 12,000 years old—and the drawings have combined to give scientists some ideas of daily life all those millennia past, which are illustrated in a life-size diorama at the visitor center. The park is open daily, 8:00 A.M. until 5:00 P.M., and at all times for campers. Admission is $3.00 per vehicle; call (915) 292–4464.

The second side trip from Del Rio is ✦**Langtry,** only 20 miles beyond Seminole Canyon on U.S. Highway 90, still in Val Verde County. The desperately lonely wild west outpost was founded in 1881, when the railroad came through, representing the junction of eastbound and westbound construction. How the town's name came about is still up for debate: Some historians believe that the civil engineer, a man called Langtry, who directed a crew of Chinese railroad laborers, is the source, but romantics stick with the story of Judge Roy Bean, who says he named the town for his favorite actress, the Jersey Lily, Englishwoman Lillie Langtry.

Worth the trip alone, the **Judge Roy Bean Visitor Center** is the preserved site of the infamous, unforgettable "Law West of the Pecos," whose 1880s rule was a masterful blend of wit and bravery. Travelers find the rustic saloon, courtroom, and pool

Judge Roy Bean Visitor Center

hall that was Bean's, along with a full-scale state visitors' travel center, staffed by counselors and stocked with loads of free brochures, maps, guides, and varied information. Outside, there's a cactus garden with indigenous southwestern plant life. Open daily from 8:00 A.M. until 5:00 P.M., the center can be called at (915) 291–3340.

Notice on your way to Langtry, about 18 miles east of town, there's a terrific **Pecos River Canyon scenic overlook,** offering a stunning view of the formidable canyon. This is an ideal place to stretch your legs, and a picnic area is right there if you've brought lunch along.

From Del Rio, you can begin making tracks to the southeast along the Rio Grande, traveling 56 miles on U.S. Highway 277 to **Eagle Pass,** the seat of Maverick County and home to 20,650 residents. An early U.S. settlement during the Mexican War, it's where the government founded Fort Duncan in 1849 and remains a gateway to Mexico today.

Have a look into that window of history at **Fort Duncan Museum,** housed in the old headquarters. There are archaeological exhibits, as well as detail on the Kickapoo tribe nearby, and eleven surviving buildings. The history told here is of the post's closing in 1900, then reopening in 1916 during the Mexican Revolution, and its use as a World War I training base. Among famous officers who spent time here were Phil Sheridan, James Doolittle, and Matthew Ridgeway. Open Monday through Saturday, 1:00 P.M. until 5:00 P.M., the museum is found on Bliss Street between Monroe and Adams streets, (210) 773–2748.

Eagle Pass extends across the border in the form of **Piedras Negras,** a Mexican sister and home to 33,000. To truly experience your border vacation, you have to find the wonderful deals to be made in the market downtown on glassware, wood carvings, woven blankets and rugs, silver jewelry, and colorful smocks and blouses. Bullfights are held in summer, and restaurants offer good, cheap Mexican dishes. You can gain access across an international bridge via Garrison Street, also known as U.S. Highway 57. Parking on the U.S. side of the bridge and walking across saves you from having to buy the required Mexican auto insurance.

From Eagle Pass, travel 50 miles east on U.S. Highway 277 and east on Farm Road 191 to Crystal City, seat of Zavala County. It may seem odd, but this seat of Zavala County and town of 8,000 is home to a big ✦**Statue of Popeye the Sailor,** found in front of city hall on the square. Well, it's not so strange after all—as this town calls itself "The Spinach Capital of the World" for its huge production of spinach. Look also for farmers selling enormous watermelons, tomatoes, onions, carrots, and peppers from their pickup trucks.

Now it's 92 miles straight south on U.S. Highway 83 to **Laredo,** seat of Webb County, with nearly 150,000 residents. Rich in history and culture, Laredo is the place for more of that beloved binational experience. Since its founding by Don Tomás Sánchez, a captain in the Spanish colonial army, on May 15, 1755, Villa San Agustín de Laredo has served as everything from a raiding site for Lipan Apaches and Comanches, a cattle and sheep ranching community, and an outpost for the expanding New Spain, to capital of the Republic of the Rio Grande and an international commerce center.

The city's chamber of commerce (2310 San Bernardo Street, 210–722–9895) offers an excellent walking-tour guide, with detail on numerous historic neighborhoods and buildings, shopping districts in both Laredo and **Nuevo Laredo,** the Mexican twin across the Rio Grande, and dining and hotel offerings. While you're looking around downtown, be sure to pay attention to **San Agustín Plaza,** bounded by Grant, Zaragoza, Flores, and San Agustín streets; here you'll see the beautiful **St. Agustín Church**, a Gothic-revival masterpiece, and several remarkable buildings in designs ranging from Mexican Colonial and Mexican vernacular to Victorian and neo-classical revival, dating from the 1700s.

Facing the plaza, ◆ **La Posada Hotel** (1000 Zaragoza, 210–722–1701) occupies the former Laredo High School, built in 1916. The hotel is nothing short of lovely, with an exquisitely blue-tiled pool surrounded by a lush courtyard. The food is fair to good in the hotel's restaurants, the best being the **Tack Room,** upstairs in an adjacent building that was once the town's telephone exchange. You'll find big steaks, spareribs, chicken, and fish on the menu.

If you happen upon Laredo in February, you may be in for a real treat during **George Washington's Birthday Celebration,** a two-week party held annually since 1898. The fiesta includes parades, pageants, fireworks, dances, a jalapeño festival, carnival, charreada, and an occasional bullfight.

For a selection of superb food and shopping, make the requisite walk across one of two international bridges to Nuevo Laredo, a busy city with a population of a quarter million. International Bridge #1 is reached via Convent Street, and International Bridge #2 is accessed from Interstate 35. Again, it's a good idea to park on the U.S. side and walk across; auto insurance for Mexico is a bother, and parking is tough in Nuevo Laredo.

The town's favorite restaurant, the Cadillac Bar, has changed hands and is now the **El Dorado**, on Belden at Ocampo streets, serving the same excellent *cabrito*, quail, steaks, and New Orleans Gin Fizzes that made its predecessor internationally famous for most of this century. More formal and simply perfect is **Victoria's 3020**, on Victoria at Matamoros streets, with a beautiful courtyard and wonderful steaks and Mexican specialties. Reservations are a good idea; to call from Laredo, dial 011–52871–33020.

Nuevo Laredo's **El Mercado,** at the intersection of Guerrero

Avenue and Belden Street, is a two-story, square-block retail center where vendors sell goods that range from jewelry, sandals, leather bags, and saddles to barware, clothing, baskets, pastries, and pottery. Prices are low to begin with, but you can bargain to the basement. A gorgeous department store, **Marti's,** at Guerrero Avenue and Victorian Street, stocks fancy gold and silver jewelry, china, crystal, antiques, designer dresses, expensive tapestries and rugs, and furniture. To call from Laredo, dial 011–52871–23137.

THE RIO GRANDE VALLEY

Back on the road, it's another 49 miles south on U.S. 83 to **Zapata,** seat of Zapata County and home to 3,500 Texans. Named in honor of Antonio Zapata, the renowned Mexican pioneer and tough Indian fighter, the town is mostly a supply point for outdoor enthusiasts embarking on an adventure at **Falcon State Park,** 28 miles south on U.S. 83, Farm Road 2098, and Park Road 46, (210) 848–5327. The shores of the enormous international lake, impounded on the Rio Grande, offer more than 500 acres for camping, picnicking, fishing, and swimming. There are groceries at the park, too, as well as a snack bar. Admission is $3.00 per vehicle; the park is open daily.

From Zapata, it's 51 miles south on U.S. 83 till you reach **Rio Grande City,** seat of Starr County, with a population of 5,700. The town came about in 1848 when General Zachary Taylor established Fort Ringgold, which was named for Major David Ringgold, the first army officer killed in the Battle of Palo Alto, opening the Mexican War. The fort remained active until 1944 and was home to Colonel Robert E. Lee when he commanded the Department of Texas prior to the Civil War.

Travelers will want to pause in Rio Grande City just to stay at ◆**La Borde House** (601 East Main Street, 210–487–5101), the 1899 home and border mercantile built by a French merchant and riverboat trader who had the house designed in Paris, then refined by San Antonio architects. Totally renovated, the home was made into a hotel years ago and contains sublime Victorian furniture and antiques. With shaded verandas, courtyard, patio, parlor, guest rooms, and restaurant, it's a showplace on the Rio Grande.

Continuing south on U.S. 83 just 12 miles, watch for Farm Road 886, which you'll turn right onto for 2 miles until you reach the Rio Grande and a sight found nowhere else on a U.S. border. The **Los Ebaños Ferry** is a wooden, two-car ferry hand-pulled by a Mexican staff using ropes and is possibly in numbered days, as plans call for its eventual replacement by a bridge. For the moment, vehicle ferry is $1.00 and people are 25 cents each.

Another 14 miles south on U.S. 83, **Mission** is an 1824 settlement where the Rio Grande Valley's famous citrus industry was begun, possibly by the original priests. Today the town of 28,000 in Hidalgo County is "Home of the Grapefruit," specifically the famous Texas ruby red. Mission is not only the citrus center but also the state's **poinsettia center** and home of the nation's only all-poinsettia show, held annually in December. Most Texans—and all Rio Grande Valley residents—will also proudly tell you that Mission is the birthplace of Tom Landry, the first (and thirty-year) coach of the World Football Championship Dallas Cowboys.

Should you join other Winter Texans for a January stay in the Valley, rest up for the seventy-year-old **Texas Citrus Fiesta**, held the last week of the month all over the area. The bash consists of a grand parade, barbecue cook-off, carnival, dances, citrus judging, arts and crafts show, sporting events, and a spectacular citrus products costume style show. For information call the Mission Chamber of Commerce at (210) 585-9724 or 585-2727.

La Lomita Chapel (on Farm Road 1016, 3 miles south of town, 210-581-2725) was first an adobe waystation dating to 1865 for Oblate padres traveling on horseback upriver from Brownsville. The present, rebuilt version, erected in sandstone in 1889, is a tiny structure with original floors, rough beamed ceilings, and outdoor beehive oven. It sits in a seven-acre park with picnic areas, barbecue grills, rest rooms, walkways, and historic site signs.

For still more outdoors, head for ◆ **Bentsen–Rio Grande Valley State Park** (6 miles southwest on U.S. 83, Farm Road 2062, and Park Road 43, 210-585-1107), nearly 600 acres of land along the Rio Grande with excellent bird watching, especially for the Audubon's oriole, hooded oriole, zone-tailed hawk, and redeye cowbird. At the park office, pick up lists and booklets on these, as well as mammals, herbs, plants, butterflies, and other flora and fauna to be seen on nature trails. Camping, picnicking, and boating are options, too. The park is open daily; admission is $2.00 per vehicle.

McAllen, 10 miles east along U.S. 83, also lies in Hidalgo County and is home to 95,000 residents. The hub of activity in the lower Rio Grande Valley, McAllen appeals to retirees from the Midwest and Canada who spend entire winters here in the subtropical environs.

McAllen International Museum (1900 Nolana Street, 210–682–1564) has a wonderful Mexican folk-art mask and textile collection, as well as contemporary American and regional prints, sculptures, and oils from sixteenth- to nineteenth-century Europe. Open Tuesday through Saturday, 9:00 A.M. until 5:00 P.M. and Sunday, 1:00 P.M. until 5:00 P.M.; admission is $1.00 for adults and 25 cents for children.

The citrus season lasts from October through April, so to pick some citrus for yourself or buy your own crates, head over to **Eggers Acres** (immediately west on Farm Road 494, 210–581–7783), a family citrus business run by the granddaughter of Dr. J. B. Webb, who discovered the ruby red grapefruit. Gift packs are sold, and an adjacent garden center offers exquisite tropical foliage. A similar business is **Klement's Grove** (Farm Road 1924 and Taylor Road, 210–682–2980), which offers you-pick-em fruit off the trees, fruit selection in baskets, and gift packs, as well as mesquite and wildflower honey, pecans, fresh pies, and fruit cake.

A side trip to take if you have a free morning or afternoon—and if it's not too awfully hot—is to ❖**Santa Ana National Wildlife Refuge** (U.S. 83 east to Alamo, south on Farm Road 907 7 miles to U.S. 281, and east to the entrance, 210–787–3079). Here, 2,000 acres of subtropical foliage provide a habitat for an astounding variety of bird species, some of which aren't found elsewhere in the United States. The species list of nearly 400 can be picked up at the visitor center, and three nature trails are offered. In the winter, a tram tour is available. Trails are open daily from sunrise until sunset, and the visitor center is open Monday through Friday, 8:00 A.M. until 4:30 P.M., and Saturday and Sunday, 9:00 A.M. until 4:30 P.M. Admission is free, but tram tours cost $2.00 for adults and $1.00 for children. Note: Use insect repellent before going out on trails.

Head north of McAllen 8 miles on U.S. Highway 281 to **Edinburg**, the Hidalgo County seat, on Saturday night to see a proud Texas tradition, the rodeo. The **Sheriff's Posse Rodeo** is a weekly offering, with cowboys demonstrating calf roping, bull riding, and quarter horse racing. The rodeo arena is 2 miles south of town on U.S. 281. Admission is free.

Just a couple of miles east of McAllen via U.S. 83, the San Juan exit delivers you to the doors of the ◆**Shrine of La Virgen de San Juan del Valle** (U.S. 83 and Raul Longoria Road, 210–787–0033). This impressive church was built to the tune of five million dollars—mostly paid for by small contributions—after the elaborate, 1954 original was destroyed when a plane deliberately crashed into it. The wooden La Virgen statue wasn't harmed, and now it has a special place at the center of a hundred-foot wall. Open daily from 6:00 A.M. until 8:00 P.M.

That next South-of-the-Border experience is just a walk across the International Bridge to **Reynosa,** reached by driving 10 miles south on Tenth Street, also known as Texas Highway 336. The city founded in 1749 is home now to more than half a million residents, and it's a great place for travelers to shop, eat, and see a bullfight or a baseball game in the Mexican League. It's best to park on the U.S. side of the bridge and walk across.

The **Zaragoza Market,** Hidalgo and Matamoros streets, is a standard market with brass, glass, wood, silver, leather, straw, and pottery gifts. Don't forget to bargain. Go to **Gabii's,** 1097 Avenida Los Virreyes, for pretty Mexican designer dresses, folk arts and crafts from Mexico and Central America, and finer giftwares.

The best food is at **La Cucaracha,** at Aldama and Ocampo streets, serving chateaubriand, lobster thermidor, and flaming desserts and offering live music for dancing. Also try **Sam's,** Allende at Ocampo streets, for cheap, reliable eats popular with tourists since 1932.

It's but 30 miles south from McAllen on U.S. 83 to **Harlingen,** a town of nearly 50,000 in Cameron County named for a city in the Netherlands. Called Sixshooter Junction for a wild time around 1910 and the Mexican Revolution, when frequent bandit raids necessitated the peacekeeping efforts of the Texas Rangers and mounted patrols from U.S. Customs. The National Guard was eventually brought in to help the Rangers when, it's said, there were more firearms than citizens in town.

Things have calmed down considerably since then, but visitors can become better acquainted with history at the **Rio Grande Valley Historical Museum Complex,** at Harlingen

Industrial Air Park, at Boxwood and Raintree streets, (210) 423–3979. The four museums here are the Historical Museum, detailing the culture of the lower Valley; a restored nineteenth-century stagecoach inn; a medical museum, with 1920s equipment; and the Lon C. Hill Home, a 1905 house built by the city founder who hosted dignitaries such as William Jennings Bryan. The complex is open Tuesday through Friday, 9:00 A.M. until 12:00 noon and 2:00 P.M. until 5:00 P.M., and Sunday, 2:00 P.M. until 5:00 P.M.

A somewhat unexpected treat is found at Harlingen's ◈**Marine Military Academy and Texas Iwo Jima War Memorial,** 320 Iwo Jima Boulevard, (210) 423–6006. The Public Affairs Office will tell you if any parades or activities are scheduled, which offer the chance to see a U.S. Marines–style private academy at work. On the campus is the original working model for the Iwo Jima Memorial bronze statue at Arlington National Cemetery, donated to the academy by sculptor Dr. Felix W. de Weldon in 1981. The figures are 32 feet high, the M-1 rifle is 16 feet long, the flagpole is 78 feet long, and the canteen could hold 32 quarts of water. The pole flies a cloth flag. The Marine placing the flag pole in the ground was Corporal Harlon Block from nearby Weslaco, who was later killed in battle.

The final leg of the Valley tour is a 26-mile stint south from Harlingen on U.S. 83/U.S. 77 to **Brownsville,** seat of Cameron County and city of 115,000 Texans. While it's a pleasant place near the ocean and a popular gateway to Mexico, Brownsville's past is tumultuous.

In 1846 President Polk ordered General Zachary Taylor to build a fort at this spot, and the Mexicans understood this to be an act of veiled aggression. Soon the Mexicans invaded Texas here, igniting the Mexican-American War, which counted among early casualties a Major Jacob Brown, for whom the fort and city were eventually named. Two important battlefields are found near town, the first being the ◈**Palo Alto Battlefield,** north of town at Farm Road 1847 and Farm Road 511, marked by a historical marker. The other is **Resaca de la Palma Battlefield** on Farm Road 1847 between Price and Coffeeport streets; a leader in this battle was Second Lieutenant Ulysses S. Grant.

Another significant battle site—this in the Civil War—is ◈**Palmitto Ranch Battlefield,** about 14 miles east of downtown via Texas Highway 4. The fight was won by Confederate forces who hadn't heard that Lee had surrendered at Appomattox a month earlier. When the Rebels learned of the South's concession, the victors were taken prisoner by the prisoners.

For a much more modern and nature-oriented attraction, look no further than the ◆ **Gladys Porter Zoo,** at Ringgold and Sixth streets, (210) 546–2177. Widely considered one of the top ten zoos in the nation, this one is special for having no bars or cages. Animals in the thirty-one-acre spread are kept separated by moats and waterways and have room to roam. There are some 1,800 birds, mammals, and reptiles representing five continents. A children's zoo offers petting opportunities and an animal nursery. There's a half-hour, narrated tour aboard a miniature train on Sunday. Open Monday through Friday, 9:00 A.M. until 5:30 P.M., and Saturday and Sunday, 9:00 A.M. until 6:00 P.M. Admission is $5.00 for adults and $2.50 for children.

If you've a hankering for some crashing waves, head just 22 miles east of town on Texas Highway 4 till you find ◆ **Brazos Island State Park,** also known as Boca Chica. There's nothing but ocean and a little swatch of sand—it's completely undeveloped, and no facilities are available, so take your own water, drinks, ice chest, snacks, towels, and sunblock. If you're so inclined, feel free to swim, camp, surf, picnic, hunt for seashells and sand dollars, or just stroll the dunes. For gulf fishing, there's a half-mile-long stone jetty at the northern end of the beach.

Finally, there's one more Tex-Mex adventure to be had: **Matamoros** is a city of half a million and Brownsville's sister across the border, reached by two international bridges. One— Gateway International Bridge—is at the end of International Boulevard, and the other is south at Perl Boulevard, also called East Twelfth Street. Both come out at Avenida Alvaro Obregon, a major thoroughfare in Matamoros. Most gringos find it's better to park on the U.S. side and walk across, then hop aboard a maxi-cab or mini-van, which are cheap and go to all the popular tourist places.

Once there, as in all the Tex-Mex border towns, you'll find the shopkeepers and restaurant servers speak plenty of English, and they'll happily take American dollars. Mexican border towns like this one extend sunny personalities and the *mañana* attitude you've become familiar with all over South Texas. Shopping is a primary reason for making a Matamoros trip, with stores such as **Barbara de Matamoros,** 37 Avenida Alvaro Obregon, heading the list of good ones. Beautiful gifts, bearing appropriate price tags, are the specialty here. Find mammoth, colorful papier-mâché parrots and macaws on brass perches, life-size brass animals, ceramic tableware, jewelry, paintings, weavings, and other crafts from deeper Mexico.

The less pricey goods are sold at **Mercado Juarez,** Matamoros at Nueve/Ninth streets. All the standard items are here, including silver jewelry, embroidered cotton blouses and dresses, baskets of every description, pottery and glassware, leather crafts, and wood carvings. You'll find the pushiest sales people here, so bargain like crazy to get the prices you want.

After all that shopping, take a load off and have a ball over drinks and dinner. For something rather elegant, head for **Garcia's,** on Obregon near the bridge, where pretty linens and regal service are part of the pleasures, as are excellent steaks, frog legs, lobster, quail, and Mexican dishes. No less fancy and long popular with Americans is the **Drive-In,** Sexta/Sixth and Hidalgo streets. Here, the crystal chandeliers and red upholstery, bird-filled aviary, and continental dishes—including shrimp, steaks, and lobster—keep crowds coming back.

THE PINEY WOODS

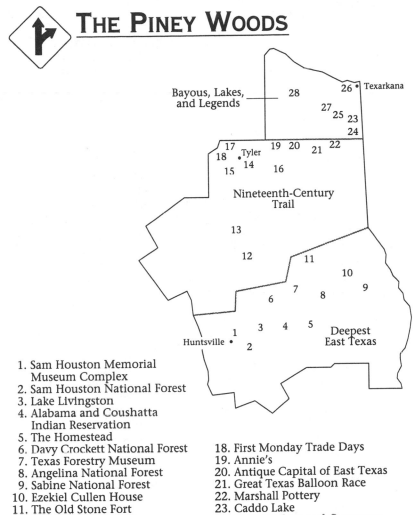

Bayous, Lakes, and Legends — 28

26 • Texarkana

27
25 23
24

17
18 • Tyler   19 20   21 22
15   14   16

Nineteenth-Century Trail

13

12   11

10

7   8   9

6

1   3   4   5   Deepest
Huntsville •   2   East Texas

1. Sam Houston Memorial Museum Complex
2. Sam Houston National Forest
3. Lake Livingston
4. Alabama and Coushatta Indian Reservation
5. The Homestead
6. Davy Crockett National Forest
7. Texas Forestry Museum
8. Angelina National Forest
9. Sabine National Forest
10. Ezekiel Cullen House
11. The Old Stone Fort
12. Texas State Railroad
13. The Texas Basket Company
14. Municipal Rose Garden
15. Edom
16. Rangerette Showcase
17. Munzesheimer Manor

18. First Monday Trade Days
19. Annie's
20. Antique Capital of East Texas
21. Great Texas Balloon Race
22. Marshall Pottery
23. Caddo Lake
24. T. C. Lindsey and Company General Store
25. The Excelsior House
26. The Perot Theatre
27. Lake o' the Pines
28. Ezekiel Airship

THE PINEY WOODS

East Texas's Piney Woods region defies so many myths held by those who don't truly know Texas: It's generously green, frequently hilly, and always lush. There are majestic millions of acres of forest—four national forests, to be exact. Rich in ancient pines, cypress, and plenty of hardwoods, this is where Texans make annual pilgrimages in autumn to see fall blazing in its radiant glory. And in spring, country paths in and out of the forest lands are sensational with brilliant explosions of magenta azaleas, frilly pink and white dogwoods, and evening primroses blooming across wild fields in lavender profusion. Amidst the legions of trees pushing skyward are lakes and more lakes, small places and big spreads of water, where lifelong lake residents share space and stories of honey holes with anglers hoping to catch even a little one—shimmering lakes where sailing and water-skiing and watching sunrises are the most important events that will occur in a day, places where timeless Indian legends tell of the Great Creator's work in watery, woodsy artistry.

Everything in the Piney Woods seems fresh and new, though the area has history dating to Texas's origins as a Republic and as a state. Vestiges of the life of Sam Houston—whose later years were spent serving his beloved Texas—are found here, and the state university in Nacogdoches, a wonderful Piney Woods town, is named for the "Father of Texas," Stephen F. Austin. A healthy population of Native Americans, the people of the united Alabama and Coushatta nations, live on a reservation near one of the state's great pioneer living-history museums. Travelers to the Piney Woods can ride restored nineteenth-century railroads or buy baskets that have been made here for more than one hundred years and pottery that has been crafted by generations of the same families, families that helped settle the region. There are no amusement parks or major league athletic teams or four-story shopping malls in the Piney Woods, but you will find a rose garden with five hundred varieties that supplies a third of the nation with its commercial roses; the state's antiques capital; Victorian mansions made over into bed and breakfast homes, some rumored to be staffed by resident ghosts; and towns offering the World's Richest Acre, the nation's first drill team, a biblical airplane, and some of the best fried alligator tail you could ever hope to savor. That's just a small taste of the Piney Woods.

DEEPEST EAST TEXAS

Begin this journey in **Huntsville,** an hour north of Houston, the Walker County seat and home to 33,000 East Texans. Settled in a very pretty setting of rolling, forested terrain at Interstate 45 and U.S. Highway 190, Huntsville was founded as a trading post in 1836, the same year Texas won its independence from Mexico. Now the home to Sam Houston State University (SHSU), the city is better known as the place to learn more about the life of Sam Houston himself. The ◆**Sam Houston Memorial Museum Complex,** on the SHSU campus at 1836 Sam Houston Avenue (409–294–1832), is a fifteen-acre spread that belonged to the Texas hero and now holds two of his homes, the furnished Woodland Home and the Steamboat House, the latter of which was his death site in 1863. Other buildings there include a law office, kitchen, and blacksmith shop displaying, among other things, some of Houston's possessions, as well as Mexican items taken at the defeat of Santa Anna at San Jacinto. Pack a lunch for this visit, as the grounds have a spring-fed pond with picnic facilities. Open Tuesday through Sunday, 9:00 A.M. until 5:00 P.M. Free admission.

You can visit Houston's burial site at Oakwood Cemetery, Avenue I and Ninth Street. **Sam Houston's Grave and National Monument** is marked by a tomb bearing Andrew Jackson's sentiment, "The world will take care of Houston's fame." Open always, there is no admission charge.

An entirely different kind of attraction is found at the **Texas Prison Museum,** 1113 Twelfth Street (409–295–2155), where exhibits include the history of the Texas prison, with Bonnie and Clyde's rifle collection; Old Sparky, the electric chair; relics from the Carrasco prison siege; and memorabilia from the famous, defunct Texas Prison Rodeo, plus music and art projects by inmates. Open Tuesday through Friday and Sunday from 12:00 noon until 5:00 P.M., and Saturday from 9:00 A.M. until 5:00 P.M. Admission is $2.00 for adults, 50 cents for children.

In warm weather Huntsville's **Blue Lagoon,** north 6 miles on Farm Road 247, then left on Pinedale Road (409–291–6111), is the place to go for dips and dives in a quarry filled with sparkling artesian water providing 40-foot visibility. There's an underwater platform at 20 feet and a submerged yacht for divers and other splashy appeal is found on beach areas. Open Monday through Friday from 10:00 A.M. until 6:00 P.M., and Saturday and Sunday from 8:00 A.M. until dark in spring, summer, and fall. Admission is $10.00 for divers and $5.00 otherwise.

To begin your tour of Texas's thick forest country, drive east on U.S. Highway 190 just 2 miles from Huntsville, and you're in ✪ **Sam Houston National Forest** (409–344–6205). Covering 160,000 acres in Montgomery, San Jacinto, and Walker counties, this forest contains 27 miles of the 140-mile Lone Star Hiking Trail. To reach this National Recreation Trail, find the trail head off Farm Road 1725 just northwest of the town of Cleveland on the forest's southern edge. For a map, see the forest ranger's offices either at Cleveland or at New Waverly, 13 miles south of Huntsville. Also in the forest, Stubblefield Lake is on the West Fork of the San Jacinto River about 12 miles north and west of New Waverly; there you can go camping and picnicking.

From the forest head east on U.S. Highway 190; you'll immediately see ✪ **Lake Livingston**, 52 miles long and lined with 452 miles of wooded shoreline with every sort of recreation. The 640-acre state park on the east shore of the lake offers campsites, screened shelters, group trailers, boat ramps, a store, floating docks and gas docks, showers, and hiking-nature trails. Fishing, swimming, and water-skiing are the most popular pastimes on the lake. For details, call the state park at (409) 365–2201. Admission is $3.00 per vehicle. Groceries, restaurants, and all supplies are available in the town of Livingston, the Polk County seat, 7 miles east of the park.

Two side trips worth your time are directly east from the lake. The first is the ✪ **Alabama and Coushatta Indian Reservation,** 33 miles east of the lake on U.S. Highway 190 (409–563–4391), home to two Native American tribes that have lived in these woods for a century and a half. Some of their ancestors fought with Sam Houston, and others were Confederates in the Civil War. The 500 people living here offer visitors a chance to observe tribal customs, such as dances and traditional craft work. You can ride a miniature train to tour a traditional village, then visit a museum, gift store, and restaurant. Open in summer Monday through Saturday from 10:00 A.M. until 6:00 P.M., and Sunday

Pickett House

from 12:30 P.M. until 6:00 P.M. In fall and spring, hours are reduced, so please call ahead. Admission is $11.00 for adults and $9.00 for children.

About 12 miles east of the reservation on U.S. Highway 190, watch for **Heritage Village,** a reconstructed pioneer community right on the highway, where the primary attraction is **Pickett House** (409–283–3946), a re-created boarding house. Family-style dining offers all-you-can-eat fried chicken, chicken and dumplings, vegetables grown here in the village, stone-ground cornbread, homemade preserves from the locally harvested fruits, and specially blended teas. Open daily March through August from 11:00 A.M. until 8:00 P.M.; September through February, open Monday through Friday from 11:00 A.M. until 3:00 P.M., Saturday from 11:00 A.M. until 8:00 P.M., and Sunday from 11:00 A.M. until 6:00 P.M.

If that's not enough food for you, take note that you're in superior home-cooking country. Just another 2 miles from the Pickett House east on U.S. Highway 190 is the community of Woodville, where you can pick up U.S. Highway 69 and follow it 8 miles south to the village of Hillister and its superb restaurant, ◆ **The Homestead** (409–283–7324). This restored 1912 house behind a white picket fence has a certain rustic charm, with its hardwood floors and walls, and rugs, wallpaper, and furniture from the period—but atmosphere isn't the main appeal of The Homestead. The cornucopia of country cooking is nothing short of outstanding, including smothered or baked chicken, steaks and roast beef, fish and ham, plus irresistible desserts. Be advised that reservations are a good idea at this small place, which serves Thursday through Saturday from 5:00 P.M. until 10:00 P.M. and Sunday from 11:00 A.M. until 3:00 P.M.

Back on Lake Livingston, ◆ **Davy Crockett National Forest** is 11 miles west from the lake on U.S. 190, then north on Farm Road 356 12 miles northwest to Sebastopol, where you'll pick up Farm Road 355 and go 14 miles north. This forest, like the other three national forests in Texas, was ravaged early in this century yet has made remarkable recovery in its hardwood and pine populations. The Davy Crockett is 161,000 acres in Houston and Trinity counties, containing the Big Slough Canoe Trail and Wilderness Area on the Neches River, and the Four C Hiking Trail, a 19-mile path linking the Neches Bluff and Ratcliff Lake. That lake has camping, picnicking, and swimming areas, plus screened shelters and canoe rentals. For maps and facilities, go to the ranger station at Crockett (409–544–2046), just west of the forest on U.S. Highway 287, or Apple Springs (409–831–2246), in the forest on Texas Highway 94.

At the ◆ **Texas Forestry Museum,** 1905 Atkinson Drive (409–632–9535), in Lufkin, 12 miles east of the forest on Texas Highway 94, the state's lumber industry is detailed, as well as the impact the forestry-products business has had on the region. Also, there's a moonshiner's still, a fire lookout tower, a blacksmith's forge, and a logging train. Open daily from 1:00 P.M. until 4:30 P.M.; admission is free, but donations are welcome.

From Lufkin head 22 miles southeast on U.S. Highway 69 to the ◆ **Angelina National Forest,** a 152,000-acre preserve spreading across Angelina, Jasper, Nacogdoches, and San Augustine counties and wrapping itself around vast **Lake Sam Rayburn.** The lake, exceptionally popular with bass and catfish anglers, has 560 miles of shoreline with numerous marinas and campgrounds. The pine-and-hardwood land gives shelter to deer, squirrel, and turkey, some of which can be seen on the Sawmill Hiking Trail, a 5½-mile path following the Neches River and stretching from Bouton Lake Park to the Old Aldrich Sawmill and Boykin Springs. Along the way you'll find ruins of an old tram line, logging camps, and bridges. Several parks line the lake, offering various concessions. For maps and information, as well as ranger-led activities, check at the ranger office next door to the Texas Forestry Museum in Lufkin (listed above); call (409) 639–8620.

From the Angelina forest, head for the ◆**Sabine National Forest** by following Texas Highway 147 to its intersection with Texas Highway 103, which leads east to this last of Texas's four national forests. At nearly 158,000 acres, covering ground in Jasper, Sabine, San Augustine, Newton, and Shelby counties, the Sabine hugs the 65-mile-long **Toledo Bend Reservoir,** which Texas shares with Louisiana. Along the lake, in the shade of southern pines and hardwoods, are seven different parks, with offerings ranging from picnicking, camping, and swimming, to boating areas and nature trails.

Fishing on Toledo Bend is a big attraction to anglers in search of bass, catfish, bluegill, and crappie. Check at the ranger offices for maps, concessions, and activities, in Hemphill, in the forest on Texas Highway 87 (409–787–2791), or San Augustine, on the forest's west side on Texas Highway 21 (409–275–2632).

San Augustine is conveniently found just 8 miles west on Texas Highway 21. A town of nearly 3,000, San Augustine is known as "The Cradle of Texas" and was settled officially in 1832, although it was a community on the Spaniards' Old Road to San Antonio, also called El Camino Real, even earlier. Because a mission was established here in 1716 (and abandoned just twenty years later), San Augustine claims to be the oldest town in Texas. Important historical residents included Sam Houston, who was a San Augustine resident while seeking the Republic presidency, and J. Pinckney Henderson, Texas's first governor.

Although much of the town burned in 1890, there are some good sites still standing, such as the ◆**Ezekiel Cullen House,** 207 Congress Street (409–275–3610). The home belonged to a judge and Texas House of Representatives member who fought for public school lands funding. This Greek-revival house was built in 1839, given to the Daughters of the Republic of Texas by Cullen's family, and is headquarters for an annual tour of homes in April. Open Monday through Saturday from 1:00 P.M. until 4:00 P.M.; admission is $1.00.

San Augustine's quiet, shady environs are likely to lull you into taking time out from the journey. Maybe it's time to check into **The Wade House,** 202 East Livingston Street (409–275–5489 or 275–2553), within walking distance of the historic downtown area. The house sleeps seventeen in six rooms with three private baths and one shared bath, and continental breakfast is offered, as is use of the kitchen.

From San Augustine, continue your tour on Texas Highway 21 36 miles to **Nacogdoches** (NACK-ah-DOE-chez), the town generally credited with being the oldest in Texas. The settlement is historically believed to have had hospitable Indians—the Caddo people—when the Spaniards came through en route to Mexico, probably around 1541 or 1542. The first permanent European settlement, however, is dated at 1716, when Father Margil founded the Mission of Our Lady of the Guadalupe of Nacogdoches; it was abandoned in 1773, when the settlers were ordered to move to San Antonio.

Several weren't happy and moved back with Antonio Gil Ybarbo to Nacogdoches; in 1779 he laid out the town and built a stone house and trading post there, which survives as ✦**The Old Stone Fort,** the town's most heritage-packed site. An exact replica of Ybarbo's structure sits today on the Stephen F. Austin State University Campus, at Griffith and Clark streets (409–568–2408). Its long and colorful history includes its service as a fort and a prison, as well as government headquarters during many attempts to establish the Republic of Texas; its function as offices for the first two newspapers published in Texas; and the place that Bowie, Thomas Rusk, Sam Houston, and Davy Crockett were administered the oath of allegiance to Mexico. Nine different flags have flown over the fort, including those from three failed revolutions. Now a museum, the Old Stone Fort offers exhibits detailing this tumultuous past and the people who left an indelible mark on the republic and the state. Open Tuesday through Saturday from 9:00 A.M. until 5:00 P.M., and Sunday from 1:00 P.M. until 5:00 P.M. Admission is free, but the museum welcomes donations.

Nacogdoches is fairly flooded with historic sites directly related to the Republic of Texas. One that must not be missed is the **Sterne-Hoya House**, 211 South Lanana Street (409–569–5426), built in 1828 by Adolphus Sterne, a prominent land owner who raised $10,000 to outfit a volunteer company to serve in San Antonio. Sam Houston was baptized there in the Roman Catholic faith in 1833 as Mexican law required at the time to become a Texas citizen. Today the home is a memorial library and museum of Texas history since colonization. Open Monday through Saturday from 9:00 A.M. until 12:00 noon and 2:00 P.M. until 5:00 P.M. Admission is free.

Nearby **Oak Grove Cemetery,** Lanana at Hospital streets, is where four of the signers of the Texas Declaration of Independence are buried. One is Thomas Rusk, secretary of war in the republic, San Jacinto hero, commander-in-chief in Sam Houston's army, and one of the first U.S. senators from Austin. Another is William Clark, the great grandfather of this author's maternal grandmother. The cemetery is always open, and there is no admission.

Today Nacogdoches—seat of the same-named county—is home to nearly 29,000 residents, some of whom have worked to make a success of several worthy downtown antiques shops, as well as the showplace known as **Millard's Crossing,** at the north end of town (6020 North Street, also U.S. Highway 59 North, 409–564–6631). Numerous nineteenth-century homes and commercial buildings have been relocated here in a village setting. Among them is the first Methodist parsonage (1900) and its chapel (1843); a rustic stone-and-log cabin (1830); and the Millard-Burrows House (1840), graced with enormous holly bushes and an iron fence with fleur de lis detail. Tours are given Monday through Saturday from 9:00 A.M. until 4:00 P.M. and Sunday from 1:00 P.M. until 4:00 P.M. Admission is $3.00 for adults and $2.00 for children.

Take time out to have a good Mexican lunch or dinner at **La Hacienda,** 1411 North Street (409–564–6450). Situated in a lovely home built in 1913, the restaurant has a long reputation for hearty Tex-Mex plates, as well as steaks, chicken, and seafood. It's open daily for lunch and dinner.

Do plan to relax for a few days at the **Llano Grande Plantation Bed and Breakfast,** a complex of three historic homes sheltered deep in the woods immediately south of town. The centerpiece is the Tol Barrett house, a pioneer farmhouse dating to 1840, named for its original owner, the oilman credited as being the first to drill a producing well west of the Mississippi. It's rustic but infinitely comfortable. Its front is framed by myriad wildflowers, and the interior is filled with period pieces. Guests cook their own breakfasts of venison sausage and homemade breads (in the stocked kitchen, of course) in this private house; other guests stay in one of the two other lovingly restored houses, within walking distance of the Tol Barrett. Guests find their hosts to be hospitable and friendly historians. Reservations and directions must be obtained in advance by calling (409) 569-1249.

THE NINETEENTH-CENTURY TRAIL

From Nacogdoches head east on the very scenic Texas Highway 21—once the famed El Camino Real—25 miles to the town of Alto, where you'll head north on U.S. Highway 69 12 miles to reach **Rusk**. Just under 4,400 people live in the Cherokee County seat, cited for having the nation's longest footbridge, measuring 546 feet, located in Footbridge Garden Park, 1 block east of the town square on East Fifth Street. The town was also the birthplace of Jim Hogg and Thomas Mitchell Campbell, the first and second native-born Texans to serve as governor.

Most visitors come to Rusk with a single purpose, that of riding the ◆**Texas State Railroad,** which has one of its two depots here. **Rusk State Park** is spread with one hundred acres of pines and hardwoods surrounding the train terminal. Not only can you catch the scenic train ride here, but you can camp, hike on trails, picnic, rent paddle boats and rowboats, turn the kids loose in a playground, play tennis, and cast for catfish, bass, and perch in the fifteen-acre stocked lake. The park is 2 miles west of town on U.S. Highway 84, (903) 683-5126; it's open at all times, and admission is $3.00 per vehicle.

The Texas State Railroad is said to be the longest and skinniest state park in the entire nation, as it offers travelers the chance to ride just under 26 miles between Rusk and **Palestine,** a town directly west. Passengers ride in vintage coaches powered by antique steam engines through gorgeous forest lands, decorated with pink-and-white dogwood blooms in spring and rust-scarlet-gold tapestries in fall. There's a snack bar aboard the train and short-order restaurants at both terminals. The train trip is exceptionally popular, and reservations are a must. In service on weekends from March through May and in October, and Thursday through Monday during summer months. Train fare is $11.00 for adults and $6.00 for children; call (903) 683–2561 or (800) 442–8951 in Texas only for reservations.

In Palestine, the Anderson County seat and home to 18,000 Texans, your sightseeing opportunities are varied. The **Howard House Museum,** 1011 North Perry Street (903–729–2511 or 729–4784), has been established in an 1851 home and offers a doll collection, an array of antique photos depicting early residents and events, and good period furniture. The home is shown by appointment but is usually open during Palestine's **Dogwood Trails,** a popular event among Texans from around the state, as it is a prime opportunity to see the delicate pink-white blooms cover the forests in a dainty blanket. The event is usually held in late March and early April and features historic homes touring, a parade in historic downtown, an arts and crafts festival, a chili cook-off, a community theater play, trolley tours, and a car show. Contact the festival headquarters at (903) 729–7275.

Travelers not returning right away on the train to Rusk will want to consider a night or two at a remote bed-and-breafast spread on a lovely East Texas Christmas tree farm near Palestine. Called **Grandma's House,** the farm has two petite guesthouses, a "bunkhouse" of sorts, and lots of acreage on which to stroll, watch deer graze, and fish. Breakfast in the hosts' farmhouse is a bounteous production of eggs, sausages, homemade breads and preserves, as well as juices and coffee or tea. For reservations, call Bed and Breakfast Texas Style in Dallas at (214) 298–8586.

Once back in Rusk via the Texas State Railroad, you can continue your journey by driving north on U.S. Highway 69 14 miles to **Jacksonville,** another Cherokee County town. Known fifty years ago for its abundant tomato crop, the modest city of 12,000 residents today is known for baskets. ◆**The Texas Basket Company,** 100 Myrtle Drive (903–586–8014), is one of a handful of such companies still in operation in the nation. Established in 1924, this outfit still uses original equipment to make baskets crafted entirely from wood cut within 200 miles of town, including sweet gum, black gum, birch, hackberry, elm, cottonwood, and sweet bay wood. Between 6,000 and 10,000 baskets are produced daily for shipment to all fifty states, as well as to Canada, Germany, and Puerto Rico. Visitors can watch craftspeople at work, and most will want to spend some shopping time in the large store, stocked with thousands of baskets in every imaginable shape and size. Open Monday through Saturday from 8:00 A.M. until 5:00 P.M. Admission is free.

Travelers who enjoy a leisurely drive filled with exquisite scenery will rejoice in the countryside surrounding Jacksonville. Take a picnic to **Love's Lookout Park,** on the roadside 5 miles north of town on U.S. Highway 69. Or just take a few soft drinks and soak in the hilly vistas of forest and water on Farm Roads 747 and 2138 wrapping around Lake Jacksonville.

For a lake of greater import, follow U.S. Highway 175 from Jacksonville 17 miles west to Frankston and catch Texas Highway 155 north, which crosses **Lake Palestine,** a 25,500-acre impoundment on the Neches River in this rolling timberland. Anglers especially will want to spend time here, as the lake is known for record catches, such as a twelve-pound striper bass and a twelve-pound largemouth bass. Water-skiing is popular here, as well. Marinas and campgrounds surround the lake, as do numerous catfish restaurants serving up the freshest local catches.

From the east side of Lake Palestine, continue north on Texas Highway 155 another 13 miles to **Tyler,** the Rose City of Texas. The Smith County seat, Tyler has over 75,000 residents. After the Civil War, nurserymen found the sandy soil and rainfall ideal for growing fruit trees and roses. The fruit trees became diseased before the turn of the century, however, and the rose business carried these growers happily into the 1900s. Today, more than a third of the nation's commercially grown rose bushes are raised within a 50-mile radius of Tyler.

Visitors revel in the glory found at Tyler's ✦**Municipal Rose Garden,** 1900 West Front Street (903–531–1370), where more than 30,000 rose bushes in 500 varieties fill a fourteen-acre park—making it the country's largest municipal rose garden. The blooming season peaks in mid-May and continues through November. The garden is open daily from 6:00 A.M. until 10:00 P.M. Admission is free.

This huge rose business gives rise to the **Texas Rose Festival**, a giant celebration held every October, complete with the crowning of a Rose Queen, a rose show featuring more than 100,000 roses, and parades, balls, antiques shows, crafts fairs, and more. Call the chamber of commerce for details at (903) 592–1661.

It's appropriate, then, that the sweetest place to stay in Tyler is the **Rosevine Inn**, 415 South Vine Avenue (903–592–2221). A 1930s-style home in a bricked-street area becoming well known for good antiques shops, the inn is surrounded by a white picket fence with well-manicured grounds. The interior is thoughtfully decorated as an inn, its cozy corners and comfortable rooms scattered with antiques and country decor. All five rooms have a private bath, and there's a hot tub on the patio. Breakfasts are gourmet affairs, and afternoons bring wine and cheese or coffee and cookies.

Tyler is a central location for various East Texas side trips. One to keep in mind is a jaunt to ◆ **Edom**, west of Tyler 15 miles via Texas 31 and Farm Road 279. A tiny artists' enclave, Edom is becoming known for its extraordinary annual Arts and Crafts show held in September, with juried works drawing artists from around the nation. Several artists—mostly crafters of pottery, leather, and brass—keep shops in town right on the main street, which is Farm Road 279. These shops don't keep regular hours, so you have to take your chances. Next to a row on shops on the road is **The Shed**, a simple country cafe serving huge lunches and dinners, with specialties including pork chops, chicken-fried steak, catfish, and enormous coconut, banana cream, and chocolate pies. The cafe's phone is (903) 852–7791.

Most travelers come to Edom, however, to stay at **Wild Briar**, a pretty modern home on twenty-three acres in the country operating as a bed-and-breakfast inn. A large den serves as a parlor, where guests gather by the fireplace before dinner or breakfast: The hosts have hosted more than a dozen weddings there. Dinners are an event, with cheese vegetable soup, eye-of-round roast beef, three fresh vegetables brought from the Farmers' Market in Dallas, grilled potatoes, black-bottom pie or peach cobbler composing a typical meal. Breakfast is nearly as elaborate. A British theme is carried throughout the inn, as the hosts have spent years traveling in England, Scotland, and Wales. For reservations, call (903) 852–3975.

Another option is an excursion to **Kilgore,** east of Tyler 25 miles via Texas Highway 31. Crude, classics, and kicks aren't what most people expect in an East Texas town of 11,000: Home to the **World's Richest Acre,** Kilgore has the mammoth success of the Great Texas Oil Field discovery in 1930 to thank for its prosperity, but the community is best known as giving the world its most famous classical pianist, Van Cliburn, who now resides in Fort Worth; it's also responsible for the phenomenon known as the drill team.

First the oil business: Head to the corner of Main and Commerce streets, a small area with one life-size derrick and twenty-three mini-derricks representing the oil boom days when more than a thousand wells were jammed into the downtown area and twenty-four wells, claimed by six different operators, were crowded onto a one-acre site, creating the World's Richest Acre, which produced more than two and a half million barrels of crude oil.

To see the industry explained in an interesting manner, visit the **East Texas Oil Museum,** Henderson Boulevard at Ross Street on the Kilgore College campus (903–983–8295), and see how a town grew from 800 to 8,000 residents in twenty-four hours. There's a working oil rig out front, with a 70-foot wooden derrick, steam boiler, rotary table, and draw works. A realistic model of a 1930s street is created inside, complete with a car stuck in the mud, board sidewalks, post office, barbershop, general store, sounds of a thunderstorm building overhead, and music from a period radio. Firsthand accounts of boom-town existence can be heard through headphones; a fifteen-minute film of actual footage is shown in a "town theater," with the theater rumbling during a gusher; and an elevator takes riders to the center of the earth. This just scratches the surface of the museum's offerings; see for yourself Tuesday through Saturday from 9:00 A.M. until 4:00 P.M. and Sunday from 2:00 P.M. until 5:00 P.M. Admission is $3.50 for adults and $2.00 for children.

For something radically different, and certainly more frivolous, walk down the street a block to the ❖ **Rangerette Showcase,** also on the Kilgore College campus, at Broadway and Ross streets (903–984–8531). In this little corner of East Texas is yet another worldwide attention getter, born ten years after the oil boom began. The Kilgore Rangerettes formed their first high-kick line in

1940, and the showcase tells the story of this famous precision-and-drill dance team of Kilgore College. Some may say it is sexist, but many will argue it's just Texas camp. The first of their kind, Red Grange called them the "sweethearts of the nation's gridiron," and they perform annually on New Year's Day at the Cotton Bowl halftime, their painted red lips matching their shirts, contrasting with little blue skirts and white boots and cowgirl hats. The group responsible for putting showbiz on the football field is chronicled through an assemblage of displays with historical films and videos and decades of newspaper clippings illustrating the team's global reach. The showcase is open Tuesday through Friday from 10:00 A.M. until 12:00 noon and 1:00 P.M. until 5:00 P.M., and Saturday and Sunday from 2:00 P.M. until 5:00 P.M. Admission is free.

Even if these attractions don't draw you to Kilgore, probably **The Country Tavern,** on Texas Highway 31 just on the western outskirts of town, will. Most patrons are from all over Texas, and many will argue that this unassuming beer joint serves the best pork ribs in the state. A juke box and dance floor are good for dancing the Texas two-step, and blue-jeaned waitresses are good for friendly local color. For exactly thirty years, this place has served up the biggest platter of ribs in memory, with sides of tasty potato salad, onions, and pickles. Open Monday through Saturday for lunch and dinner, the tavern's phone is (903) 984-9954.

Still another side trip from Tyler is **Mineola** (minny-OH-lah), north 27 miles on U.S. Highway 69. It's a modest but respectable collection of antiques shops that brings folks to Mineola but it's the ◆**Munzesheimer Manor,** at 202 North Newsom Street (903–569–6634), that makes them stay. The remarkable 1906 home—with stained-glass windows, seven fireplaces, wraparound porch, and footed tubs—has been thoroughly restored and spread with English and American antiques. It's a huge, comfortable home, perfect for settling in with a cup of tea and a good novel. Breakfasts during the week are continental, while weekends are full affairs with such treats as fresh berries and German Pancakes.

The final side trip from Tyler—this one to **Canton**—may well be the best. Head west of Tyler 40 miles on Texas Highway 64, and you'll wind up directly at the Van Zandt County Courthouse Square, just a few yards beyond your actual destination, ◆**First Monday Trade Days.** If you arrive early and are lucky, you may be able to find a parking spot on the square or nearby, then just walk the block east to the one-hundred-acre fair-grounds, where some 5,000 vendors are spread out with their goods for sale. This, of course, occurs the Friday, Saturday, and Sunday preceding the first Monday of each month. Since the middle of the nineteenth century, country folks have been traveling here to buy and sell everything from kitchen wares, clothes, farm equipment, furniture, and toys to baby carriages, jewelry, home-made jellies and jams, and books. Collectors of Depression glass, quilts, iron beds, and china find this a great place to hunt bargains. Food booths are set up everywhere, too, selling burgers, barbecue, pastries, and cold drinks. It's a colorful experience well worth taking in even for visitors who aren't in the market to buy anything. Trade Days gates open at 7:00 A.M. and close at dark; for information, call the chamber of commerce at (903) 567–2991.

This last side trip done, you'll want to head on from Tyler to **Big Sandy,** 30 miles north on Texas 155. A burg of just 1,100 in Upshur County, Big Sandy is home to ◆ **Annie's,** an unusually busy complex for such a tiny town. What started as a kitchen-table business of mail-order sales of needlework patterns in the 1970s has exploded into a retailing and hospitality industry spread over several buildings splashed with pastel paints and endearing Victorian appeal. First, there's Annie's Tea Room, at U.S. Highway 80 and Texas Highway 155, a sweet place to have breakfast, lunch, or tea; offerings typically include cold strawberry soup, cream-cheese-stuffed French toast, chicken salad, and orange muffins. It's open Sunday through Friday from 9:00 A.M. until 5:00 P.M. and is closed Saturday. Call (903) 636–4952 for information. Next door, there's a gift shop and needlework-catalog publishing business. Directly across the street is Annie's Country Inn, a bed-and-breakfast house with thirteen rooms. It's all lacy and frilled, with small but comfortable rooms. The parlor downstairs usually winds up being a good place to meet fellow travelers over a cup of tea or a glass of wine. For reservations, call (903) 636–4355.

From Big Sandy, it's only 10 miles east on U.S. Highway 80 to the ◆ **Antique Capital of East Texas,** seen on the map as **Gladewater,** a town of 6,000 Texans in Gregg County with more than 250 antiques dealers scattered around in sixteen antiques malls and sixteen individual shops. Most of the shopping is con-centrated in Gladewater's vintage downtown area, all within easy walking distance from one point to another. One of the shops is **Miss Lou Della's,** at 111 South Main Street (903–845–2655), a place to find nineteenth- and early twentieth-century collectibles. In the rear of the store, the Soda Fountain is a yesteryear relic of huge marble-top counters, carved mahogany bar backs, checkerboard floor, and parlor chairs and tables. Delectables here include apple dumplings topped with ice cream and peach-amaretto flavoring and pecan-honey butter, chicken-salad sandwiches, old-fashioned burgers, and cherry phosphates. The soda fountain is open Tuesday through Sunday, 11:00 A.M. until 5:00 P.M.

From Gladewater, continue east to **Longview,** 13 miles east on U.S. Highway 80. The unassuming town of 70,000 is the Gregg County seat and has a heritage of railroad, agriculture, lumber, and oil businesses that left it somewhat undistinguished. This has changed, however, in recent years, as the popularity of the ◆ **Great Texas Balloon Race** has skyrocketed. For a three-day weekend in early July, hundreds of brightly colored hot-air balloons can be seen scattered throughout the sky in early morning or evening as pilots from around the nation compete in tests of skill. The contest involves a pilot's ability to maneuver the balloon between points and drop a marker on a designated target—all of which is determined by the winds. Besides the flights, there are on-ground events during the festival, such as arts and crafts fairs, aircraft exhibits, evening concerts, and other fun for spectators. The party is held at the Gregg County Airport; information is available from the chamber of commerce, (903) 753–3281. Admission is free, but parking fees are charged.

Two other diversions are worth investigating in Longview. First, the **Gregg County Historical Museum** is a modest but interesting collection of area memorabilia detailing the growth of the county from the late nineteenth century through World War II. The bank building, built in 1910, makes a handsome home for the museum, lending itself to exhibits such as a period bank president's office and vault. A hands-on area is good for children. Find the museum at 214 North Fredonia Street (903–753–5840). Admission is $2.00 for adults and $1.00 for children; the museum is open Tuesday through Saturday from 10:00 A.M. until 4:00 P.M.

There's also the **Stroh's Brewery Tour,** offering a look at the largest brewery in Texas, producing nearly four million barrels of beer each year. Tours last forty minutes; they cover the

113

brewing and packing areas, end with sampling in the hospitality room, and are conducted Monday through Friday at 10:00 A.M., 11:00 A.M., 1:00 P.M., 2:00 P.M., and 3:00 P.M. Stroh's is found at 1400 West Cotton Street (903–753–0371). Admission is free.

The suds may work up your appetite, so head for **Bodacious Barbecue**, 227 South Mobberly, an East Texas institution famous for its chopped-beef sandwiches, as well as sliced beef brisket, ribs, and spicy links. Open for lunch Monday through Saturday.

With bellies full, try to find the strength to push on to **Marshall,** 23 miles east on U.S. Highway 80. The Harrison County seat, with almost 24,000 residents, has a deep southern heritage imbued with plantations and Civil War history—in fact, more than 150 historical markers are found throughout Harrison County. So strong is its legacy that newsman Bill Moyers, Marshall's favorite son, hosted a PBS broadcast titled "Marshall, Texas, Marshall, Texas" in his *A Walk Through the 20th Century with Bill Moyers.*

People whose artistic tendencies run toward throwing clay may have already heard about Marshall's famous retailer, ◆**Marshall Pottery,** an old-fashioned business celebrating its centennial in 1995. Found at 4901 Elysian Street, the pottery is the largest manufacturer of red clay pots in the nation, but it retains every bit of its friendly country charm. Master potters—some of whom are third- and fourth-generation potters—can be observed at their craft, some painting the cobalt-blue decoration commonly seen on the glazed bowls, pitchers, mugs, and dinnerware. These items are all for sale and are always reasonably priced. Under the same roof are twenty shops with savings on baskets, silk flowers, linens, candles, and other decorative housewares. Outside, a "seconds" yard is filled with slightly misshapen or barely chipped pottery—look for real steals here on many things that don't appear to be damaged at all. Next to the main building, a Victorian cottage houses the Hungry Potter, a cafe open for lunch daily. Soups, salads, and sandwiches are better than average, but the pies, cobblers, and other sweets are worth a long look. Open Monday through Saturday from 9:00 A.M. until 6:00 P.M. and Sunday from 12:00 noon until 6:00 P.M. Admission is free; the phone number is (903) 938–9201.

Artistic expression of a different nature is in the **Michelson-Reves Art Museum,** 216 North Bolivar Street (903–935–9480), a small treasure house of works by French impressionist Leo

Michelson (1887–1978). His work is also displayed in museums in Baltimore, Jerusalem, Paris, San Diego, and Tel Aviv, among others. Traveling exhibits fill the gallery, as well. Open Tuesday through Friday from 12:00 noon until 5:00 P.M., and Saturday and Sunday from 1:00 P.M. until 4:00 P.M.; admission is $2.00 for adults and $1.00 for children.

The folks in Marshall are big on celebrations, and the **Fire Ant Festival,** held annually on the second weekend in October, is a fine example. Some 50,000 people have been known to pour into town for a party dedicated to a truly aggravating insect, so you know this is a place with a sense of humor. Costume contests, fire ant calling contests, a chili cook-off, the World Championship Pizza Crust Fling, and a parade are among the wild and woolly events. Things calm down a bit in time for the holidays, and Marshall lights up like a Christmas tree—literally. The Wonderland of Lights is focused on the historic county courthouse, which is covered with four and a half million tiny white lights, and area businesses and homes are aglow, as well, from Thanksgiving until New Year's Day. For information on special events, call the chamber of commerce at (903) 935–7868.

The chamber of commerce is also a good source to find the right bed-and-breakfast home for you. One of the finest houses in town is a B&B, **La Maison Malfaçon,** at 700 East Rusk Street (903–935–6039); the first floor of the Greek-revival mansion was built in 1866, and the second floor was added thirty years later. The antique pieces throughout are magnificent, especially in the Shakespeare Room, a guest room with an 1840s hand-carved bed and dresser; and in the Plantation Room, with its 200-year-old four-poster bed covered with a nineteenth-century quilt. Several other good B&Bs are in town, and even the ones said to be occupied by ghosts are very popular. Call the chamber at (903) 935–7868.

BAYOUS, LAKES, AND LEGENDS

From Marshall, you need travel only 14 miles northeast on Texas Highway 43 to find one of the state's greatest natural assets, ✦**Caddo Lake.** The only lake in Texas not created artificially, the 35,400-acre lake is characterized by seven-century-old cypress trees draped in an ethereal manner with heavy curtains of Spanish moss. The effect nature has wrought is one of a haunting beauty, appropriate for a place whose creation is a mystery. One legend holds that the reservoir was formed when a resident Caddo Indian chief was warned by the Great Spirits to move his people to a higher ground or watch them die in a terrible earthquake and flood. It seems he ignored them and chose to take his warriors hunting, as they returned to find that a mighty shake had occurred and their village had been replaced by a huge lake. Some part of the story could be true, as recorded history shows that an earthquake in 1811 in New Madrid, Missouri, is estimated to have had a force that would register 8.9 on today's Richter scale—and it's possible that that tremor created a logjam in the Red River that dammed Caddo Lake, lapping a bit across the Louisiana state line.

Naturally, photographers and painters are captured by Caddo's ancient beauty, best seen on boat tours led by lake experts. These sloughs and canals are terribly confusing to anyone unfamiliar with its shrouded paths, but the fishing and wildlife watching are far too wonderful to pass up. One tour option is **Sarge's Barge,** departing Curley's Lodge, near **Caddo Lake State Park,** on Texas Highway 43, on the lake's south shore (903–679–3834 or 789–3352). Tours cover 15 miles of lake area, last a little more than an hour, and include plenty of history and local color. Call ahead for reservations.

At the state park, on Farm Road 2198, just 1 mile east of Texas Highway 43 (903–679–3351), several rock cabins are available for rental, but they are reserved for weekend stays up to ninety days ahead, so call early or try for a weeknight stay. Shaded by towering pines near the water, these are nice places to kick back for a while. Canoe rentals are offered in the park, as is camping, fishing, hiking, picnicking, and nature study.

Adjacent to the park is the tiny community of **Uncertain**—and no one's certain how the name came about. One theory says that when the hamlet was contemplating incorporation, a poll was taken to choose a town name, and "Uncertain" was frequently listed on the third-choice line. Of one thing you can be sure, there is a cluster of little businesses offering rustic accommodations, marina and fishing guide services (helpful in navigation and landing big catfish and bass), cafes, and good humor. Among these multi-service places are Shady Glade (903–789–3295) and Crip's Camp (903–789–3233).

A little side trip into history from Caddo is a short drive away at ◆ **T. C. Lindsey and Company General Store,** found by following Farm Road 134 13 miles east in the town of Jonesville. In business since 1847, it's still a family-owned, no-frills country store. With high ceilings and creaky wooden floors, this general store is obviously the real McCoy. Shelves are stacked with groceries, fabrics, and feed, while a room off to the side is now a makeshift museum. You'll find farm tools, ancient hunting traps, horseshoes, massive iron skillets, and other relics from another time. Glass cases in front hold antique eyeglasses, glass bottles, toiletries, and household items used by our grandparents and great-grandparents. Snacks, candies, cold drinks, and slices from a massive wheel of cheese will tide you over until supper. The store is open Monday through Saturday from 8:00 A.M. until 4:30 P.M. Admission is free; call the store at (903) 687–3382.

From Caddo Lake, your next destination could be the old bayou town of **Jefferson,** a town packed with charm and romance, reached west from the lake 13 miles on Farm Road 134. The Marion County community of 2,200 is rapidly growing in stature around the state for its perfect balance of historical preservation and hospitality.

A good place to call home during a few days of relaxation and exploration is ◆ **The Excelsior House,** at 211 West Austin Street (903–665–2513). The second-oldest hotel in Texas, the Excelsior has been in continuous operation since 1858 and has hosted dignitaries such as Ulysses S. Grant, Rutherford B. Hayes, W. H. Vanderbilt, Oscar Wilde, and Lyndon B. and Lady Bird Johnson. A beautiful place with ornate furniture and heavy, baroque French frames around paintings, crystal chandeliers, oriental carpets, a grand piano, Italian marble mantles, and pressed-tin ceiling, it's a showplace, as well as a delightful setting in which to have a plantation breakfast—by reservation, of course. The fourteen rooms and suites are in demand on weekends, so call ahead or try for a mid-week visit.

The Excelsior's 1961 restoration spurred revitalization throughout the town, which had fallen into a quiet decline after its riverboat days were long past. In the nineteenth century, steamboats churned the waters of the Big Cypress Bayou from Jefferson, via Caddo Lake and the Red River, all the way south to New Orleans. Today's visitors can still tour the bayou aboard the *Bayou Queen*, an open-air boat departing Jefferson Landing four times

117

Jefferson

daily in spring, summer, and fall for one-hour, narrated tours. Call (903) 665–2222 for hours; admission is $4.50 for adults, $3.00 for children.

Another way to see the water and woodsy environs is aboard the **Jefferson and Cypress Bayou Railroad,** a narrow-gauge railroad powered by an antique steam locomotive winding along the bayou on a scenic, 5-mile route; this is another great way to gain an overview of the town. Tours are offered Friday, Saturday, and Sunday at 1:30 P.M. and 3:30 P.M. Admission is $6.50 for adults and $4.50 for children. Call (903) 665–8400 for details and schedule updates.

For more background on the town and area, head for **Jefferson Historical Museum,** 223 West Austin Street (903–665–2775), where history lessons are made fun. Housed in a former federal courthouse and post office (1888), this big red gem of the past contains three floors of the historical society's collected memories. More than 30,000 visitors come annually to see the dress Lady Bird Johnson (from nearby Karnack) wore to a State dinner for the West German chancellor, sterling silver flatware that belonged to Whistler's mother; and personal belongings of Sam Houston and Annie Oakley. Admission is $1.00 for adults and 50 cents for children.

Dozens of antiques shops are found along the brick streets of downtown in historic commercial buildings. Some beautiful nineteenth-century homes are open for tours year round, while eight designated homes are chosen annually to be on show during the **Jefferson Pilgrimage,** always held the first weekend in May. The weekend features not only the homes but also the **Diamond Bessie Murder Trial,** a wonderful melodrama based on the story of a former prostitute who was thought to have been murdered by her rich diamond-merchant husband. For Pilgrimage information, contact the chamber of commerce, (903) 665–2672, or the Jessie Allen Wise Garden Club, event hosts, at the Excelsior Hotel, (903) 665–2513.

Many of Jefferson's lovingly renovated houses—more than forty, in fact—are open as bed and breakfast lodgings. Many of these are showplaces, some are romantic hideouts, and others are good for families. Count on warm hospitality and excellent breakfasts. For a complete listing, inquire at the chamber of commerce, 116 West Austin Street, or call (903) 665–2672.

For a detour into curiosity, take an hour's drive north from Jefferson on U.S. Highway 59 to **Texarkana,** sometimes called the State Line Cities, as it's part Texas, part Arkansas—hence, the name. Of particular interest here is ◆ **The Perot Theatre,** at 221 Main Street (903–792–4992), an Italian Renaissance theater opened as The Saenger in 1924. Seating 1,600 patrons, it was among the most famous showplaces in a four-state area in its heyday. In the late 1970s, Texarkana native, now Dallas billionaire, Ross Perot donated two million dollars to restore the theater to its former magnificence with glistening chandeliers, royal-blue and gold interiors, and marble floors. A symphony series, plays, musicals, and pop music concerts are staged here from September through May. Tours are by reservation, depending on scheduled events.

Most unusual in Texarkana is the **Bi-State Justice Center,** at 100 North State Line Avenue (903–798–3000), a building straddling the Texas-Arkansas line and, therefore, shared by two cities, two counties, and two states. It is thought to be the world's only post office and federal building with a state line bisecting it. As was appropriate, the building was crafted from both Texas pink granite and Arkansas limestone. The building is open Monday through Friday from 8:00 A.M. until 5:00 P.M.; tours are free and by appointment.

From Jefferson, there is still much to be seen in the way of outdoor beauty. To sample this bounty, drive west from Jefferson on Farm Road 729 for 17 miles and you'll find yourself at the shores of shimmering ✪ **Lake o' the Pines,** surrounded by lush hardwoods and pines, a scene that's splendid in autumn, as the leaves make quite a show of changing to crimson, burnt orange, and amber. The lake is 18,000 acres, with excellent fishing for large-mouth bass, white bass, and spotted bass; swimming, water-skiing, and sailing are favorites here, too. Campsites abound, as do picnic areas and nature trails. The Army Corps of Engineers, (903) 665–2336, offers more information.

About 10 miles north of the lake via U.S. Highway 259, the town of **Daingerfield,** Morris County seat and home to 2,500 Texans, offers supplies, groceries, lodging, and an excellent array of cheesecakes and other sweets at Main Street Bakery. Check out the offerings available at the chamber of commerce, 208 Jefferson Street, (903) 645–2646.

At **Daingerfield State Park,** immediately east of town on Texas Highway 11, 550 acres of pine-blanketed land surrounds a lovely, eighty-acre, spring-fed lake. Photographers have traveled from around the state to capture the color riot in autumn, and spring's demonstration is just as dramatic, as redbuds, dogwoods, and wisteria explode in shades of pink and purple. Hiking trails, fishing, camping, cabins, playgrounds, and picnic areas make this a place to stay for more than a day. For information and reservations, call the park office at (903) 645–2921.

From Daingerfield, travel west 16 miles on Texas Highway 11 to **Pittsburg,** the Camp County seat and home to 4,000 residents. Its economy is based on a significant poultry business—Pilgrims Pride alone produces more than 600 million pounds of chicken yearly—but Pittsburg's moderate fame is due to the ✪ **Ezekiel Airship,** a replica of a 1902 flying craft that, while undocumented, is said to have been airborne a year before the

Wright Brothers made their first flight. Its inventor was a sometime Baptist preacher who took his idea of an airship from the prophet Ezekiel, who described in the Bible an apparatus that flew. The preacher raised $20,000, selling stock in his company, and built his ship. Unfortunately, it was destroyed during shipment to the St. Louis World's Trade Fair in 1904. A 26-by-23-foot replica, created from historical notes and a photo, is displayed at Warrick's Restaurant, 142 Marshall Street (903–856–7881). The restaurant serves dinner nightly, and there's no charge to see the airship.

The chicken business may be big here, and there is a Spring Chick Festival held in Pittsburg in late April, but the primary food found here is the **Pittsburg Hot Link.** The not-too-spicy sausage made from beef and pork is, appropriately, served up hot at the Pittsburg Hot Links Restaurant, 136 Marshall Street (903–856–5765). Patrons place their orders at the counter in back, ordering links by the link or having other specialties, such as beef stew, chili, burgers, or chicken-fried steak. The restaurant is open Monday through Saturday from 9:00 A.M. until 6:00 P.M.

Before heading back to your cabin at Daingerfield, your campsite at Lake o' the Pines, or your cozy corner in Jefferson, consider another detour, this time to **Winnsboro,** a pleasant hamlet just 22 miles west of Pittsburg on Texas Highway 11. There's another pretty lake here for a dip in summer, but the primary attractions come after the weather begins changing. Fall foliage is a cause for big celebrations, hence the **Autumn Trails Festival,** held every weekend in October. The chamber of commerce hosts an antique car show and a homes tour; driving maps to see the best in fall's color parade are offered, too. And the Christmas season brings folks from all over East and North Texas to choose a special tree from one of the several area Christmas tree farms; hot apple cider is a bonus offered by the farmers while customers find the prettiest evergreen. For details, contact the chamber of commerce, 201 West Broadway Avenue, (903) 342–3666.

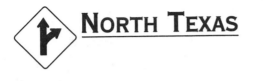

NORTH TEXAS

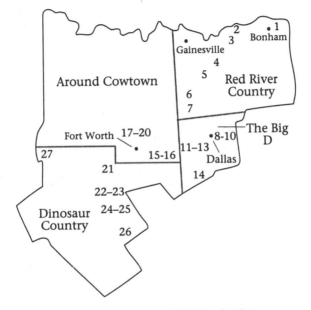

Gainesville

2
3
Bonham 1

Around Cowtown

4
5
Red River Country

6
7

Fort Worth 17–20
15-16
11–13 •8-10 ┌The Big D
•
27
21
Dallas
14

22–23
24–25

Dinosaur Country
26

1. Sam Rayburn Library
2. Lake Texoma
3. Hart's Country Inn
4. Clark's Outpost
5. Little Chapel in the Woods
6. Ranchman's Cafe
7. Texas Lil's Diamond A Ranch
8. The Museum of African-
   American Life and Culture
9. Deep Ellum
10. The Mesquite
    Championship Rodeo
11. Farmers' Market
12. Belo Mansion
13. The Dallas World
    Aquarium

14. Waxahachie
15. Caelum Moor
16. Ballpark in Arlington
17. Cultural District
18. Cattleman's Museum
19. Sundance Square
20. Stockyards National
    Historic District
21. Acton State Historic Site
22. The Nutt House
23. *Granbury Queen*
24. Inn on the River
25. Dinosaur Valley State Park
26. Clifton
27. Possum Kingdom Lake
    State Park

NORTH TEXAS

North Texas mirrors the Lone Star State's uncanny ability to wear a vast number of different hats. Denying any one classification or description, the region exhibits a broad range of personalities. Big D, as Dallas is proudly called in the Southwest, was built largely from the fruits of the oil and cattle industries and is known as well as a major fashion, electronics, and motion pictures center. Further, Dallas boasts having more restaurants per capita than any city in the nation, and the city joins Fort Worth in being home to teams competing in every professional sport. Together the two are called the Metroplex. Fort Worth, 30 miles east, is also called Cowtown, and it is famous for a curious mix of Wild West and world-class fine arts. In addition, Fort Worth has a restored stockyards area where Butch and Sundance hid out and where today you can "scoot a boot" in the world's largest honky tonk.

Travelers to the North Texas region find that in perfect balance to this unusual cosmopolitan–Wild West mix are the small towns where a simpler way of life is still valued. Communities that gave the world such dignitaries as Sam Rayburn and Dwight D. Eisenhower are special places that continue to live in yesteryear, where historic houses and pretty lakes—instead of shopping malls and symphonies—are the draws. Exotic wildlife ranches, a quiet Norse community, a rustic ranch where city folks can play cowboy for a day, an ancient riverbed where dinosaur tracks are plainly visible—these are the places where people go to escape fax machines and voice mail.

RED RIVER COUNTRY

Oldest town in the Red River Valley and home to more than 6,600 residents, the Fannin County seat of **Bonham** was settled in 1837 by a former Arkansas sheriff who brought settlers to a land grant he received from the Republic of Texas. The community was eventually named for James Butler Bonham, the Alamo's courageous messenger, whose statue stands before the courthouse.

But Bonham's greatest claim to fame is Sam Rayburn, the political legend who spent forty-nine consecutive years, or twenty-five terms, in the U.S. House of Representatives—seventeen of those as speaker of the house. Mr. Sam, as he was fondly called, is remembered at the ❖**Sam Rayburn Library** (800 West Sam Rayburn Drive, 903–583–2455), which holds a perfect replica of his Capitol Hill office, with all furnishings. A host of his memorabilia is displayed here, including a gorgeous white marble rostrum that was used by every House speaker from 1857 until 1950. Other interesting artifacts are a collection of political cartoons, gavels, and a 2,500-year-old Grecian urn Rayburn received from the Athens Palace Guard. The library was donated to the University of Texas, whose students come to use it for research. It's open Monday through Friday, 10:00 A.M. until 5:00 P.M.; Saturday from 1:00 P.M. until 5:00 P.M.; and Sunday, 2:00 P.M. until 5:00 P.M. Admission is free.

Rayburn, who was born in Tennessee in 1882, moved to Texas with his parents in 1887. The **Sam Rayburn House,** 1 mile west of town on U.S. Highway 82 (903–583–5558), is a fourteen-room home he built for his parents in 1916. Modest but comfortable, it's been restored, along with the grounds, to the look it had upon his death in 1961. It's open Tuesday through Friday 10:00 A.M. until 5:00 P.M., Saturday from 1:00 P.M. until 5:00 P.M., and Sunday 2:00 P.M. until 5:00 P.M. Admission is free. Rayburn's funeral was attended by President Kennedy, Vice President Johnson, and former presidents Truman and Eisenhower; the speaker is buried in Bonham's **Willow Wild Cemetery,** on West Seventh Street at Texas Highway 121. The large monument there bears the impression of a gavel and the simple epitaph, "Mr. Sam, 1882–1961." The cemetery is never closed, and no admission is charged.

If you happen onto Bonham in October, see if you're in time for the **Fannin County Fair,** a wonderful tradition over a hundred years old, with livestock shows, baking and other homemaker contests, a carnival, and entertainment. Call the chamber of commerce at (903) 583–4811.

From Bonham, follow U.S. Highway 82 west 15 miles, then head north on U.S. Highway 69 another 13 miles to **Denison,** a town of 21,000 in Grayson County. It's best known for being the gateway to ❖ **Lake Texoma,** created from the mighty Red River by the building of Denison Dam, the nation's largest rolled earthfill dam upon its completion in 1944. The enormous reservoir on the Texas-Oklahoma line covers 89,000 acres and has fifty parks, more than one hundred picnic areas, and plenty of recreation facilities along 580 miles of shoreline. Travelers come from a three-state area to the resort hotels and motels and marinas surrounding these waters, and anglers spend time on the lake catching record black bass, striper bass, crappie, and lunker catfish. Many of today's vacationers head for the 14-mile Cross Timber Hiking Trail that hugs the water. See the Denison Chamber of Commerce for specific information at 313 West Woodward Street, (903) 465–1551.

Interesting that the same year the dam was completed, Denison's most famous son became an all-time American hero. Five-star general and two-term U.S. president Dwight D. Eisenhower is remembered at the **Eisenhower Birthplace** at 208 East Day. The two-story frame house saw the birth of the great soldier and leader on October 14, 1890, and it's been restored to that period. The family moved a short time later to Abilene, Kansas, but there is an Eisenhower family quilt displayed in the bedroom where Ike was born. His large bronze statue makes a great place for souvenir photos of the family. People interested in taking the "Ike Hike" on the ten-acre reserve should make reservations. Open daily from 10:00 A.M. until 5:00 P.M. Admission is $2.00; for information call (903) 465–8908.

Delve a little deeper into the past at **Grayson County Frontier Village,** found in Loy Lake Park via U.S. Highway 75 south to Farm Road 691 west and Farm Road 131 north 1 mile, (903) 463–2487. The meticulously restored pioneer settlement offers a look at homes, buildings, and the instruments of daily life in the mid-1800s. One house dating to 1839 displays bullet holes in its walls, left from an Indian raid. Look in the museum, kept in a restored log cabin, for more memorabilia from the period. In late September, an annual picnic is held here, and the annual Old-Fashioned Christmas staged here in early December gives a glow to yesteryear. A craft shop offers gifts, and a lake, fishing pier, and picnic area are within the park. Open Wednesday through Saturday from 10:00 A.M. until 5:00 P.M. and Sunday 2:00 P.M. until 5:00 P.M., the park offers free admission.

Sherman, 9 miles south of Denison on U.S. Highway 75, is the Grayson County seat and a city of 31,000 people. Settled in 1846, it was named for Sidney Sherman, a Battle of San Jacinto leader and hero credited with the well-known cry, "Remember the Alamo! Remember Goliad!" To see some of the lovely homes and buildings from Sherman's late nineteenth-century boom, grab a map from the chamber of commerce (1815 South Sam Rayburn Freeway, 903–893–1184), which covers places dating from 1883.

Austin College, at 900 North Grand (903–892–9101), is the oldest college in Texas operating under an original charter. Several firsts include being the state's first college to grant a graduate degree, the first to start a law school, and the first to have a national fraternity. A bell hanging in the chapel was a gift from Sam Houston, one of the first trustees of the college. Plays and concerts are staged by the theater and music departments, and monthly art exhibits are held.

Directly across the street from Austin College, ◆**Hart's Country Inn,** at 601 North Grand Street (903–892–2271), occupies a lovely Victorian home that was a hospital upon its erection in 1898. It became a home when the Naylor family bought it in 1905 (and this author's grandfather was raised there), and after loving restoration, a bed and breakfast in 1988, now with five individually decorated guest rooms, including a bridal suite. The inn is filled with antiques, many of which guests may buy.

For still another look at history, stop in at the **Red River Historical Museum** (301 South Walnut Street, 903–893–7623), which occupies a wonderful 1914 Carnegie Library building, listed on the National Register of Historic Places. Among exhibits are a room of furnishings and artifacts from Glen Eden, the main house of a grand Red River plantation that was dismantled upon the creation of nearby Lake Texoma; a 1900 country store; and an excellent collection of World War II aircraft models. Open Tuesday through Friday, 10:00 A.M. until 12:00 noon and 1:00 P.M. until 4:30 P.M., and Saturday and Sunday from 2:00 P.M. until 5:00 P.M. Admission is $2.00.

Now you may want to head west on U.S. Highway 82, stopping 33 miles down the road at **Gainesville**, the Cooke County seat and home to 14,000 people. Some of their ancestors were Forty-Niners headed to California during the gold rush, and some of these were free-thinkers in their day: When most Texans wanted secession in the 1860s, Cooke County folks were against it, and some of them created a secret society supporting the Union.

The surrounding area is now renowned for its rich quarter horse ranches, seen on country drives from town. Downtown, however, is a charming, bricked square with its nineteenth-century appeal intact, augmented by a cluster of antiques shops, one of which contains a cute little tea room.

Most shoppers today, however, are arriving in droves to spend time and money at the spectacular new **Gainesville Factory Shops,** Interstate 35 at exit 501, (817) 668–1888. The retailers with wholesale or better prices—anywhere from 25 to 75 percent off is the norm—number above sixty and include such topnotch names as Nine West and Guess?. Plan to go early, as there are more places worth looking into than at the usual outlet mall.

Food of the fast variety is available at that shopping center, but you'll find a far more interesting taste experience down the road in **Muenster,** about 14 miles west of Gainesville via U.S. Highway 82. In this minute German town, you'll easily find the **Center Restaurant & Tavern** right on U.S. 82, (817) 759–2910. It's open for breakfast, lunch, and dinner daily, from 6:00 A.M. until 10:00 P.M.; specialties are outstanding pork schnitzel, German potato salad and sauerkraut, homemade sausages, and apple strudel.

If German fare doesn't grab you, and the idea of fantastic barbecue piques your interest (and taste buds), you'll want to head for **Tioga,** south from Gainesville on Interstate 35 for 10 miles, then east on Farm Road 922 for 17 miles. Another super-tiny town, this one is on the old M-K-T rail line and is in the heart of that rolling, multimillion-dollar horse ranch country.

The object of this drive is to have a lunch or dinner that will remain long in your memory at ⓟ **Clark's Outpost,** on Texas Highway 377 at Gene Autry Lane, (817) 437–2414. Looks can be deceiving, and this little brown roadhouse appears to be leaning a bit to one side, but the interior is warm and homey, as is the service. Find smoked brisket, ribs, turkey, and river trout, plus lots of vegetables, great barbecue sauce, and sensational homemade pies. The walls are covered with photos of championship horses from nearby ranches, as well as celebrities—supermodel Christie Brinkley is just one—who love this Texas chow. It's open Monday through Thursday from 11:00 A.M. until 9:00 P.M., Friday and Saturday until 9:30 P.M., and Sunday until 8:30 P.M.

From Tioga, drive about 20 miles south on U.S. Highway 377—skirting scenic Lake Ray Roberts—to U.S. Highway 380, and go west about 7 miles to **Denton,** seat of the county bearing the same name and home to 66,000 residents. Besides being home, too, to the University of North Texas, Denton is the site of Texas

Women's University, where you'll find ◆**Little Chapel in the Woods,** at Bell and University streets. Designed and built in 1939 by noted architect O'Neil Ford, it's considered one of the country's finer architectural achievements. Art melds with nature, as the stained-glass window (designed by students) depicts "Woman Ministering to Human Needs." Open daily from dawn to dusk; telephone (817) 898–3615.

For some cultural contrast, check out **Evers Hardware Store,** 109 West Hickory Street, on the south side of the courthouse square, (817) 382–5513. Measuring 25 feet wide, the front of the store is exactly as it was at its opening in 1885. You'll find the merchandise stacked floor to ceiling, with clerks using old rolling ladders to get to top shelves. Open Monday through Saturday, 8:00 A.M. until 5:30 P.M.

Let's hope it's time to eat again, as this ranch country has plenty of good eats to share. From Denton, head 4 miles west on U.S. 380, then take Farm Road 156 south another 4 miles to the hamlet of **Ponder,** home to an excellent steak joint called ◆**Ranchman's Cafe,** right on Farm Road 156, (817) 479–2221. A legendary favorite of North Texans, this family place serves a mean steak dinner. The St. Louis beef is cut when you order your steak, cooked exactly to order, and served with salad and baked potato—if you had the foresight to call ahead and reserve your very own spud. Do not, under any circumstances, get too full for dessert: Ranchman's is famous for its homemade pies and cobblers, good enough alone to draw people from Fort Worth and Dallas, both an hour away. The cafe's open daily 8:00 A.M. until 10:00 P.M.

If a cowboy's experience is what you want after Ranchman's, ◆**Texas Lil's Diamond A Ranch** at Justin, just 7 miles south of Ponder on Farm Road 156, is your destination. A dude's day on this expansive ranch is filled with horseback riding, hayrides, fishing, swimming, campside or ranchhouse dining, and a variety of entertainment, even golf. Kids have a petting zoo and a playground. Call ahead for rates and information, (800) LIL–VILL or (817) 430–0192.

THE BIG D

The way to **Dallas** is easy from Justin: Travel east on Farm Road 407 for 19 miles, then pick up Interstate 35-E South; downtown

Dallas is 25 miles ahead. (Note: Do *not* take Interstate 35-W South—that goes to Fort Worth, which we'll see on this tour later.)

Stay on Interstate 35 all the way into the city and watch for Interstate 30 East, which you'll be upon when you see downtown and the unmistakable **Reunion Tower**—that big silver ball atop a tall tower. Take Interstate 30 East, avoiding morning or evening traffic hour if possible, and continue a short distance to the exit for **Fair Park.** Follow the directional signs a few blocks until you reach entrances on Parry Street or Cullum Boulevard.

Inside the park, your destination is **⬥ The Museum of African-American Life and Culture,** 3536 Grand Avenue, (214) 565–9026, a new, six-million-dollar storehouse/showcase of ethnic artifacts. The only one of its kind in the entire Southwest, the grand building of ivory-colored stone with a huge rotunda and four vaulted galleries contains a library and research center, as well as remarkable changing exhibits that typically include the work of nineteenth-century black masters: wood carvings, contemporary paintings, photography, and sculpture. Closed Mondays, the museum is open Sunday and Tuesday through Thursday from 12:00 noon until 5:00 P.M., Friday 12:00 noon until 9:00 P.M., and Saturday 11:00 A.M. until 5:00 P.M. Admission is free.

Nearby are other important buildings worth a look. For example, the **Hall of State,** 3939 Grand Avenue, (214) 421–4500, is one of the fantastic Art Deco buildings erected for the 1936 Texas Centennial exhibition held at Fair Park. Inside, find heroes of Texas's fight for independence honored in bronze, including William B. Travis, General Sam Houston, and Stephen F. Austin. Several fascinating murals illustrate the state's history from the pioneer period to the centennial year. The hall is open Tuesday through Saturday, from 9:00 A.M. until 5:00 P.M., and Sunday from 1:00 P.M. until 5:00 P.M. Admission is free.

From Fair Park it's just a quick drive of a few blocks to **⬥ Deep Ellum,** taking First Avenue off of Parry Street out of the park and under Interstate 30. Soon you'll be crossing Commerce Street, then Main Street, and Elm Street, the three big thoroughfares in this unusual and very culturally infused district. Its name comes from the African-American people—many of whom produced landmark blues music—who lived here in the early twentieth century and placed a somewhat southern twist on "elm."

Today, it's a sensational neighborhood in which to find odd, unique, and always imaginative dining, clothes, jewelry, home furnishings, artwork, and lots of live music. Vintage brick buildings have been elaborately restored, and interiors have been doused with massive creativity. Whether you're in search of a Native American-designed bed, an early seventies lava lamp, an antique electric fan, a handmade water pitcher, 1920s lace-up boots, post-modern cowboy art, sumptuous barbecued pork ribs, a vegetarian sandwich, a Manhattan on the rocks, a four-layer double-fudge chocolate cake, an oversized cup of caffe latte, or an earful of alternative rock or moody jazz, you will have no trouble finding it in Deep Ellum. Businesses are usually open daily, and most restaurants and nightclubs keep very late hours.

For radically different entertainment in spring, summer, and early fall, make a detour by heading east again on Interstate 30 about 10 miles to Interstate 635, which you'll take south 3 miles to the Military Parkway exit. Just ahead on the right you'll see a big, covered arena, home to the ◆**Mesquite Championship Rodeo,** at 118 Rodeo Drive (214–285–8777). Since 1958, cowboys have considered this a top place to make a name at bull riding, calf roping, and steer wrestling, and spectators have been ever enthusiastic. A barbecue pavilion offers supper—that's what dinner is called in many parts of Texas—at 6:30 P.M. on performance nights. The rodeo is staged for 6,000 fans every Friday and Saturday night from April through September at 8:30 P.M. Tickets are $8.00.

Another attraction that's been a favorite for several generations of Texans is found back in downtown Dallas at the ◆**Farmers' Market,** a rich country tradition deep within the heart of the nation's eighth-largest city. Head back to town on Interstate 30 West and take the downtown exit marked Pearl Street. You'll find the 4-block, open-air market at 1010 South Pearl Street, best if visited early in the day. Some farmers personally bring their produce from around the state, while other vendors are locals who buy from farmers or wholesale nurseries and then sell to the public. Even if you're not in need of fresh fruits, vegetables, herbs, flowers, or plants, the sensory experience is pure invigoration—be sure to load the camera. The market is open daily from 5:00 A.M. until 7:00 P.M. in summer, and 6:00 A.M. until 6:00 P.M. in winter. The phone number is (214) 670–5879.

Next stop is also downtown, at the ◈ **Belo Mansion,** 2101 Ross Avenue. This extraordinarily opulent house was designed by noted architect Herbert Green and completed in 1900. It's the only residence still existing in the city's Central Business District and was home to Colonel Alfred H. Belo, founder of the venerable *Dallas Morning News.* Mr. Belo died in 1901, and the family retained ownership, leasing it out as a funeral home from 1926 until 1977, when it was purchased by the Dallas Bar Association. Now open as the Dallas Legal Education Center, it's available for free tours by appointment; just call (214) 969–7066.

A few blocks west, find ◈ **The Dallas World Aquarium,** at 1801 North Griffin Street, a spectacular new offering. Bearing the look of a small European museum, it showcases a 65,000-gallon array of saltwater marine life including sharks, stingrays, and reef fish in a reconstructed coral reef ecosystem. Then there are tropical blackfoot penguins in their own terrarium world. A restaurant, called the Eighteen-O-One, is open daily for lunch and Sunday brunch. The aquarium is open Monday through Friday, 11:00 A.M. until 6:00 P.M.; Saturday, 10:00 A.M. until 6:00 P.M.; and Sunday, 12:00 noon until 6:00 P.M. Admission is $5.00 for adults and $3.00 for children. Telephone (214) 720–2224.

Having found the aquarium, you're already in what's known as the **West End Historical District,** a wildly popular place for shopping and dining. Interest in the latter will keep you here for lunch or dinner, and there's an oasis of serenity found at **Lombardi's 311,** at 311 Market Street at Ross (214–747–0322). Let everyone else crowd into the rollicking beer, spaghetti, steak, or enchilada joints; this delightful Italian cafe provides a welcome respite from the party scene outside. Languish over freshly crafted dishes from Italy's provinces, furnished by unobtrusive, polished servers. The focaccia bread is a favorite, and live jazz is offered most evenings. Open from 11:00 A.M. Monday through Friday, and from 5:00 P.M. Saturday and Sunday, the restaurant closes between 10:00 P.M. and 11:00 P.M. except on Friday and Saturday when it is open until midnight.

Leave your car wherever it's parked and walk down Market Street (south) 4 blocks to Main Street, then turn right (west) and proceed another long block. To your left at the intersection of Main and Houston streets, is **Old Red,** the imposing red sandstone building that originally was Dallas County's courthouse when erected in 1892. It's quite a spectacle in all its Richardsonian Romanesque glory, complete with scary gargoyles scowling down at you from the corners. This is a great photo for anybody with a zoom lens.

Right in front of the courthouse, bounded by Houston, Commerce, and Elm streets, is **Dealey Plaza,** a small and very scenic little park with a reflection pool, trees, and a statue honoring early *Dallas Morning News* publisher and civic leader George Bannerman Dealey. Since November 22, 1963, however, Dealey Plaza has been known as the place where President Kennedy was assassinated. No matter the time of day or night when you visit, you won't be alone: More than thirty years after the tragedy, people of all ages and nationalities still show up to look around, perhaps wondering if some answer could ever be known.

The life, death, and heritage of President Kennedy is detailed in an educational and historical exhibit across the street from the park, the **Sixth Floor: John F. Kennedy and the Memory of a Nation,** a remarkable museum on the sixth floor of the former Texas School Book Depository from which Lee Harvey Oswald allegedly shot the president. Opened in 1988, the exhibit contains historic pictures, artifacts, forty minutes of documentary films, and an award-winning audio tour. Open daily from 10:00 A.M. until 5:00 P.M., the Sixth Floor's address is 411 Elm Street (214–653–6666). Admission is $4.00 for adults and $2.00 for children.

Before leaving the Dallas area, consider a worthwhile side trip. Head exactly 30 miles due south of Dallas on Interstate 35 to ◆ **Waxahachie**, the Ellis County seat and home to 20,000 citizens. Waxahachie (WOCKS-uh-hatch-ee) is a charming Victorian town built on the rich cattle and cotton businesses here at the turn of the century. Some 170 of the original, ornate homes with extensive gingerbread detail survive, giving the community its "Gingerbread City" nickname. For a map of historic places on both walking and driving tours, ask at the chamber of commerce, 102 YMCA Drive, (214) 937–2390.

You won't dare miss the **Ellis County Courthouse,** easily the most fabulous of all Texas's many magnificent courthouses. Located at Main and College streets, the 1896 masterpiece is noted for a spectacular clock tower, balconies, arches, and gargoyles. An intriguing story that's survived the past century says that one of the artisans brought from Italy to craft the stonework became enamored with a Waxahachie beauty and modeled the lovely face above the east entrance after her; she did not return his love, however, and in his anger he created monstrous faces on the rest of the detail.

Waxahachie's celebrated Victorian veneer has appealed to Hollywood in a big way: Among the excellent films shot here are *Places in the Heart, Tender Mercies, The Trip to Bountiful,* and *Bonnie & Clyde.* A brochure outlining the movie sites is also available from the chamber.

The exquisite architecture is exhibited in grand style annually on the first Saturday and Sunday in June during the **Gingerbread Trail.** The special tour showcases several homes, the courthouse, two museums, and a fine auditorium. For information and tickets, contact the chamber of commerce at (214) 937–2390.

Another annual event bringing throngs to Waxahachie is **Scarborough Faire,** a re-created sixteenth-century English village spread over thirty-five acres of open countryside. It's an impressive production, consisting of more than 400 actors and musicians portraying royalty, peasants, jesters, knights and ladies, and minstrels. Among activities and entertainment are jousting competitions, juggling, sheep-dog demonstrations, magic, and comedy shows. Arts and crafts—some of which aren't entirely Old World—are available, as are all kinds of foods and drink. The faire is held on eight weekends from late April until mid-June; if you go in summer, dress for hot weather. Admission is $12.00 for adults and $5.00 for children. Call (214) 937–6130 for details.

Don't fill up on the faire's junk fare, however; you need to save room for the wonderful southern cooking at Waxahachie's **Catfish Plantation,** 814 Water Street (214–937–9468). The delightful 1895 house is said to be haunted, but that seems to simply enhance the good dining experience found here. Besides the signature fresh catfish, enjoy sweet potato patties, fried corn, fried chicken, black-eyed peas, bread pudding in rum sauce, and cobbler. It's open Thursday from 5:00 P.M. until 8:00 P.M.; Friday, 11:30 A.M. until 2:00 P.M. and 5:00 P.M. until 9:00 P.M.; and Sunday from 11:30 A.M. until 8:00 P.M.

AROUND COWTOWN

From Waxahachie your destination is **Arlington,** a fast-growing place of more than a quarter-million residents that has the highest average income per household in the state. You'll find it by traveling 42 miles northeast via U.S. Highway 287, to the intersection of Interstate 20; once there, go east just about 5 miles, and you'll soon see something that reminds you more of Britain than Texas. ✛**Caelum Moor,** a 540-ton collection of stones designed by sculptor Norm Hines, is spread across a five-and-a-half-acre park on the access road immediately north of the interstate, just to the west of the Matlock exit. Resembling Stonehenge, the twenty-two blocks of Texas pink granite from the Hill Country town of Marble Falls (the same granite source as the State Capitol in Austin) were designed to look like Celtic ruins; artist Hines had ancient Scottish sites in mind. The stones—in heights from 15 to 34 feet—are arranged in five groupings, and the overall effect creates a very pleasant place for taking time out to read a book, scribble some post cards, or just meditate.

Maybe just as unexpected for a busy city involved in incredible growth is Arlington's **Antique Sewing Machine Museum,** at 804 West Abram Street (817–275–0971). Find it by driving east on Interstate 20 just to Cooper Street and taking that north to Abram Street. Inside the museum there are more than one hundred sewing machines in this private collection, one of which is an 1858 Wheeler-Wilson. Several of the other models were made by Elias Howe, who received the patent for the first practical sewing machine. The museum is open Tuesday through Saturday from 9:00 A.M. until 5:00 P.M. and Sunday from 1:00 P.M. until 5:00 P.M. Admission is $2.00 for adults, $1.00 for children.

That stop puts you closer to the new pride of the Metroplex, one Arlington worked hard to wrestle from the grasp of Dallas, which already claims professional football and basketball teams. The stunning new ✛**Ballpark in Arlington,** home to the Texas Rangers Baseball Club, is situated on Interstate 30 at the Pennant Drive exit. Opened in time for the Rangers' 1994 season, this masterpiece is crafted from the popular Texas pink granite and red brick to look like a vintage stadium from baseball's glory days much earlier in this century. The stadium boasts multiple tiers as well as friezes around the facade detailed with Texas longhorns and Texas Rangers, the lawmen, and an interior hall of fame honoring baseball greats. Billed as being revolutionary and unique to the industry, the ballpark has restaurants, sidewalk cafes, bars, various shops, and other kinds of businesses—even a dentist. Around the stadium an expansive park includes Little League fields, picnic areas, a riverwalk, and an amphitheater. The ballpark is the site for the 1995 Major League All-Star Game, too. For tour information—which varies according to the season—and Rangers tickets, call (817) 273-5100.

It's time for a megadose of serious, albeit very enjoyable, culture, so head on into **Fort Worth,** taking Interstate 30 West for 20 miles. You'll pass downtown and exit University Drive, heading north on that street less than a mile to the ✦ **Cultural District,** a highly unusual place where four unforgettable, very independent museums are clustered within a 5-block area.

From University Drive, turn left at the Lancaster Avenue light, and you'll quickly see the **Kimbell Art Museum,** 3333 Camp Bowie Boulevard (817-332-8451). Designed by the famous architect Louis Kahn, the museum was founded by industrialist and entrepreneur Kay Kimbell, who left a wealth of art and money to begin the nation's second-richest privately endowed museum, surpassed only by the Getty in Malibu, California. Within the beautifully vaulted, gray-white building are vast galleries filled with paintings by El Greco, Velázquez, Rembrandt, Cézanne, Picasso, and others, plus varied pieces of pre-Columbian art. World-class exhibits make appearances here on worldwide tours; for information, call the museum.

If possible, plan a stop at the Kimbell around lunchtime, as the museum's cafe offers an inspired array of salads, soups, and desserts—so good, in fact, that the cafe published its own cookbook. The wonderful museum store sells various books, notecards, prints, and gifts; a whole Christmas shopping list can be taken care of in one stop here. The Kimbell is open Tuesday through Friday from 10:00 A.M. until 5:00 P.M., Saturday from 12:00 noon until 8:00, P.M. and Sunday from 12:00 noon until 5:00 P.M. Admission is free.

Just a block west, the **Amon Carter Museum,** 3501 Camp Bowie Boulevard (817-738-1933), is known for its outstanding collection of western art, particularly by Frederic Remington and Charles M. Russell, willed to the city along with a foundation by millionaire Amon G. Carter, the founder of the *Fort Worth Star-Telegram* and dedicated promoter of Fort Worth. Today's Carter Museum collection includes works by such noted American artists as Winslow Homer, Grant Wood, and Georgia O'Keeffe. A sensational bookstore is found here, too. Open Tuesday through Saturday from 10:00 A.M. until 5:00 P.M. and Sunday from 12:00 noon until 5:00 P.M.; tours are given at 2:00 P.M. daily, except Monday. Admission is free.

Right across the street, the **Modern Art Museum of Fort Worth,** 1309 Montgomery Street (817–738–9215), is the city's oldest museum, begun in 1901 as a gallery at the Carnegie Library. Noteworthy in that it's one of a very small number in the United States with a collection devoted to twentieth-century artists, the museum houses a permanent collection including works by Warhol, Picasso, and Rothko. There's another museum bookstore here. Open Tuesday through Friday from 10:00 A.M. until 5:00 P.M., Saturday from 11:00 A.M. until 5:00 P.M., and Sunday from 12:00 noon until 5:00 P.M. Admission is free.

Next door, you'll find Fort Worth's best children's attraction, the **Museum of Science and History,** 1501 Montgomery Street (817–732–1631), also important for being the largest repository of its kind in the entire Southwest. Numerous exhibits—many of which appeal to children and adults alike—include those on Texas history, fossils and geology, the human body, medical history, and computer science. At the museum's Noble Planetarium, shows include astronomy and lasers; and the Omni Theater houses a domed screen 80 feet in diameter, a projector weighing almost a ton and casting the largest film in history, and seventy-two speakers hugging the audience with unbelievable sound. Shows are sensational, dealing with earth science in a thrilling format. Omni shows are offered several times daily; admission is $5.50 for adults and $3.50 for children. Planetarium shows cost $3.00; call for times and information. Museum admission is $3.00 for adults and $1.00 for children. Open Monday from 9:00 A.M. until 5:00 P.M., Tuesday through Thursday from 9:00 A.M. until 8:00 P.M., Friday and Saturday from 9:00 A.M. until 9:00 P.M., and Sunday from 12:00 noon until 8:00 P.M.

The entire Cultural District is electrified from mid-January until early February when the **Southwestern Stock Show and Rodeo** is held at **Will Rogers Coliseum,** facing the Carter and

Kimbell museums at 3301 West Lancaster Avenue (817–877–2400). This terrifically Texan event—which includes the world's largest indoor rodeo—will celebrate its centennial in 1996. Annual attendance is edging close to one million, with attractions ranging from shows of more than 15,000 animals, livestock auctions, and sales of every sort of western wear, western art, Texas souvenirs, and food, to pig races, goat-milking contests, and a carnival. Rodeo tickets sell out early, so order in advance if possible. Grounds admission is $5.00.

For a dining experience that isn't exactly the norm for Fort Worth, walk across the street from the Will Rogers and the museums to **Sardine's,** 3410 Camp Bowie Boulevard (817–332–9937), an Italian bistro that seems transplanted directly from Chicago or New York. Dark, lively, and infused with terrific live jazz, Sardine's has become a Fort Worth institution appealing as much to locals—plenty of residents celebrate engagements and weddings here—as to visitors. Veal, steak, seafood, and pasta dishes are plentiful and filling. Open daily from 5:00 P.M. until 11:30 P.M.

A concise look at the industry that originally put Fort Worth on Texas's map is available at the ✪**Cattleman's Museum,** 1301 West Seventh Street (817–332–7064), just 2 miles east of the Cultural District. The Texas ranching and cattle business is documented from its earliest days through audio and visual and hands-on exhibits, plus historic photographs of such distinguished Texas citizens as Charles Goodnight and Captain Richard King. Admission is free, and the museum is open Monday through Friday from 8:30 A.M. until 4:30 P.M.

Continue east on West Seventh Street to downtown, turning left on Main Street, which leads to historic ✪**Sundance Square,** a collection of carefully restored historic buildings adjacent to the infamous section of town once called Hell's Half-Acre. Brick streets course through the 6-block area bounded by West Second Street on the north, Houston Street on the west, West Fourth Street on the south, and Commerce Street on the east. Among the beautiful buildings is the Knights of Pythias—the first such temple ever built—at 315 Main Street. The Chisholm Trail mural on the south side of 400 Main Street is a spectacular work giving the illusion of dimension to a flat painting. This technique is used on several other buildings on Houston Street, too, seen on your own walking tour or from a horse-drawn carriage.

The beautiful **Tarrant County Courthouse,** 100 Weatherford Street at Main Street, is at the north end of Sundance and is worth a good look at the 1893 Renaissance-revival architecture, crafted again from marble and that wonderful Texas pink granite. Sundance Square is filled with boutiques, gift shops, art galleries, an eleven-theater movie complex, cafes, restaurants, and lively nightspots, particularly the **Caravan of Dreams,** where the bill is often filled with jazz greats such as Wynton Marsalis. Admission varies; call (817) 877–3000 for details.

Take Main Street north from downtown, around the courthouse, just 3 miles to a new-old showplace, Fort Worth's ◊**Stockyards National Historic District,** North Main Street at Exchange Avenue (817–625–5082). At one time in the cattle heyday, these were the largest stockyards in the world, a square-mile area valued at twenty-five million dollars. Historic buildings to see are the Stockyards Hotel, in a 1907 building; the Cowtown Coliseum, opened in 1908 and site of the world's first indoor rodeo; and the Livestock Exchange, erected in 1902. For tour information and maps, visit the Stockyards Visitors Center at 130 East Exchange Avenue, or call (817) 625–9715. The yards remain active, though in a much smaller way today; rodeos are still held spring, summer, and fall at the Coliseum; and the hotel, at 109 East Exchange Avenue (817–625–6427), is a dandy of a place to stay. Wander around the entire area, especially if you're in search of a pair of cowboy boots or an authentic, custom-made cowboy hat, saddle blankets, a duster (that's one of those long cowboys coats), or a great steak or plate of Tex-Mex food.

New to the Stockyards is **Stockyards Station Market,** facing the Coliseum on Exchange Avenue. It's where more than eighty-three million head of hog and sheep were sold during the area's heyday and is adjacent to a terminal for the **Tarantula Train** that runs sightseeing tours. Train tickets are $8.00 for adults and $4.50 for children; call (817) 763–8297. The market is filled with shops such as the Jersey Lilly, where you dress up in vintage clothing and have an old-fashioned, sepia-toned picture taken; Riskey's Barbecue, with beef sandwiches, salads, and grilled chicken; the Trading Post, stocked with blankets, baskets, art, and gifts; and the King Ranch Saddle Shop, selling the great ranch's signature line of bags, briefcases, and luggage with the ranch's Running W brand.

Walk a half block west of Main Street to **Miss Molly's Hotel** at 109½ West Exchange Avenue (817–626–1522) for a cozier night's stay than can be remembered. Opened as a small hotel in the late nineteenth century, it became a bordello for a few years, and is now a place for sweet dreams. All eight rooms are filled with Old West antiques.

Nobody should leave the Stockyards without a visit to **Billy Bob's Texas,** a block north of the Stockyards Hotel at 2520 Rodeo Plaza (817–624–7177). Famous as the world's largest honky tonk, Billy Bob's has an ongoing schedule of country music on two stages, with a huge dance floor, souvenir and western-wear shops, plenty of bars and cafes, and an indoor rodeo. Call for schedules, hours, and ticket prices.

DINOSAUR COUNTRY

From Fort Worth, the next destination is **Granbury,** a charming 1800s town that was restored in the 1970s to its original Victorian glory. You can reach Granbury by driving south 30 miles from Fort Worth on U.S. Highway 377; note, however, that a slight but most worthy detour can be found 5 miles shy of Granbury. ◆**Acton State Historic Site** is just 2 miles away on Farm Road 4, which intersects U.S. Highway 377. The Acton Cemetery holds a lovely monument to Elizabeth Crockett, widow of Alamo hero Davy Crockett, who moved here after he was killed. The statue rising above her grave shows her with her hand to her brow, watching and hoping he will come home. If you arrive during spring, the cemetery—and all this countryside—will be blanketed in vibrant bluebonnets.

Continue to Granbury then, following signs directing you to the historic downtown, which has been listed on the National Register of Historic Places. The town, after its 1890s heyday, fell into a decline but was grandly resuscitated by a town project in the 1970s that became a model for all Main Street renovation projects in the state. The of 5,000 is the Hood County seat and a charming escape for a day, but most people stay at least a weekend.

First stop is at ◆**The Nutt House** on the Granbury Town Square (817–573–5612), named, of course, for the Nutt family who originally owned the building when it was a mercantile in 1893. If ever there were a laid-back country inn, this is it: Rooms have screen doors and ceiling fans, even though the hotel's air-conditioned; a large upstairs landing has tables for playing cards and writing letters; and an excellent restaurant—drawing diners from all over North Texas—is downstairs. The hotel's popularity necessitated the addition of extra rooms, which are found a block away in the Annex, also on the square, stationed in an old law office.

Specialties at the Nutt House restaurant are fried chicken, chicken and dumplings, hot-water cornbread, fresh cobblers, and buttermilk pie. Meals are served at lunch Tuesday through Friday, 11:30 A.M. until 2:00 P.M., and Saturday and Sunday, 11:30 A.M. until 3:00 P.M.; and at dinner Friday and Saturday, 6:00 P.M. until 8:00 P.M.

Facing the Nutt House is the **Hood County Courthouse**, built in 1890 and containing its original Seth Thomas clock; past that is **Granbury Opera House,** 116 East Pearl Street, built in 1886 and a very popular stage for a variety of musical productions from February through December. For show information and tickets, call (817) 573–9191.

Off the north side of the square, the **Hood County Jail,** 208 North Crockett (817–573–1622), is an 1885 Old West jail crafted of hand-hewn stone. Used as a jail for ninety years, it's now home to the chamber of commerce, but visitors are welcome to look at the old cellblock and hanging tower.

Granbury is known by North Texas weekend explorers for its abundance of reasonably priced antiques stores, tea rooms offering wonderful lunches, and bed-and-breakfast lodgings. To get a list, a few good maps, and information, see the Granbury Convention & Visitors Bureau at 100 North Crockett Street (817–573–5548).

The Brazos River cuts its path diagonally across North and Central Texas and in Granbury is impounded to make the 8,700-acre Lake Granbury that nearly wraps around the city. In addition to more than one hundred miles of shoreline with parks, swimming beaches, and marinas, there's the ⚓ *Granbury Queen,* a Mississippi paddlewheeler replica. Sightseeing and lunch and dinner cruises are offered spring through fall. Check into live music-dance cruises, too, which are usually offered on weekends only. Ticket prices range from $6.00 to $25.00. The *Queen* docks just off of Texas Highway 144, 1 mile south of U.S. Highway 377; call (817) 573–6822 for information and schedules.

Dinosaur Valley State Park

From Granbury, follow Texas 144 17 miles south, and you'll find the bucolic town of **Glen Rose.** Founded in 1849 as a trading post, it is now the Somervell County seat and home to 2,000 people. From the 1920s through the 1930s, however, this was a thriving health resort for people who came to sanitariums here to take the rejuvenating waters. One still standing has been transformed into a lovely place to stay today, the ✦**Inn on the River,** at 206 Barnard Street (817–897–2101), an extravagantly renovated and decorated nineteen-room bed-and-breakfast lodge. Built in 1919, the inn backs up to the serene Paluxy River and is a romantic place to spend the weekend. Gourmet breakfasts and dinners are offered to guests, and sometimes to nonguests, by reservation only. The four-course dinners are $30 prix fixe for all diners.

Glen Rose is known best, though, for something much older—actually prehistoric. ✦**Dinosaur Valley State Park,** 4 miles west of town on Farm Road 205 (817–897–4588), is the site of the

142

best-preserved dinosaur tracks, some experts say, in the world. In the solid limestone bed of the Paluxy River, just above its confluence with the Brazos River, the unmistakable prints have been found to be those of the sauropod, a gargantuan creature that ate plants, measured longer than 55 feet, and weighed more than 30 tons. Other tracks have indicated that the duck-billed dinosaur and the theropod also lived in this area. Near the river, a fenced-off area contains two life-size models of the T-rex and the brontosaurus, fiberglass models left over from the Sinclair Oil Corporation's dinosaur exhibit at the 1964–65 New York World's Fair. The park is about 1,500 acres and offers a wild but enchanting shrubby terrain of bluffs and water, ideal for picnicking, camping, and hiking. A dinosaur exhibit at the visitor center is open daily from 8:00 A.M. until 5:00 P.M. Park admission is $3.00 per vehicle.

North Texans also come to Glen Rose throughout the year for the numerous **bluegrass festivals** hosted by Oakdale Park, on Texas Highway 144 about 3 miles south of U.S. Highway 67 (817–897–2321). There are camping facilities, cabins, a swimming pool, and a pavilion here, as well.

From spring through fall, outdoors lovers flock to this part of the Brazos River for **canoeing** near Tres Rios Park, 2 miles east of town on County Road 312 (817–897–4253). Canoe trips can last a day or a week, depending on your wishes. The park offers information, as well as cabins and camping.

Three miles southwest of town via U.S. Highway 67 (817–897–4588) is the fascinating, renowned **Fossil Rim Wildlife Ranch.** More than a thousand endangered animals from five continents call this 3,000-acre conservation center home. There's a 9-mile driving tour through the ranch, where visitors see animals roaming at will, among them the white rhino, cheetah, gray zebra, and wildebeest. The scenic overlook near the route's end is an excellent place for photos and reflection, and a restaurant, petting zoo, nature hiking trail, riding stables, and picnic areas are close by. The ranch is open daily from 9:00 A.M. until two hours before sunset. Admission is $9.95 for adults, $8.95 for seniors, and $6.95 for children.

The ranch also offers the **Foothills Safari Camp,** a luxury wildlife safari providing guests with posh tents and gourmet meals. For inquiries and reservations, call (817) 897–3398.

From Glen Rose, depart on Texas Highway 144 heading south 23 miles, to pick up Texas Highway 6 in the town of Meridian, and follow it south another 12 miles. This places you at the tiny community of ◆ **Clifton,** settled in 1854 on the banks of the pretty Bosque (BOSK-ee) River, today the largest town—with just 3,000 residents—in Bosque County. Fishing is a popular pastime here on the Bosque River and nearby at Lake Whitney.

Scandinavian traditions are still observed in Clifton by descendants of the original Norwegian settlers. To see the terrain of this heritage, drive into what's known as Norse Country, along Farm Road 219 west from town and Farm Road 182 north from town. Tours are given by appointment by Dan and Mary Orbeck, who can be reached at (817) 675-8733. The Norse church, sitting alone in the countryside, is really special.

To explore more of this Norse community, check out the **Bosque County Memorial Museum,** at Avenue Q and West Ninth Street (817-675-3845), a small but informative place with exhibits detailing the founding and growth of the Norse Capital of Texas. You'll see excellent examples of "rosemaling," the Norwegian craft of painting or carving intricate floral detail on all sorts of wooden furnishings. The museum is open Sunday and Thursday from 2:00 P.M. until 5:00 P.M., and Friday and Saturday from 10:00 A.M. until 5:00 P.M. Admission is $2.00.

Your next destination from Clifton takes you along some roughly scenic prairie and ranch land, gently rolling into the west. Drive north along Texas Highway 6 36 miles to the town of Hico (HY-koe), stopping for a robust breakfast, lunch, or dinner at the **Koffee Kup Kafe,** at the intersection of Texas Highway 6 and U.S. Highway 281 (817-796-4839). Don't try to resist the extraordinary meringue pies—it's impossible.

From Hico, drive north on U.S. Highway 281 47 miles, touring through more rolling, tree-dotted ranch country, until you arrive in **Mineral Wells,** a pretty old town of 14,000 in Palo Pinto County, a wonderful place to pause in your approach to West Texas. Here's another town that saw a boom—this one in the 1880s—thanks to its mysteriously healing waters. Since no one could explain why this mineral-laden water, which didn't have an appealing scent, would make people feel better, it became known as Crazy Water, and everything in town was named similarly, such as the Crazy Hotel, the Crazy Park, and a radio show called "The Crazy Gang."

The boom was highlighted by the building of the elaborate, luxurious Baker Hotel in 1929, but the Depression ended the boom, and today the grand Baker Hotel—which was a copy of the famous Arlington Hotel in Hot Springs, Arkansas—stands deserted. Nevertheless, it's a great photo site rising above the skyline in the middle of town. **The Crazy Water Hotel,** North Oak Street at Northwest Third Street (817-325-4441), is a popular retirement home. Visitors are often allowed access to the seventh-story terrace, from which a good view of the town and the Palo Pinto Mountains just north is available. Mineral Wells's downtown streets have a few good antiques shops with most reasonable prices.

The best place to spend a few days in this area is at ◆ **Possum Kingdom Lake State Park,** reached by driving west of Mineral Wells on U.S. Highway 180 for 38 miles until you reach the settlement of Caddo. Then head north 17 miles on Park Road 33, which ends at the park entrance; the park's phone is (817) 549-1803. Near the entrance, look for some not-too-shy longhorn cattle; they are part of the official state herd.

The massive lake, a 22,000-acre reservoir formed by damming the beautiful Brazos River, has depths up to 150 feet and the clearest water in the Southwest, making it a popular site for scuba diving, water-skiing, and sailing. Campsites, cabins, marinas, and cafes sit around the 300 miles of shoreline, but the state park's offerings are generally the best. Sitting on the south shore, the 1,500-acre park has superb hiking trails, nice if small beaches, shady and scenic campsites, a playground, canoe rentals, simple cabins, a small store, a long and lighted fishing pier, and countless good places for bank fishing.

Your best stop for all supplies is **Caddo Mercantile,** on U.S. Highway 180 at the turnoff to the state park (817-559-6844). It looks like little more than a gas station, but it offers groceries and bait, local folks discussing the news and fishing and hunting, plus a good little grill serving fresh breakfasts and hearty lunches. The store and grill are open from 6:00 A.M. until 5:30 P.M. daily.

THE TEXAS PANHANDLE

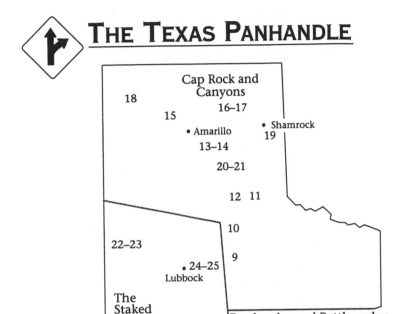

18

15

Cap Rock and Canyons
16–17

• Amarillo
13–14

• Shamrock
19

20–21

12 11

10

22–23

• 24–25
Lubbock

9

The Staked Plains

26

Fandangles and Rattlesnakes
8   6
5   1–2
3 • Abilene

27

7
Sweetwater

4

1. The Old Jail Art Center
2. Fort Griffin State
   Historical Park
3. Dyess Air Force Base
4. Buffalo Gap Historic Village
5. Anson
6. Stamford
7. Avenger Field
8. White Buffalo Statue
9. Silver Falls Park
10. Punkin Days
11. Hotel Turkey
12. Caprock Canyons State Park
13. Livestock Auction
14. Cadillac Ranch

15. Cal Farley's Boys Ranch
16. Alibates National Monument
17. Lake Meredith National Park
18. XIT Museum
19. Blarney Stone
20. Panhandle Plains Museum
21. Palo Duro Canyon State Park
22. National Mule Memorial
23. Muleshoe National
    Wildlife Refuge
24. Ranching Heritage Center
25. Llano Estacado Winery
26. Garza Theater
27. Comanche Trail Park

THE TEXAS PANHANDLE

Romance and longing? For the Texas Panhandle? Why not? The pioneers who settled here came with a dream that—with plenty of muscle and heart—they made come true. Although the earth and the elements had their hard edges, the South, Staked, and High Plains also offered sweet repose. Anyone who read the Pulitzer Prize–winning *Lonesome Dove* (or watched the fine television mini-series) will have a sense of déjà vu upon arrival. The *llano estacado* (staked plains) stretches north toward the Cap Rock Escarpment, later yielding to the High Plains. The Canadian River should look familiar—that's the area where a lone Gus used his horse as a fort to fight the Kiowas and where he rescued the tortured Lorena from Blue Duck.

The sixteenth-century Spanish conquistadors were enamored with the endless grasslands and countless buffalo of the Panhandle, as were the Apaches, who were followed by the war-loving Comanches and young American pioneers, determined to find a future. Some would-be Gold Rushers jumped off the Fort Smith–Santa Fe Trail in the Panhandle, and ranchers came sometime after the Comanches were conquered and sent to the Oklahoma Territory. By 1888, thirty-three ranches spread to occupy a land the size of Ireland.

Yucca plants shoot sharply skyward, nettles sprout white blooms, and challas burst with pink blossoms after a rainy spring. It's not unusual to drive an infuriatingly straight highway, then find it inexplicably winding and climbing a bluff before the monotonous view suddenly falls off into a green and red valley blanketed in yellow flowers. Purple-red firewheels scale rocky hillsides, also lined by paths etched by the collared lizard, whose skin ranges from neon green to dusty yellow. Watch out for bushes with three-inch thorns, but rest assured it's okay to eat the tart sumac berries—Indians made their version of Kool-Aid from the stuff.

Barbed-wire fences—which originated on ranches in this region—stretch for thousands of miles, attempting to corral this great openness. The sky grows larger every day. A few of the scarce trees have elongated, gnarled arms that surely were loved by those who administered outlaw justice. And hilly rises where there were once no trees are now populated by the tenacious mesquite.

Just a fews years after the buffalo hunters and ranchers came to Texas a century ago, the Indians and buffalo had been exterminated. Indeed, Panhandle cattle empire builders were successful in their work; for a period, there were three cows to every person. Poking around the same plains today, it's easy to trace history. Little has changed, for one matter, and the region's children are accomplished at preservation and continuation, for another. You'll come away wondering why all Westerns aren't filmed here—it's so utterly Texan that other places in the state seem almost fraudulent by comparison.

FANDANGLES AND RATTLESNAKES

Most likely, your Panhandle tour will pick up where our North Texas trail left off. But whether you're approaching the northwest section of Texas from Possum Kingdom Lake, just west of Fort Worth, or coming directly from the Dallas–Fort Worth area, you'll want to follow U.S. Highway 180 west from the Metroplex. First stop is Albany, seat of Shackelford County and home to 1,900 Texans, west of Fort Worth 120 miles on U.S. Highway 180.

Albany earned the handle "the home of the Hereford" for being the place where the favorite cattle breed was introduced in Texas's young days. The western heritage associated with the town endures: Hereford and other cattle represent some 90 percent of Shackelford County's agriculture business; historians point out that one of Albany's more famous sons was Edwin Dyess, for whom the Air Force base at Abilene is named; and one of its more infamous guests was prisoner John Selman, who later killed gunman John Wesley Hardin in El Paso.

First stop on the Albany tour is ◈ **The Old Jail Art Center,** South Second Street near Walnut Street (915-762-2269), which has achieved status as one of the finer small art museums in the Southwest, having gained a great deal of stature since its 1980 opening. Its staff enjoys bragging that this museum has a larger storage vault than Fort Worth's esteemed Kimbell Art Museum. Several wings have been added to the original structure, which was built in 1877. Some of the masons were paid by the stone, and their initials are visible on many of the large rectangles of stone. The jail once housed the keeper's office, cells, and exercise room, also known as a runaround. Today, it contains the remarkable pre-Columbian collection donated by a Mineral Wells resident. Of note are the Chinese terra-cotta tomb figures, dating to 206 B.C., and a Buddhist prayer book from Cambodia dating to the sixteenth century.

In the several new wings added to the jail are such interesting items as art deco doors from the Old Town Drug Store; an exceptional jade and amethyst collection; Picasso drawings; Italian ballroom chairs; and small Henry Moore bronzes. There also are exquisite furnishings such as a grand piano crafted from tiger-eye oak in 1895. The museum's courtyard is a pretty place for reflection and for the myriad parties held there. Commanding attention in the center is a blockish contemporary windmill carved from native stone by artist Jesus Morales. The museum is open Tuesday through Saturday from 10:00 A.M. until 5:00 P.M. and Sunday from 2:00 P.M. until 5:00 P.M. Admission is free.

Just a block away in the City Park on South Main Street at South First Street, the **Georgia Monument** is a touching site. The stark stone memorial commemorates the five companies of volunteers who made the journey from Georgia to fight with the Texans in their revolution. Sadly, the majority were killed with Colonel James Fannin in the famous massacre at Goliad; nearly twenty years later the Georgia legislature invoiced Texas for $3,000 for guns but waived payment if the Lone Star State would erect a monument to the victims. Thanks to the citizens of Albany, that was finally accomplished in 1976.

Also downtown at City Park, the **Ledbetter Picket House** occupies the corner of South Main and South First streets. The restored 1870s frontier ranch has been relocated from near Fort Griffin so people can better inspect the interior, with items from the Ledbetter Salt Works, built in 1860. "Picket" is the term used for the construction style in which walls are built with vertical rather than horizontal boards. To tour this place, make an appointment with the chamber of commerce, (915) 762–2525.

When it's time for a meal, **Fort Griffin General Merchandise Restaurant,** just west of the Albany square on Texas 180 (915–762–3034), is not only a good place to dine but also a self-contained point of interest. Chef and co-owner Ali Esfandiary is a petite, jovial man who is retired from Dyess Air Force Base, but who comes originally from Iran. Ali is all smiles and jokes, and as he talks with patrons, it's obvious that he's quite a local favorite.

The restaurant is all roadhouse upon first impression, but its interior surprises with homey touches such as curtains and antiques. The menu is fashioned after an old-time newspaper, full of noteworthy items and lore from the past century. Atmosphere and details aside, the rib-eyes are fork-tender and simply the best in memory, the beautiful prime rib is the size of most placemats, and red snapper and fresh zucchini strips are other delights from the mesquite grill.

Stick around and relax the night away at the **Ole Nail House Inn** on the courthouse square, (915) 762–2928. The comfortable bed and breakfast occupies the upstairs of a 1914 home whose former resident was Robert Nail, creator of the town's Fandangle—which we'll soon cover. The three guest rooms are made soft and pretty with flowers, antiques, and fruit baskets. Sunporch breakfast spreads are usually something wonderful such as pecan waffles, bacon, and fresh fruit.

From town, head 15 miles north on U.S. Highway 283 to ◆ **Fort Griffin State Historical Park** (915–762–3592), occupying 500 acres along the Clear Fork of the Brazos River. The fort was established in 1867 during the federal reoccupation of Texas after the Civil War, and the cavalry stationed here fought Kiowa and Comanche and helped end their domination of North Texas. Some people know the park chiefly as the home of the state longhorn herd, whose story is as impressive as any in the state. Fort Griffin was along one of the routes through which some ten million head of Texas longhorns were driven north to the beef markets a century ago. The longhorn was nearing extinction around 1920, and western author J. Frank Dobie was among a handful of men who helped preserve the stock. Descendants of the Dobie herd live at Fort Griffin, while other animals in the state herd live at state parks including Possum Kingdom, Palo Duro Canyon, and LBJ. By loan agreement, University of Texas mascots bearing the name Bevo are obtained from the Fort Griffin herd.

The park grounds also hold a restored bakery, replicas of other fort buildings, and some ruins, with a model of the fort and an exhibit on fort history inside the visitor center. In addition, there are nature and walking trails, restrooms, showers, a picnic area, a playground, and campsites, some with water and electricity.

The Chisholm Trail's Western Trail split off and came through Fort Griffin, and, like Fort Worth, this town was one of the

West's wildest for gunslingers, gamblers, and outlaws—and that's where the **Fort Griffin Fandangle** comes in. The grand outdoor musical has been staged by locals for more than fifty years and is one of the more endearing annual events in Texas. Lawlessness and the fortitude it took to endure that, as well as isolation and Indian scares, are celebrated in song, dance, and pageantry, with longhorns and horses helping to create the mood. Close to a quarter of the townspeople—about 300—are involved in the spectacle, which takes place the third and fourth weekends in June. The show begins at 8:30 P.M. on pageant nights, with a barbecue dinner taking place earlier. For reservations and information, call (915) 762–3642.

If you go back through Albany, then west 8 miles on Texas Highway 6 and south 27 miles on Texas Highway 351, you will arrive in **Abilene,** the Taylor County seat and home to 106,000 residents. A sizeable stop on Interstate 20, Abilene is best known as the location of ◈**Dyess Air Force Base,** Interstate 20 at U.S. Highway 277 (915–696–5609 or 696–2196), which is a closed base requiring you to obtain a pass at the main gate to enter. Having done that, head for Dyess's **Linear Air Park,** where twenty-five World War II, Korean, and Vietnam War aircraft displayed outdoors include the C-47 Skytrain and B-17 Flying Fortress, plus B-1 bombers for training and combat. If you come in late April or early May, you may happen upon an air show featuring the USAF Thunderbirds. Admission is free, and the air park is open during daylight hours.

For another collection, head for the **Museums of Abilene,** situated at Grace Cultural Center, 102 Cypress Street (915–673–4587), a cluster of three museums. In the Children's Museum, kids learn in a participatory way scientific principles and technology's uses and applications in daily life; at the Fine Arts Museum, exhibits generally include classical to abstract art, using various media; and the Historical Museum profiles Abilene's history, with emphasis on the recent past. Numerous traveling exhibits make stops at this museum center annually. Admission is $2.00 for adults, $1.00 for children; the museums are open Tuesday through Saturday from 10:00 A.M. until 5:00 P.M. and Sunday from 1:00 P.M. until 5:00 P.M.

To find western artistry of a slightly different nature, head for **Art Reed Custom Saddles** at 904 Ambler Street (915–677–4572). The saddlemaker has been at his craft for more than three decades, building custom saddles from the saddle tree up. Along with western saddles—mostly crafted for ranchers and other cowboys, starting at around $1,500—Mr. Reed makes tack, chaps, and belts. His work is so popular he typically accepts orders for up to six months in advance of delivery. Open Monday through Friday, 9:00 A.M. until 5:00 P.M.

It won't take quite as long to claim a pair of custom-made boots at **James Leddy Boots,** 926 Ambler Street (915–677–7811), one of the renowned names in Texas cowboy boots. Order now, and you should have your eel, snakeskin, calfskin, lizard, or other exotic leather boots within two or three months. Prices start at around $450 and top out at about $3,500. Don't forget to order a belt or wallet to match. Open Monday through Friday, 8:30 A.M. until 5:00 P.M.

Chain motels are plentiful, but you may find a cozier stay at **Bolin's Prairie House Bed & Breakfast,** 508 Mulberry Street (915–675–5855). Four affordable guest rooms sleep eight guests, with two shared bathrooms. A full breakfast is offered, giving travelers a chance to get to know the hosts and fellow guests.

Knowledgeable Texans carry on over the steaks served in Abilene's restaurants. Many claim to have the best, but diners in the know generally vote first for **Royal Inn Steak House,** at 5695 South First Street (915–692–3022). Non-beef-eaters will find fish, chicken, and salads, too, and everyone enjoys the sumptuous surroundings, complete with chandeliers. The restaurant is open for breakfast, lunch, and dinner daily.

Another excellent place to find great cuts of beef is the **Perini Ranch Steakhouse,** situated in ◆ **Buffalo Gap Historic Village,** about 6 miles south of the Abilene city limits on Farm Road 89. In this rustic setting, diners enjoy sixteen-ounce roast rib-eyes with cowboy potatoes and ranch beans, or baby-back ribs cooked over mesquite. Open for dinner Wednesday and Thursday and lunch and dinner Friday through Sunday. Call (915) 572–3339 for reservations.

Spend time before dining exploring Buffalo Gap, a restored frontier complex that was once a stopping place along the famous Dodge Cattle Trail, containing relocated historic buildings such as the Taylor County Courthouse and Jail, circa 1879, a railroad depot dating to 1881, Abilene's first blacksmith shop, and Buffalo Gap's own Nazarene Church, built in 1902. A charming trip back in time, Buffalo Gap is open mid-March through

Fort Phantom Hill

mid-November Monday through Saturday from 10:00 A.M. until 7:00 P.M. and Sunday from 12:00 noon until 7:00 P.M.; and mid-November through mid-March Friday and Saturday from 10:00 A.M. until 6:00 P.M. and Sunday from 12:00 noon until 6:00 P.M. Admission is $4.00 for adults and $1.75 for students. Call the village at (915) 572–3365. The last weekend in April brings the Buffalo Gap Arts Festival, staged in the oak tree shade and featuring art booths and an auction, as well as entertainment ranging from mariachis to barbershop quartets, and square dancing.

Another look at history is found north from Abilene 14 miles on Farm Road 600, where the **Fort Phantom Hill Ruins** consist of monolithic, cactus-crowded crumbled masses of stones. These ruins have a particular poignance about them, especially in the day's first or last light—it's easy to imagine that desertion was a problem here because of monotony and loneliness. Dramatic as its name, Fort Phantom Hill was established in 1851 for protection against the Comanches as the westward settlement activity spread. The fort was abandoned in 1854, as the water supply was insufficient; although it mysteriously burned shortly afterward, the fort was later used as a Texas Rangers outpost and as a U.S. Army outpost during the Indian Wars of the 1870s. The ruins lie on private property today, but the owner keeps the site open to the public daily from dawn until dusk. Admission is free.

For fishing or a picnic, head back toward Abilene on Farm Road 600 just 4 miles to **Lake Fort Phantom,** more than 4,200 acres, with 29 miles of shoreline dotted by marinas, boat ramps, primitive campsites, a swimming beach, and an airfield for model planes. Call (915) 676–6217 for information.

Abilene serves as a good pivot point to reach two more marvelous pockets of the Old West. First is ✦**Anson,** 24 miles northwest of Abilene via U.S. Highway 83/277, the seat of Jones County. The town was long known and widely criticized until a few years ago for banning dancing—except at the Christmas Ball—for religious reasons. Times have changed slightly, but most citizens still choose only to go dancin' in Anson for the three days every December when Anson hosts its historic Cowboys' Christmas Ball. Usually held the weekend prior to Christmas, Anson has quite a time letting its citizens cut a rug, and western crooner Michael Martin Murphey has put into song and video the century-old poem honoring the ball, written by rancher Larry Chittenden. If you miss the dancin', check out the other element that drew the locals' ire: The Depression-era mural in Anson's post office offended folks at its 1941 unveiling, as some townspeople felt it was wrong to illustrate the fun people were having on the dance floor. (This *is* the Bible belt, remember.) See the mural depicting the Christmas Ball in the post office on tiny Main Street; (915) 823–2241.

Now point your car to our next side trip, to ✦**Stamford,** 17 miles north of Anson on U.S. Highway 277, still in Jones County and with a population of 3,800. You're in true cowboy country here, as Stamford is home to the Texas Cowboy Reunion held for three days over the weekend closest to July 4. Begun more than sixty years ago, it hosts unquestionably the world's greatest amateur rodeo, drawing more than 500 competitors and thousands of fans. The festival includes chuck wagon meals, a huge western art show, and lots of music. Call the chamber of commerce at (915) 773–2411.

For a better understanding of Stamford's cowboy history, head to the **Cowboy Country Museum,** 113 South Wetherbee Street (915–773–2411). Well-known cowboy artists have paintings and prints displayed here, and other exhibits include ranch and farm artifacts from a century ago, as well as a blacksmith shop. The museum is open Monday through Friday from 8:00 A.M. until 12:00 noon and 1:00 P.M. until 4:00 P.M.; admission is free.

There may not be a better place to capture on film the heritage of this region than at the **Mackenzie Trail Monument,** at the intersection of U.S. Highway 277 and Texas Highway 6. This immense, sand-colored stone marker was hand carved to depict the days of the famous Mackenzie Trail (1874–1900) and the buffalo, Indians, pioneers, and early ranchers who figured into this history. Open at all hours.

Now, we're off to rattlesnake country: Head west from Abilene on Interstate 20, following it 42 miles to **Sweetwater,** seat of Nolan County and home to 12,000 salty Texans. The community came about when buffalo hunters in the 1870s camped on Sweet Water Creek simply because they preferred the sweet, clear water there over the area's other, gypsum-flavored streams. The humble beginnings continued with the opening of a dugout trading post in 1877; then the town charter—first established in 1884—failed twice due to blizzard, drought, and resulting evacuation. After the 1902 incorporation held, the area grew during World War II, when the Women's Air Force Service Pilots training program was based at the local ◆Avenger Field. The world's first and only all-women military flying school produced just over a thousand pilots out of 25,000 applicants. The thirty-nine who died in service are honored with a bronze statue and a walk of fame on the campus of Texas State Technical College–Sweetwater at Avenger Field, on Interstate 20 West at Sweetwater Municipal Airport, (915) 235–8441. Open during daylight hours.

Plan your arrival in time for lunch, as you wouldn't want to miss a chance to use your boarding-house reach at **Allen's Fried Chicken**, not unlike Sunday dinner with a big family. For $6.50, you eat family style from a long table spread with a plastic tablecloth and set with unmatched plates. For lunch your table will be filled with plates and bowls weighted down with not only fried chicken, but also cream gravy, beef brisket, buttered potatoes, candied sweet potatoes, potato salad, turnip greens, green beans, stewed summer squash, corn, English pea salad, pinto beans, fruit salad, rolls, peach cobbler, and iced tea. The restaurant has been a favorite for forty years and will soon be one of yours. It's at 1301 East Broadway Street, (915) 235–2060. Open for lunch only, Tuesday through Sunday.

If good fortune was in your planning, you'll have arrived in Sweetwater on the second weekend in March—that's when the town is jumping, thanks to some 20,000 or 30,000 folks who show up for the annaul **Rattlesnake Roundup.** Some six or seven tons of rattlesnakes are gathered during this, the world's largest such event. Several other Texas towns have followed suit, but Sweetwater's is the oldest, having begun in 1958 when the Jaycees pitched in to help local ranchers and farmers deal with their tremendous rattlesnake problem. The roundup became a festival, and the rest—as is widely said in the western reaches of this state—is history. The weekend is filled with a parade, the Miss Snake Charmer Queen Contest, real hunts for western diamondback rattlers, professional snake-handling demonstrations, snake-milking for medical research, a 10-K run, a dance, a tour of rattlesnakes' natural habitats, and a rattlesnake-eating contest. Fried rattlesnake is available, as are numerous other—and less exotic—snacks. And there's a weigh-in and prize ceremony for the most snakes captured and the largest. All the fun takes place at the Nolan County Coliseum at the north end of Elm Street. Call (915) 235–5488 for schedules, details, and ticket information.

Now it's time to head into the Panhandle Plains, taking Interstate 20 west 8 more miles till you pick up U.S. Highway 84, following it 30 miles north to **Snyder,** found right at the U.S. Highway 180 West exit. This is the seat of Scurry County, with a population of 12,000 and—more important—a monument saluting a rare beast, the ◆ **White Buffalo Statue,** on the courthouse lawn at College and Twenty-fifth streets. One of the many,

many buffalo hunters who killed off the valuable herds here claimed that among the 22,000 buffalo he killed was a rare albino, shot near Snyder. To honor the herds, Snyder's townspeople put up this life-size replica of the albino buffalo. Some say the beast began as a bull buffalo but respect for delicate sensitivities rendered it a cow instead.

Also to amuse you is the **Scurry County Museum,** on the campus of Western Texas College on Texas Highway 350 South (915–573–6107). Regional history covers progress from earliest Indian civilization through the oil boom, marked by the county's production of the billionth barrel in 1973. You'll learn more about the buffalo-hunting days, as well as the tumultuous period when the 1876 trading post was plagued by outlaws, a range war raged between ranchers and homesteaders, and cowboys locked up the sheriff in his own jail. Things eventually calmed down early in this century, just to become upset again when the oil boom nearly quadrupled the population in the early 1950s, and shantytowns popped up at an alarming rate. Decency prevailed, the concerned citizens cleaned up Snyder, and their hometown was declared an All-America City in 1969 by the National Municipal League.

On the lighter side of Snyder, there's the **House of Antieks** at 4008 College Street (915–573–4422), an excellent place for clock hunters. Shopkeepers are knowledgeable about the many antique clocks, victrolas, tables, chairs, cabinets, and other home furnishings stocked. Open Monday through Saturday, 9:00 A.M. until 6:30 P.M.

CAP ROCK AND CANYONS

Now we head into some of the most physically compelling country, if regarded with respect to those who spent lifetimes trying to tame it. Taking country roads at this point is the way to best drink in the often parched land, fascinating to anyone with an eye for prehistoric aesthetics. From Snyder, take Texas Highway 208 north 57 miles to the town of Spur, passing through Clairemont. Now skirting the Cap Rock's eastern edge, head north 20 miles on Farm Road 836 to U.S. Highway 82, then go west just another 6 miles, driving actually onto the famous escarpment. Watch for a roadside park on the left, and you'll have found ◆**Silver Falls Park,** a stop said by many to be the finest of all roadside parks in the vast state. The White River courses through this part of the Cap Rock and its canyon land on its way south to join the Brazos River, and state engineers were wise enough to place picnic tables and carve riverside hiking paths here for journeymakers like yourself. Perhaps you've picked up snacks or sandwiches on the way; this is a perfect place to stretch your legs and take some scenery photos.

It's just another 4 miles west to the town of **Crosbyton,** seat of Crosby County and home to 2,000. It's in the heart of an agricultural land, and the local Associated Cotton Growers is said to be the world's largest cotton-processing plant of stripped cotton, serving more than 500 cotton companies in a 50-mile area. Crosbyton is also home to the **Pioneer Memorial Museum** at 101 Main Street (806-675-2331. Inside, the pioneer lifestyle is illustrated with home replicas and admirable collections of vintage housewares, arts, and farm equipment. Indian relics and artifacts relevant to the local ecology are exhibited, too. Open Tuesday through Saturday from 9:00 A.M. until 12:00 noon and 1:00 P.M. until 5:00 P.M.; admission is free.

From here, head north 23 miles on Farm Road 651 to **Floydada**, seat of Floyd County, home to 3,900 Texans and the undisputed Pumpkin Capital of the United States. If it's autumn, you've no doubt seen some awesome pumpkins—they call the hundred-pounders Big Macs—at markets and along roadsides in Texas, and you can bet they came from here. The town's annual ◆ **Punkin Days** is a festival held on the courthouse square the weekend closest to Halloween. Stop in for some pumpkin bowling, pie tastings, seed-spitting contests, and carving competitions. Most events are free. Find the fun at Main and Missouri streets; for details, call (806) 983-3434.

Now it's time to cross the Cap Rock again, heading east on U.S. 62/70 from Floydada 24 miles to Matador, where you'll pick up Texas Highway 70 north, following it 28 miles to **Turkey,** a Hall County town and site of the **Bob Wills Museum,** intriguing to anyone with even a passing interest in the music called Texas swing. Found on Sixth Street at Lyles Street (806-423-1033), the collection dedicated to the King of Texas Swing—who was born just outside of town and whose daughter has moved back to Turkey to run the foundation—includes fiddles, boots, hats, recordings, sheet music, and photos belonging to or representing the Texas Playboys. Open Monday through Friday from 8:00 A.M.

159

until 10:00 A.M. and 1:00 P.M. until 5:00 P.M. and weekends by appointment. Admission is nominal. Inquire, too, about Bob Wills Day, usually held the last weekend in April, with a parade, fiddlers contest, dances, and performances by members of the original Texas Playboys.

The town is home to, naturally, the ✪ **Hotel Turkey,** Third and Alexander streets, (806) 423–1151. A couple from North Texas bought the seventy-year-old hotel—now listed on both the Texas Historical Property register and the National Register of Historic Places—in the late 1980s and spent the years since giving it a face-lift. The comfortable hotel draws plenty of Bob Wills fans, as he played here in the late 1920s, as well as people who simply enjoy old hotels. Guest rooms are filled with original furniture and wallpaper adorned with hand-sewn decorations, while the front parlor downstairs is furnished with century-old sofas, chairs, and tables. The forty-seat dining room is decked out with antique photos of Turkey's residents. Some 1,200 guests stay here each month, and the owners frequently receive gifts such as vintage clothing, gloves, hats, and knickknacks from past guests.

From Turkey, turn west on Texas Highway 86 and travel 13 miles to Ranch Road 1065, following it north for just over three miles till you reach ✪ **Caprock Canyons State Park,** just inside Briscoe County and 3 miles beyond the tiny town (population 500) of Quitaque (KIT-a-KWAY). You may want to stock up on some groceries and camping goods in that town or back in Turkey, as this little-known park is an ideal place to kick back a while and savor this rugged country. The views here of mountains, canyons, streams, and indigenous flora and fauna are simply breathtaking, and a visitor center offers an interpretive area plus an archaeological site, with artifacts representing the canyon for some 250 million years. There's a hundred-acre lake for swimming, fishing, and boating, but the real draw—besides the vistas, of course—is the hiking trails, 25 miles of paths coursing through the mountainous, 14,000 acres of parkland. Be on the lookout, especially on mountain trails, for buffalo and antelope, among several species of wild animals. Joining you on the paths may be horseback riders or campers who brought their own mounts. Camping is in both primitive and improved campsites. The park is always open, and admission is usually $5.00 per vehicle. Call (806) 455–1492 for information and reservations.

After the relaxation, you can get to **Amarillo,** seat of Potter County and home to 160,000 people, by driving north from the Caprock park on Texas Highway 86 not quite 9 miles and taking Texas Highway 256 west another 9 miles till you reach Texas Highway 207 north, which will put you on a scenic route across the majestic **Palo Duro Canyon,** which we'll explore in detail later. For now, stay on Texas 207 48 miles till you reach U.S. Highway 287 at the town of Claude, and follow that highway west 28 miles to the Amarillo city limits.

Amarillo's humble beginnings date to its 1887 establishment as Ragtown, a railroad workers' tent camp. Today it's a mammoth center of cattle trade, and there are wonderful places to buy western artwork and clothing. Some lovely historic homes are on view, as are an art museum and a well-known science and technology museum.

To get a taste of Amarillo's tremendous cattle heritage, make your first stop at the city's ✦**Livestock Auction,** held in the stockyards at 100 South Manhattan Street (806–373–7464) every Tuesday from 8:00 A.M. until 5:00 P.M. As you walk in, the auctioneer's rhythmic patter with odd inflections meets your ears as assorted cows and bulls are moved quickly for viewing through the main room's bottom, from which rise bleachers for spectators and bidders. Outside, the purchased cattle are herded into pens one at a time, usually by a few no-nonsense cowgirls, who are the only indication that anything has changed in the past one hundred years. To understand the significance of this place, note that more than 300,000 cattle are sold here every year, making this the largest individually owned auction in the state. It's the world's largest weekly livestock auction, and annual sales are close to seventy-five million dollars. Even if you miss auction day, you can look around the place; admission is always free.

At the adjacent **Stockyard Cafe,** also at 100 South Manhattan Street (806–374–6024), you can fill up on cheap but big steaks, home-cooked vegetables, sandwiches, and home-baked pies, sitting down with cowboys and ranchers. It's open for breakfast and lunch Monday through Saturday and for dinner Friday and Saturday only.

Newer to Amarillo but just as important historically is the **American Quarter Horse Heritage Center** at 2601 Interstate 40 East (806–376–5181). The magnificence of the quarter horse is studied from its days as the working ranch horse of the American West to the equine competitor of the modern world. Its life is examined from the seventeenth century, when the breed was developed in the Western Hemisphere, to the present day. The complex is also the international headquarters of the American Quarter Horse Association, the world's largest horse registry. Open in summer daily from 9:00 A.M. until 6:00 P.M., and in winter Monday through Saturday from 10:00 A.M. until 5:00 P.M. and Sunday from 12:00 noon until 5:00 P.M. Call ahead for a guided tour. Admission is $4.00 for adults, $2.50 for children, free for age five and under.

For a day of cowboy life, head for the **Bar H Dude Ranch,** an hour's drive east of the city via U.S. Highway 287 in Clarendon (806) 874-2634. Ride horses or haywagons, do a little work with the cowboys, pitch horseshoes, fish, take square dancing lessons, and even stay the night if you like. Call ahead for reservations and prices.

Explore Amarillo's high-tech side at **Don Harrington Discovery Center and Planetarium,** in the fifty-acre Amarillo Garden Center at 1200 Streit Drive (806-355-9547). Named for a local oil mogul and philanthropist, the complex presents *Panhandle Promise*, a slick, twenty-five-minute show incorporating thousands of slides that illustrate a century of history. "Cowboys are as real as weather," the narrator's voice says, supported by vivid images showing pioneers and the lives through the years that brought drought, devastating winters, the railroad from Fort Worth, the Depression, Bob Wills, and the legendary Route 66, all in rapid, dramatic bursts. The Discovery Center also presents Smithsonian traveling exhibits and several interactive displays that are enjoyed by children and adults alike.

And in tribute to Amarillo's standing as chief helium producer in the United States, a leggy, four-pronged **Helium Monument** stands in front of the Discovery Center. The structure functions as a futuristic sundial, and its limbs are time capsules filled with newspapers, a Sears catalog, and a piece of apple pie sealed in helium. The Discovery Center is open Tuesday through Saturday from 10:00 A.M. until 5:00 P.M. and Sunday from 1:00 P.M. until 5:00 P.M. Admission is free, except in summer when it's $5.00 for adults and $2.50 for children. Planetarium shows cost $1.00 extra.

The quintessential, Texas-size experience is found in lunch or supper at the **Big Texan Steak Ranch,** 7701 Interstate 40 East at Lakeside exit (806–372–6000). Resembling a circus arena, the cavernous interior is fun and fascinating, with a giant wooden Indian and a stuffed grizzly greeting you at the entrance and big game trophies covering every wall. Chairs and benches are fashioned from horseshoes, of course. The menu is laden with buffalo, rattlesnake, rabbit, calf fries (the most private of calf parts), chicken-fried steak, and rib-eye steak. The fanfare, however, surrounds the presentation of a seventy-two-ounce prime steak dinner that's free if the diner eats the whole thing—with the accompanying salad, shrimp cocktail, baked potato, bread, and butter—in one hour. Some do it, but it's a true challenge. The luckiest diners happen by when the Kawahadi Indian Dancers are scheduled for a performance. The restaurant is open daily for lunch and dinner.

In addition to several hotels and motels, Amarillo offers bed and breakfast lodging at **Galbraith House,** 1710 South Polk Street. Built in 1912, the 4,000-square-foot mansion exhibits gorgeous interior work in walnut, oak, and mahogany, as well as oriental rugs and antiques. Rooms to be enjoyed by guests include the solarium, library, dining and living rooms, in addition to three balconies. There are five guest rooms with private baths, and generous breakfasts may feature casseroles, biscuits and gravy, and pastries. To make reservations, call (806) 374–0237.

Just outside of town, 7 miles to the west on Interstate 40—also the epic Route 66— ◆ **Cadillac Ranch** is the unique creation of Stanley Marsh 3 (as he is faithfully called), land and broadcasting baron and easily one of the more powerful of all the personalities of modern Texas. Known always for his noteworthy and eccentric ways, he made his contribution to pop culture in a cotton field with a lineup of ten Cadillacs buried nose-down, exhibiting tail-fin designs from between 1949 and 1963 diagonally into the air. Worth noting is that the cars are buried at precisely the same angle to the ground as the great Cheops pyramids. Graffiti artists have made their own contributions, as the art display—called Amarillo's "bumper crop"—is always open. No admission is charged.

Cadillac Ranch

You can take a side trip from Amarillo 38 miles northwest of town on Farm Road 1061 and U.S. Highway 385 to reach ✛ **Cal Farley's Boys Ranch,** 2 miles north of U.S. 385 on Spur 233. This 10,000-acre spread was established in 1939 as a ranch home for troubled and needy boys. Now more than 400 boys between the ages of four and nineteen attend classes, live in comfortable dorms, and work in the ranch's dairy, horticulture, custodial, and farming divisions. Nonresidents are welcome to join the boys—who are unfailingly polite and winning—at lunch and for a short tour of the impeccable grounds. A wildlife zoo is open, too. Call ahead for reservations, (806) 372–2341. Admission is free. There's a Labor Day Boys Ranch Rodeo (admission is $4.50 for adults and $3.50 for children), drawing some 10,000 spectators to watch the boys take part in their biggest annual function.

The ranch grounds are on the site of **Old Tascosa,** a boom town that busted in 1887 when railroad planners chose to skip it. If the name seems familiar, it's because this was a haunt of outlaws and gunfighters such as Billy the Kid, Pat Garrett, and Len Woodruff. As part of your ranch visit, tour the museum housed in the Old Tascosa Courthouse, where displays illustrate West Texas's role in the days of the Wild West.

From the ranch take Texas Highway 136 north 38 miles to ◈ **Alibates National Monument,** a mostly undeveloped site popular with hikers and archaeology buffs. The area atop a high ridge overlooking Lake Meredith contains an ancient quarry of flint, unique for its amazing colors. Farmers and Indians distributed Alibates flint over the Southwest and Great Plains from 10,000 B.C. until the last century. The quarry itself is overgrown with grass and shrubs, so you won't know you've found it until you're in it. The stones are flat, somewhat smooth, and shaded with muted blues and grays, black, maroon, and orange. Nearby, great pits of buffalo bones have been found, along with pottery dating to A.D. 1250. An Indian village was excavated in a 1938–39 project, and pictographs were found in huge dolomite boulders. Ranger-led walks, extremely helpful for visitors, conclude with flint-chipping instruction. Free tours are offered at 10:00 A.M. and 2:00 P.M. during summer and by appointment for the balance of the year. Admission is always free, and the monument is open during daylight hours. Call (806) 857–3151 for information and reservations.

The monument lies on the south shore of Lake Meredith, site of ◈ **Lake Meredith National Park.** Fashioned from the Canadian River, the lake is 2 miles wide in places and 14 miles long, offering 100 miles of shoreline. The national park service has created eight recreation areas with lake and swimming-pool swimming, fishing, sailboating, and water-skiing. There are places to play golf and tennis, too. If you've picked up provisions in Amarillo or in nearby Fritch, you can pick a place from several bluffs and canyons around the lake for picnicking and camping. Open at all times, admission is typically $5.00 per vehicle. Call (806) 857–3151 for information.

One of Amarillo's better side trips takes you to **Dalhart,** seat of Dallam County, home to almost 69,000 residents. To reach it from the north side of Lake Meredith, follow Ranch Road 1319 north about 11 miles to Texas Highway 152, follow it west 20 miles to Dumas, and then go west on U.S. Highway 87 39 miles to Dalhart. Or, the route from Amarillo is north on U.S. Highway 287 49 miles to Dumas and west on U.S. Highway 87 39 miles to

Dalhart. The reason for this journey is to explore the heritage of the world-renowned **XIT Ranch** and today's ❖**XIT Museum.** Here you'll discover the considerable history of the XIT, which was in the 1880s the largest ranch in the world under a single fence, which stretchs 6,000 miles. It was created when investors from up north were contracted to erect the three-million-dollar granite capitol building in Austin in exchange for this three million acres of land. The ranch spread across an area that today covers nine counties and was 27 miles in average width and 200 miles long between north and south fences.

The XIT Museum, at 102 East Seventh Street (806–249–5646), tells the whole story, which involved the employ of 150 cowboys and the running of 150,000 head of cattle. The investors lost interest, however, and sold off the cattle and split the ranch into pieces. The museum lies inside a renovated art deco building and contains photographs, documents, an antique gun collection, and reconstructed period rooms such as a parlor, bedroom, and kitchen. Native American relics and Peter Hurd paintings are exhibited, as well. The Pioneer Chapel, created from pieces of Dalhart's first six churches, is frequently the site of today's weddings. The museum is open Monday through Friday from 10:00 A.M. until 5:00 P.M. Admission is free.

To see more of the XIT legacy, drive to a traffic island adjacent to the underpass at U.S. Highway 87 North and U.S. Highway 385. There you'll find the **Empty Saddle Monument,** honoring all XIT cowboys. The story behind it concerns an XIT cowboy who died just before the annual reunion; his widow requested that his horse be allowed to participate in the parade, and today's parade is always led by a saddled horse without a rider.

Plan your arrival in Dalhart to coincide with the first Thursday, Friday, and Saturday in August, and you'll enjoy the **XIT Rodeo and Reunion,** held in Rita Blanca Park, U.S. Highway 87 South at Farm Road 281 West. This is the world's largest amateur rodeo and features a free barbecue on six tons of beef. The parade, junior rodeo, nightly dance, antique car show, and 5-K run add to the revelry. For information and ticket prices, call (806) 249–5646.

The final side trip from Amarillo is a bit ambitious but may be worth it to those who have Irish blood coursing through their veins. **Shamrock**, a town in Wheeler County of 2,200 residents, is located 86 miles east of Amarillo via Interstate 40. This is the site of Texas's own ✦ **Blarney Stone,** in Elmore Park, 400 East Second Street. Someone in this town convinced the keepers of the original in County Cork, Ireland, to donate a small piece of their famous rock; it sits on a pedestal and is offered at all hours to anyone who cares to kiss it. Legend holds that those who do are given the gift of eloquence. The Irish celebration of St. Patrick's Day is held annually on the weekend closest to March 17 all over town. There's a carnival, bazaar, old settlers' reunion, beard contest, fiddling contest, chili cook-off, dances, cowboy roping contests, and a Miss Irish Rose pageant. Call the chamber of commerce for ticket information at (806) 256–2501.

Now it's time to make a trek back down the Panhandle, stopping first at **Canyon**—just 16 miles south of Amarillo via Interstate 27—seat of Randall County, home to 11,000 Texans and site of the exceptional ✦ **Panhandle Plains Museum.** Found on the campus of Texas A&M West University, 1 block east of U.S. Highway 87 at 2401 Fourth Avenue (806–655–7191), the museum holds the honor of being the state's largest historical center. Up front, the building's busy 1933 art deco exterior offers friezes depicting an array of Texana designs from spurs to brands. Inside, a time-line approach is used to relate the geological, social, cultural, industrial, and financial development of northwest Texas. Murals in the main hall overwhelm onlookers with an overview, and dinosaurs liven up the geological displays. Pioneer life, Indians, and Texas ranching have individual exhibit areas, and the three-floor annex is outfitted with a 1925 cable tool drilling rig. Other oil-patch relics piece together the story of oil and gas discovery and development in West Texas. An art gallery offers permanent and traveling exhibits, and a good gift shop sells souvenirs. Open Monday through Saturday from 9:00 A.M. until 6:00 P.M. and Sunday from 1:00 P.M. until 6:00 P.M. Admission is given in exchange for a small donation.

Then you'll want to continue east of town 12 miles on Texas Highway 217 to ✦ **Palo Duro Canyon State Park.** Here the Panhandle's arid climate, chilly mornings, cool evenings, and clean air are pleasingly exaggerated during spring, summer, and fall in the spectacular chasm, cut 120 miles long by a branch of the Red River. Rich in geological, Native American, and pioneer history, the canyon's rock formations rise and fall a little over 1,000 feet, showing ninety million years of earth formation, baring brilliant walls

167

colored ochre, red, and coral by the spirits of time. The Coronado expedition took shelter here in 1541 while looking for the fabled Quivira, and they decided *palo duro*—meaning hard wood—was appropriate for the tough juniper trees that still flourish here. What's so surprising and invigorating about the Palo Duro Canyon is its green trees and even greener meadows when the rain's been plentiful. Most of the canyon's beauty secrets are revealed in the state park, covering a 16,400-acre portion of the canyon.

An 8-mile paved road takes you rim to floor and affords unforgettable vistas. Hiking, camping, picnicking, and horseback riding are loads of fun, but don't miss the **Sad Monkey Railroad.** The miniature train on a narrow-gauge railroad takes a 2-mile, narrated tour through flora, fauna, and otherworldly formations of the area. Sunsets here make memories lasting a lifetime. Open daily from 6:00 A.M. until 10:00 P.M. in summer and 8:00 A.M. until 10:00 P.M. the rest of the year; admission is $5.00 per vehicle. Call (806) 488-2227 for reservations and information.

On summer nights, lightning and thunder explodes, horse hooves pound, Indians dance, and eighty voices sing against a 600-foot canyon wall during *TEXAS! A Musical Drama*, a flashy production now thirty years old. Nearly a hundred thousand people come annually to see the outdoor spectacle, with audience members representing all fifty states and almost a hundred foreign countries. In song and dance, the story presents the struggle, heartbreak, joy, and politics of Panhandle pioneers, and a barbecue dinner is offered prior to the show just outside the canyon floor's amphitheater. The musical begins at 8:30 P.M. nightly except Sundays, from early June until late August. Reservations are necessary and can be made by calling (806) 655-2181. Tickets are generally between $6.00 and $12.00 for adults and $3.00 and $12.00 for children.

Another splendid way to enjoy Palo Duro Canyon from May until September is at **Cowboy Morning Breakfasts,** booked in Amarillo but enjoyed here at the canyon. The Christian family of the Figure 3 Ranch offers their perch on the canyon's rim for you to enjoy a taste of real ranch life. Cowboys drive a mule-team wagon for a twenty-minute ride in earliest morning light through pasture to the canyon edge. The camp cook prepares sourdough biscuits in iron kettles to go with a spread of other edibles made in skillets over open fires. The food is filling and never runs out. Most partakers can't resist a hike after breakfast, which is best—simply because you can't leave the canyon until you've been in it. The ranch family indulges every tourist's whim, and it's enjoyable to watch a European visitor who's never been near a cowboy or a horse be saddled up for a little walk atop a gentle sorrel. Kids are given a chance to try some roping, and branding exhibitions are followed by cow-chip–tossing competitions. The morning will slip away quickly, but you can always go back for steak dinners on the canyon rim. Required reservations are made by calling (806) 944–5562 or (800) 658–2613; morning trips are $19 for adults and $14.50 for children, and evening trips are $22.50 for adults and $14.50 for children.

You can stay in a motel or book a room at **The Hudspeth House**, Canyon's bed-and-breakfast place at 1905 Fourth Avenue, (806) 655–9800 or (214) 298–8586. A famous former resident was the late artist Georgia O'Keeffe, who taught at the local university. There are six bedrooms, some with private baths and fireplaces, and decor includes beautiful antiques, tins, plates, dolls, grandfather clocks, and musical instruments. The breakfast table is set with linens, china, and crystal, so you'll enjoy a lavish breakfast or brunch in elegance. A spa, fitness room, sun deck, and gazebo are on the property, as well. Call well in advance for reservations.

THE STAKED PLAINS

From Canyon, follow U.S. 60 southwest 30 miles and then take U.S. Highway 385 south 40 miles. At U.S. Highway 70, head west 24 miles to reach **Muleshoe,** seat of Bailey County and home to the peerless ✦**National Mule Memorial**—what else? Found at the intersection of U.S. Highway 84 and Main Street, the memorial to the West's original draft animal is a fiberglass model measuring fifteen hands in height. The mule's statue was built in 1965 thanks to donations from people all over the country—even a mule-driver from the former Soviet Union sent a twenty-cent contribution.

Another 20 miles south on Texas Highway 214, you'll see ✦**Muleshoe National Wildlife Refuge,** the oldest such refuge in Texas, founded in 1935. As it is situated on a central flyway between Mexico and Canada, hundreds of thousands

Ranching Heritage Center

of waterfowl stop by during migration between September and March. The park consists of about 5,800 acres of rolling, mostly treeless sandhills planted with sorghum and wheat (bird food) punctuated by lakes, occupied during the season by the country's largest concentration of sandhill cranes. Observation areas are available in the refuge, and picnicking and camping are allowed. Admission is free, and the refuge is open Monday through Friday from 8:00 A.M. until 4:30 P.M. for day visitors. Call (806) 946–3341 for information.

Just south of the refuge, pick up Farm Road 37 and follow it almost 20 miles to U.S. Highway 84, which will lead 46 miles to **Lubbock**, nicknamed Hub City, or hub of the Panhandle. Seat of Lubbock County, the city is home to 186,000 people and the expansive Texas Tech University. On its campus, you'll find the remarkable ◆**Ranching Heritage Center** at Fourth and Indiana streets (806–742–2498), a living, authentic center of ranching in the American West. Each year 100,000 people visit here to tour the twelve-acre grounds filled with more than thirty restored structures, dating from 1838 until 1917. Among them you'll find one of seven division headquarters of the XIT Ranch; a century-old schoolhouse; milk and meat houses; a granary; a blacksmith shop; log cabins; a grand Victorian ranch home; a bunkhouse; a barn; and a train depot. There are horseshoeing, breadmaking, sheep-shearing, spinning, and weaving demonstrations, and changing exhibits include saddles, bronzes, and western art, plus wagons and branding irons. As was the case a century ago, windmills are more plentiful than trees, and the ranching center offers windmills of varying designs. A gallery has been created from a room at the enormous 6666 Ranch, complete with ornate mantle, saddle, brass bed, oriental rug, grandfather clock, and family portraits. Open Monday through Saturday from 10:00 A.M. until 5:00 P.M. and Sunday from 1:00 P.M. until 5:00 P.M.; admission is free.

Among Lubbock's other interests is that of music, since the city gave the world rock 'n' roll pioneer Buddy Holly. You'll find the **Buddy Holly Statue and Walk of Fame** at Eighth Street and Avenue Q, where an outdoor park honors Holly and other West Texans—including Mac Davis, Waylon Jennings, and Jimmy Dean—who made significant contributions to musical entertainment. It's open twenty-four hours and is free. Buddy Holly's grave is found in the Lubbock Cemetery at East Thirty-fourth Street at Quirt Street. Marked by a small, plain stone, the site is visited by a steady procession of fans, many from the United Kingdom.

Head for **Lubbock Lake Landmark State Historical Site,** North Indiana Street and Loop 289 (806–741–0306), one of the largest and most productive archaeological excavations in North America and thought to be the continent's only place where deposits relate to all cultures known to have lived on the Southern Plains. Covering the periods of the Clovis Man and the Folsom Man, Texas residents of 10,000 to 15,000 years ago, the site's digs have turned up remains of the mammoth, extinct horse, camel, and bison, plus a giant armadillo. Follow a three-quarter-mile trail through the twenty-acre excavation area and look for interpretive signs along the way. A new interpretive center offers exhibits, a children's center, a gift shop, and an auditorium. Open Tuesday through Saturday from 9:00 A.M. until 5:00 P.M. and Sunday from 1:00 P.M. until 5:00 P.M.; admission is $2.00 for adults and $1.00 for children.

Children also get a kick out of **Prairie Dog Town,** within Mackenzie State Park at Fourth Street and Avenue A (806–762–6418). One of the last remaining colonies of its kind in the whole country, it's home to cute little critters who are playful and endlessly amusing, and who share their habitat with burrowing owls and a few rabbits. The park also has Joyland, an amusement park; a golf course; picnic areas; and the Yellowhouse Canyon Lakes, where you can enjoy waterfalls, foot bridges, fishing, and hiking trails. Open until midnight; admission is free. (Hours at Joyland vary; call 806–763–2719 for information.)

Texas's oldest and most award-winning winery is here in Lubbock. Find ◆ **Llano Estacado Winery** just over 3 miles east of U.S. Highway 87 on Farm Road 1585 (806–745–2258). Winery founders discovered ideal conditions in the loose, sandy soil, hot days, and cool nights of the Panhandle Plains. Some fifteen or more varieties are grown at a time, and eleven or twelve different wines—plus one champagne—are bottled each year. Plan to spend an hour here touring the winery and tasting four wines. Open Monday through Saturday from 10:00 A.M. until 5:00 P.M. and Sunday from 12:00 noon until 5:00 P.M.; tours are free and are offered every half hour, with the last tour at 4:00 P.M. daily.

Southeast of Lubbock 42 miles on U.S. 84, the town of **Post**—seat of Garza County and one of Texas's more famous speed traps—is located, thanks to cereal magnate C.W. Post, who bought nearly a quarter of a million acres here and founded Post City in 1907 with the intent of developing his own utopia. He built a sanitarium, hotel, business district, cotton gin and textile plant, and farm homes, but his project never saw true success because he couldn't make it rain, and the lack of water during the 1911 drought was devastating. He died in 1914, but his statue on the courthouse lawn keeps something of his memory alive.

Post is home to the ◆ **Garza Theater,** 226 East Main Street (806–495–4005), which was one of the first movie houses in West Texas when it opened in 1920 with silent films. It was adapted to sound in 1929 but closed in 1957. In 1986 it was renovated and reopened for use by a local theater production group. Musicals and plays are presented some weekends, and a barbecue dinner is usually offered, as well. Call for schedules and ticket information.

About 6 miles southeast of town on U.S. Highway 84, find the **Llano Estacado Marker,** one that helps travelers more easily understand the geography of this remarkable area. It details the flat-topped mountains of the Cap Rock Escarpment and the Staked Plains, or llano estacado.

From Post, you can trace the lowest reaches of the Cap Rock as it unwinds to the Panhandle's reach into deep West Texas. Follow Farm Road 669 as it meanders along mesas and buttes, about 70 miles south to **Big Spring.** This is the Howard County seat and home to 23,000, and where a nice resting spot is ✦ **Comanche Trail Park.** Find this beauty at Whipkey Drive off U.S. Highway 87, immediately south of Farm Road 700 (915–263–3026). A large spring indeed is the focus of this 480-acre park, which offers a swimming pool, lighted tennis courts, an eighteen-hole golf course, small fishing lake, playground, hiking and biking trails, nature trails, a flower garden, and improved campsites. In summer, you'll especially enjoy the huge amphitheater, cut from native limestone during the Depression, which hosts summer concerts. Admission is free, and the park is open from dawn until 10:00 P.M. daily.

WILDEST WEST TEXAS

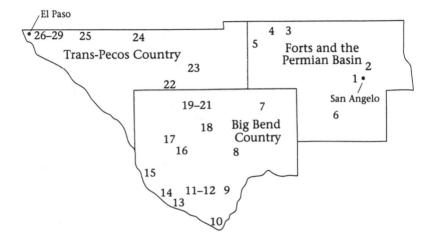

1. Fort Concho
2. Cowboy and His Horse Statue
3. Confederate Air Force Flying Museum
4. Globe Theatre of the Southwest
5. Monahans Sandhill State Park
6. Crockett County Museum
7. Paisano Pete
8. Gage Hotel
9. Big Bend National Park Headquarters
10. Mariscal Canyon
11. Study Butte
12. Terlingua
13. Lajitas on the Rio Grande
14. El Camino del Rio

15. Fort Leaton State Historic Site
16. Marfa Ghost Lights
17. El Paisano Hotel
18. Museum of the Big Bend
19. The Limpia Hotel
20. Fort Davis National Historic Site
21. McDonald Observatory
22. Balmorhea State Park
23. West of the Pecos Rodeo
24. Guadalupe Mountains National Park
25. Hueco Tanks State Park
26. El Paso's historic missions
27. Tigua Indian Reservation
28. Indian Cliffs Ranch
29. Juarez

WILDEST WEST TEXAS

Life in West Texas wasn't easy, and seeing the land even today is proof. The land is lonely, honest, tough—like the pioneers who conquered it, the cowboys who worked it, the people who call it home. Everywhere you look, the long histories of Native Americans, cavalry units posted at forts to protect pioneers and settlers, and oil-field discoveries bringing startling fortunes are unfolded.

The country wasn't always harsh. Sixteenth-century explorer Cabeza de Vaca wrote in his diary that he walked around completely unclothed in the soothing surroundings, and the earliest ranchers wrote that grasses here grew as high as cows' bellies. But herds of several thousand head of cattle were allowed to graze uncontrolled, and the ground was left bare. Apaches didn't mind the desolation, and outlaws were grateful for it. The open skies and spaces of West Texas invited pioneers to forge a new existence. Those hardy settlers who didn't find this part of the Rio Grande utterly impassable assigned names to spots like Camp Misery and Murder's Cove. They were preceded, of course, by the Comanches, whose war trails can still be seen. In 1882, the Southern Pacific Railroad connected the Trans-Pecos towns of Alpine and Marfa to its line, and Terlingua, a bit south, became the quicksilver (mercury) mining center of Texas. Faint remains of those and other long-past ventures can be found in the area.

West Texas's great wealth of natural history is defined, revealed, and studied in the sensational form of Big Bend, a name for a region, a national park, and—for many—a state of mind. Within the elbow of the Rio Grande, where it pushes deeper into Mexico, 800,000 acres were set aside by the national park service in 1944 for preservation of a complex array of huge canyons, numerous clusters and stretches of mountains, and exotic plant and animal life. Many who live here say it claims a place in the soul, and even geology textbooks found in area shops contain descriptions with mystical undertones; one Indian legend holds that after the Great Creator made the Earth with its stars, fish, sea, and birds, he threw all his leftover stony, dusty materials into one heap—the Big Bend. Because it's such a long way from anywhere, the Big Bend is one of the ten least visited parks in the nation, and that's what makes it all the more desirable.

So it's time to embrace the Chihuahuan Desert—roll down the windows and smell the cool scent of sagebrush. Walk around, but watch your step and keep quiet so deer will appear. Wear sturdy boots for protection and train an eye to the roadsides, rattlers may dart out and recoil just as rapidly; that other brownish streak of movement into the brush was the regional mascot, the road-runner. Low-slung mountain ranges, bearing names from Christmas to Chisos to Chinati, first appear like little more than bluish shadows nudging the horizon. Broomweed lies low in oversized patches of vivid yellow in fall, robust bluebonnet blooms spring forth with zeal in February. Rafters floating along the Rio Grande marvel at the changing purples, tangerines, and corals in massive canyon walls, and formations of tuff, a hardened ash from volcanic activity millions of years ago, rise like deformed sand castles, followed by layered pink and gray rock cliffs, interrupted with soft carpets of grassy hills. Travelers from as far away as Japan and Germany, as well as those from far-flung corners of Texas, express awe at towering hills of rock, mountain lion warning signs, tough gray-green scrub land, and lush riverside grasses and palms.

Names of places and life forms often ring of the Spanish-Mexican culture or are pioneer impressions of the land itself—to wit, Rosillos Mountains, Mesa de Águila, Dagger Flat, Dugout Wells, Mule Ear Peaks. And there is such diverse vegetation; most eye-catching are the sotol, century plant, Spanish dagger, and ocotillo, the latter featuring tall spines sprouting bright green, tiny leaves just after the late summer rainy season and brilliant scarlet blooms in spring. The lechuguilla blooms pinkish orange in spring, too, progressing from top to bottom. In some contrast, the Davis Mountains north of the Big Bend wrap comforting arms about you, and the Limpia River is still the crystal, gentle vision it was when settlers arrived 130 years ago. Frontier life is present in a hotel and a distinguished cavalry post. Just don't try to rush through this generous corner of the state, because it takes time to feel and see. West Texas is by turns dusty and sensual, sweltering and refreshing—but always gratifying in a deeply spiritual way.

FORTS AND THE PERMIAN BASIN

You'll likely pick up this reach into the Texas "badlands" where you left off at the end of the Panhandle, striking southeast from

Big Spring on U.S. 87—better stock the cooler with cold drinks and snacks, as this is the first of several somewhat long but always satisfying hauls. Drive 86 miles on this one highway, leaving Howard County, crossing Sterling and a corner of Coke counties, to ease into Tom Green County and its seat, **San Angelo.** Home to 85,000 thousand Texans, the town grew from the exceptional ◆ **Fort Concho,** founded in 1867 where the north and middle branches of the lovely Concho River meet. Local lore holds that one of the town's first personalities was the Fighting Parson, who held church in the town's gaming halls; the only time anyone ever objected, the parson gave the protester a knock in the head with the butt of his six-shooter. An early cattle and sheep ranching center, San Angelo today is the country's largest primary wool and mohair market and a significant livestock auction site.

Old Fort Concho is one of the state's best preserved frontier military forts, a forty-acre National Historic Landmark with twenty-three original and restored buildings quite close to downtown. It served for twenty-two years for the army, stationed here to keep peace on the frontier. Among the cavalry and infantry forces there were the heroic Buffalo Soldiers, black troops named as such out of admiration by their Native American enemies. The fort today contains three museums, featuring frontier life exhibits, officers' quarters, enlisted men's barracks, and a chapel. Throughout the year, special events and demonstrations and reenactments are held at the fort. Christmas at Old Fort Concho is a particularly colorful event, with artists, dancers, and musicians adding to the celebration. Open Tuesday through Saturday from 10:00 A.M. until 5:00 P.M. and Sunday from 1:00 P.M. until 5:00 P.M. Admission is $1.50 for adults, $1.25 for seniors and active military personnel, and $1.00 for children six and up. Fort Concho is located at 213 East Avenue D, (915) 657–4441 or 657–4444.

Still in the frontier vein but more expressive in some ways is **Miss Hattie's Museum,** 18 East Concho Street (915–655–2518). One of several bordellos that thrived along this street, it was opened in 1896 and was a successful "gentlemen's social center" until the Texas Rangers closed it in 1946. Still in its original location, Miss Hattie's has been restored to its former glory, complete with furnishings, plus clothing worn by the girls and the cowboys, soldiers, and businessmen who were patrons. Open

Tuesday through Saturday from 10:00 A.M. until 5:00 P.M. Admission is $2.00.

A different sort of cultural experience is found at the **Old Chicken Farm Art Center,** 2505 North Martin Luther King Drive (915–653–4936). Converted some twenty years ago, this chicken farm is now the showplace of a dozen artists in residence, whose works in photography, paints, metal, wood, and glass, among other media, are on display. Chances are you will come across some of the artists at work. Open Tuesday through Saturday from 10:00 A.M. until 5:00 P.M. Admission is free.

The pretty Concho River is the setting downtown for the **River Walk,** a landscaped and lighted stretch of more than 4 miles of river winding beneath huge pecan trees through parks, gardens, gorgeous homes, fountains, and waterfalls. If you're looking for nine holes of golf, miniature golf, children's play areas, hot-air balloon races, walkathons or marathons, this is the place to find them.

Consider a night or two spent in comfort at **Chaparral Ranch Bed & Breakfast,** 32 miles directly east of San Angelo in Paint Rock, which you can reach via Ranch Road 380. The hosts, who live on the property, can accommodate up to fifteen guests on sleeper sofas and beds in three rooms, each with a private bath. There's continental breakfast, or you can fix your own full breakfast in a separate kitchen—everything's supplied. Call (915) 732–4225 for reservations.

Nearby are the **Painted Rocks,** a collection of Indian pictographs thought to be more than a thousand years old displayed in their natural setting. Call ahead to reserve tours (915–732–4376 or 732–4418) and to see if river excursions, taking in both pictographs and native wildlife, are scheduled.

An interesting side trip to make while you're in the neighborhood—relatively speaking, as the neighborhoods out here are pretty big—is one for a photo op at the town of **Ballinger,** 36 miles northeast of San Angelo via U.S. Highway 67 in Runnels County. The county seat and town of 4,000 is worth finding for the ◆ **Cowboy and His Horse Statue** on the courthouse lawn, at the intersection of U.S. Highway 83 and U.S. Highway 67. The handsome memorial was sculpted by the acclaimed Pompeo Coppini, who was commissioned by the family of Charles H. Noyes, a local cowboy killed in a range accident.

179

From San Angelo, the next destination is **Midland,** on Interstate 20, 112 miles northwest via U.S. Highway 87 and Texas Highway 158. The seat of Midland County, with a population of about 90,000, Midland lies on the old Chihuahua Trail, the Emigrant Road to California, and the Comanche War Trail. Its name came from its position between Fort Worth and El Paso. Founded in 1885 by midwestern farm families, agriculture was its means of support until the 1923 discovery of oil in the region's lucrative Permian Basin. The skies over this incredibly flat land are pointed up by skyscrapers built on the oil booms and by those boom-producing oil derricks.

First stop is **Permian Basin Petroleum Museum, Library and Hall of Fame,** 1500 Interstate 20 West (915–683–4403), a complex devoted to fossil fuel origins, discovery, and resulting industries. This is where you can understand the significance of the wealthy Permian Basin, told in paintings and exhibits. There's a marine diorama of the prehistoric Permian Sea containing 200,000 replicas of sea creatures; a recreated 1920s boomtown; an assortment of antique rigs; and a display on oil and gas well fires. Open Monday through Saturday from 9:00 A.M. until 5:00 P.M. and Sunday from 2:00 P.M. until 5:00 P.M. Admission is $3.00 for adults, $2.50 for seniors, and $1.50 for children.

Midland is also home to the beloved ✪ **Confederate Air Force Flying Museum,** at Midland Airport, 9600 Wright Drive (915–563–1000). Widely considered the nation's best and most complete collection of flyable World War II combat aircraft, this moving museum was founded by dedicated pilots who wanted to make sure future generations would understand the importance of such astounding American air power. The museum is committed to acquiring, restoring, and preserving at least one example of each type of World War II plane. The array today includes—among many—the P-40 Warhawk, P-38 Lightning, P-47 Thunderbolt, P-51 Mustang, P-36 King Cobra, F4F Wildcat, F6F Hellcat, F4U Corsair, plus the British Supermarine Spitfires, a German Messerschmitt, and several Japanese planes. Also find a B-17 Flying Fortress, B-29 Superfortress, and a D-47 Skytrain. The second weekend in October, you can see these craft in flight demonstrations at the CAF "Airsho," and don't miss the museum's thirty-minute film on the Ghost Squadron, shown daily at the museum. Open Monday through Saturday from 9:00 A.M. until 5:00 P.M. and Sunday from 12:00 noon until 5:00 P.M. Admission is $4.00 for adults, $3.00 for seniors, and $2.00 for children.

Before any more travel, take a break for eats at the **Blue Star Inn,** 2501 West Wall Street (915–682–4231). The town's oldest restaurant has long been a reliable standby for excellent Cantonese dishes and excellent charbroiled steaks—a combination not altogether unusual in West Texas. Open daily for lunch and dinner.

Hitting the road again, we go 20 miles west on Interstate 20 to Midland's sister city, **Odessa,** seat of Ector County, with a population also of 90,000. Established in 1881, Odessa was named by railroad workers from the Ukraine for their home city, which this prairie land resembled.

Lest you think oil country is without culture, Odessa offers its very own ◆ **Globe Theatre of the Southwest,** at 2308 Shakespeare Road (915–332–1586), on the Odessa College Campus. A nearly perfect replica of William Shakespeare's Globe Theatre in London, this one also was built specifically to host only plays by the Bard. His works are performed throughout the year, with much celebration made of the Spring Shakespeare Festival, held close to his birthday, April 23. Another replica, the Anne Hathaway Cottage, is home to a Shakespeare library and archives. Free tours are given by appointment only.

Odessa has another distinction in its **Presidential Museum,** 622 North Lee Street (915–332–7123), the only facility in existence dedicated solely to the office of the U.S. presidency. The campaign and election processes are both studied, and collections of campaign memorabilia and presidential medals and an array of first-lady inaugural gowns in miniature replicas are all quite interesting. Traveling exhibits are almost always on show, as well. Open Tuesday through Saturday from 10:00 A.M. until 5:00 P.M.; admission is free.

Ostrich ranching in Texas has become big business, now that export from Africa is prohibited. A good place to see the industry in action is at **Yellow Rose Ostrich Ranch,** on Farm Road 1787, just off U.S. Highway 385, 12 miles south of the city limits (915–333–5222). You'll get an overview of the reasons for ostrich breeding by calling ahead for a tour.

For a downhome meal, Mexican-style, a good suggestion is **Tejas Tacos and Burgers,** 1407 North Grant Street (915–335–0166). A tidy, pleasant *taquería* that doesn't look like much at first delivers real taste delights (they're cheap, too) in the way of quesadillas, flour tortillas filled with cheese, tomatoes, onions, and chile peppers. The fajita tacos made with beef or chicken are also highly recommended. Open Monday through Friday from 11:00 A.M. until 6:00 P.M. and Saturday from 11:00 A.M. until 3:00 P.M.

Before departing this area, take a side trip west via Interstate 20 just 30 miles to ✦**Monahans Sandhill State Park,** immediately north of the interstate (915–943–2092). Wind-sculpted sand dunes resembling those in the Sahara spread over a 4,000-acre park area but also extend into New Mexico. Most of the dunes are still active, growing and assuming various shapes, and are odd also for their proliferating Harvard oak forest, covering 40,000 acres in all. The trees aren't immediately seen, as they grow no more than 3 feet in height, yet their roots reach some 90 feet into the ground. The park's interpretive center offers illustrations of the dunes' history, as well as that of the ranchers, Native Americans, and oil prospectors who once called this area home. There's a 2-mile drive around the dunes, plus a quarter-mile nature trail allowing you on the dramatic mountains of sand. The park is open daily from 8:00 A.M. until 10:00 P.M. and the center is open from 8:00 A.M. until 5:00 P.M. Admission is $5.00 per vehicle.

Now it's time to venture south a while, traveling down U.S. Highway 385 for 53 miles to the town of McCamey, where you'll pick up Farm Road 305 for 19 miles, then make a 4-mile jaunt west on U.S. Highway 190 to Interstate 10. Now head back southeast 33 miles via Interstate 10, Texas 349, and Texas Highway 290 to our destination, ✦**Fort Lancaster State Historic Site.** The site is worth finding if you like ruins, as this briefly occupied fort has a poignancy lingering amidst its rubble. Founded in 1855 to protect the many settlers traveling the San Antonio–El Paso road, it was abandoned during the Civil War and only momentarily used again after the war's end. It had an important role, however, on the frontier, a story told in the modern interpretive center on site. Open Wednesday through Sunday from 8:00 A.M. until 5:00 P.M.; admission is free.

If you're a real fort fan, continue east another 30 miles on Interstate 10 to the lonely town of **Ozona,** the Crockett County seat, with a population of 5,000. Unique for being the only town in the county—a county that's larger than the state of Delaware, by the way—and the largest unincorporated town in the nation, Ozona also offers the ◆ **Crockett County Museum,** 404 Eleventh Street (915–392–2738). Housed there are artifacts and relics pertaining to Indians, the Spanish, and pioneers that were found at Fort Lancaster. Open Monday through Friday from 2:00 P.M. until 5:00 P.M. and by appointment. Admission is free, but donations are welcome.

BIG BEND COUNTRY

West of Fort Lancaster 67 miles via Interstate 10 is **Fort Stockton,** seat of Pecos County. This town of 8,500 residents began with the establishment of Camp Stockton in 1858 by troops forming from the First and Eighth infantries of the U.S. Army. The town grew into its modern form after the Yates oil field discovery in 1925 in the eastern part of the county. The massive drilling rigs are still part of the skyline, but historical sites are the reason for stopping.

The first thing to catch your attention in town, however, is the unforgettable ◆ **Paisano Pete,** pure Texas kitsch on Main Street immediately south of U.S. Highway 290 at Farm Road 1053. *Paisano* means "companion" in Spanish, and this statue of a roadrunner is 11 feet tall and 22 feet long, making Pete the largest companion of his kind in the world. You'll see these creatures everywhere in West Texas, but you will never see another like Pete, so take this photo now—otherwise, no one back home will believe you.

To explore the admirable local history, have a look around the **Annie Riggs Memorial Museum,** 301 South Main Street (915–336–2167). Housed in an 1899 hotel and a popular stop on the Overland-Butterfield Stage line, the museum was named for a colorful local figure—a twice-divorced, hard-working woman who ran the hotel for more than twenty-five years. The building, called territorial in design, features adobe brick and wood with a wraparound veranda and heavy gingerbread trim. The local historical society assembled the collection here, but the salt cedar that Annie planted in the courtyard was already in place. The parlor boasts one of the first pianos brought west of the Pecos River, as well as a giant cranberry-glass chandelier made in Ohio

Paisano Pete

before the Civil War. The hotel's fifteen rooms are filled with relics, such as an 1880s baby christening gown, a man's collar box, furniture, lanterns, and a profusion of kitchen and outdoor cooking gadgets, as well as artifacts relating to the area's archaeology, geology, ranching, and religion. Open in summer Monday through Saturday from 10:00 A.M. until 8:00 P.M. and Sunday from 1:30 P.M. until 8:00 P.M.; and the rest of the year Monday through Saturday from 10:00 A.M. until 12:00 noon and 1:00 P.M. until 5:00 P.M., and Sunday from 1:30 P.M. until 5:00 P.M. Admission is $1.00 for adults and 50 cents for children.

One of Texas's premium vineyards is found at **Ste. Genevieve**

Wines, about 25 miles west of Fort Stockton via Interstate 10 (915–395–2417 or 395–2484). Tastings and tours are held at 10:00 A.M. on Saturday or by special appointment. Tour buses depart Fort Stockton Chamber of Commerce, 222 West Dickinson Street (915–336–8525, ext. 208) on Saturday morning by reservation. Tickets are $8.00 for adults and $6.50 for children.

Before leaving Fort Stockton, don't forget to have a sturdy Mexican plate lunch or dinner at **Sarah's,** 106 South Nelson Street at West Dickinson Street (915–336–7124). It's now the oldest restaurant in town operating in the same location, with friendly service and super tacos, enchiladas, chalupas and nachos. Open for lunch and dinner Monday through Saturday.

Now to delve deeper into the land of the Big Bend, follow U.S. Highway 385 south 58 miles, cutting through the Glass Mountains and arriving in the Brewster County town of **Marathon,** with a population of 800. This is definitely a place to set a spell, as we sometimes say in West Texas. And there's no place better to do that than at the ◆ **Gage Hotel,** right in the middle of town on U.S. Highway 290 (915–386–4205). This 1927 creation by West Texas architect Henry Trost exudes the Old West in mood and looks, with a recent updating that delivered all sorts of decor for rooms and public areas, such as branding irons, chaps, saddles, horseshoes, and spurs. A new adobe wing added rooms, all of which are as immeasurably comfortable and inviting as the original building's. The dining room is worth writing home about, be assured: Southwestern dishes with sophisticated treatment include the cabrito enchiladas. Watch the sun fall from the sky on a front-porch rocker or ask the management to arrange a raft, jeep, or hunting trip for you.

If you'd rather camp nearby and save your money for later Big Bend adventures, consider **Stillwell's Store,** the only camping option near the park's northern entrance. It's 40 miles south of Marathon via U.S. Highway 385, then 6 miles southeast via Farm Road 2627 (915–376–2244). Here, you'll find 25,000 acres for primitive camping, as well as RV hookups. Camping is anywhere from $3.50 to $15.00, and the store has plenty of provisions. An on-site bonus is **Hallie Stillwell's Hall of Fame,** a great little collection of Big Bend antiques and artifacts from the turn of the century, kept in a building next to the store. Admission is free— you just ask the storekeepers for a key. Stillwell's Store is generally open daily from 7:00 A.M. until 8:30 P.M., but you might call ahead just to be sure.

Rested up? Then make the big move to the incomparable Big Bend National Park. The northern entrance is where U.S. 385 reaches its southern terminus, 40 miles south of Marathon. On your drive down, note the Woods Hollow Mountains encroaching on the highway from the east. This image of purplish blue mountains slumping low against the horizon will become very familiar to you as you explore this magnificent region.

Once inside the park boundaries, you'll immediately come upon **Persimmon Gap Visitor's Center,** but lately it hasn't been open due to government budget cuts. If that is still the case, continue another 26 miles to **Panther Junction,** site of ✦ **Big Bend National Park Headquarters** (915–477–2251) and the point at which the park's three main paved roads meet. You'll stop here for a variety of reasons: The required $5.00-per-vehicle fee is paid here; an abundance of free and inexpensive vital pamphlets and brochures regarding roads, sightseeing, flora and fauna, hiking, camping, lodging, and ranger-led activities is offered; necessary backcountry permits are issued; and a huge relief map of the park helps you better understand the undertaking ahead of you. This is also the place to inquire about weather, river, and road conditions. Less than a mile west, you'll find a gas station–convenience store.

Having gathered the copious amounts of information that define the park, you are ready to dig in. From Panther Junction, your most immediate option for exploring is to head east on the paved road. It ends at **Rio Grande Village,** near Boquillas Canyon; here you'll find flat, grassy stretches of RV camping with full hookups and a shower house, and a store selling snacks, camping permits, and bottled water.

About 3 miles upriver, 2 miles off the main road, is an abandoned resort called **Hot Springs,** a place that was all the rage in the 1920s. The drive down here cuts through dry, white limestone and shale shelves, and the road finally turns to white, powdery sands. The rest can be seen on foot. Out of nowhere appears a long-abandoned, white-washed stone structure bearing a sign, POST OFFICE. Past that, a vacant rock lodge shaded by a grove of palm trees looks down the sandy path to the river and the therapeutic hot springs on the river's edge. Several healthy cows will probably stare vacantly at you from across the river in Mexico, but pay them no mind and go on exploring the few remains of the bathhouse in the water. When the river is low, those 108-degree waters still soothe tired bones. Ease down onto a small sitting area and feel the gush of hot water—moving at a rate of 250,000 gallons daily—revive your body and spirit.

Boquillas Canyon points up the Sierra del Carmen, rising 8,500 feet into the Mexican sky, blanketed by pine and fir forests. A great two-hour hike into the canyon delivers sensational views and a wonderful sand dune to play on. Across the river, the Mexican village of **Boquillas** welcomes you for a diversion in another culture altogether. Park on the Texas side, tip the kind Mexican attendant with a dollar or a spare Coke or sandwich, then follow a little path to the river, where you'll hop in a rowboat to be ferried across. The fare is $2.00 per person. Once in Mexico, you mount a donkey (that's $3.00) for a ride into the adobe village above you. Most tourists enjoy a simple meal of bean-and-cheese quesadillas at Don Jose Falcon's and a look around. People are friendly, and this is a nice break from life.

Other options to consider exploring in the park's eastern area are those off-road adventures, such as hiking or biking. It's a good idea to make sure your vehicle is ready for the dirt roads first, and rangers can supply you with that information. Some excursions include the trek into **Dagger Flat,** reached from the Old Ore Road that splits off from the main road into the park from the north. It's a little sought delight on a graded dirt road and an excellent primer to the extraordinary desert vegetation so abundant here. The 7-mile road leads to a strange grove of massive dagger yucca, shooting nearly a dozen feet into the air; these are stunning, especially when topped with blossoms in spring. Hike around here if you're armed with a guidebook.

Another detour to make off the main road is into **Dugout Wells,** reached by leaving the road that took you to Rio Grande Village. Here is a microcosm of the diverse Big Bend, as hardwoods comingle with all sorts of desert plants, in the company of a windmill and desert critters that are most commonly spied at sunup or sundown. Watch for the marker for the Chihuahuan Desert Nature Trail, a simple half-mile path bearing descriptive signs regarding the odd plants you see.

Heading west to the park's center by paved road, you will reach

Chisos Basin, situated in a 1,500-foot depression—hence, the basin. It rests right in the middle of the mile-high Chisos Mountains and is the busiest part of Big Bend National Park, since this is where the park's only lodging and dining facilities are. It's also the coolest part of the park, and in summer everyone comes here for relief from the heat. The Basin's **Chisos Mountain Lodge** (915–477–2291) is often booked months in advance, and the comfortable rooms with spectacular views are the reason. The restaurant here offers above-average food for breakfast, lunch, and dinner daily. The adjacent store sells candy, some camping supplies, drinks, bandanas, and postage stamps.

The Basin also has lots of campsites up numerous hillsides, but those, too, are often booked far in advance; for spring break, the park's busiest period, reservations are made a year in advance. The only in-park horseback rides are offered here at the **Chisos Remuda,** (915) 477–2374. All-day rides cover the Basin's 7,200-foot South Rim, and overnight trips can be arranged.

Hikers will enjoy the route from the Basin to the South Rim and to the popular Lost Mine Trail, which can be a two- to four-hour hike but the easiest in these mountains. This is an area where extensive wildlife is sighted, including the black bear. Rangers advise hikers to take along one gallon of water per person. Photographers will take a special interest in **The Window,** a narrow slit of a gorge through which all Basin drainage flows to a 75-foot fall below. When there is heavy rain in the mountains and rocks rush and bounce through The Window, it's easy to see how the Basin was formed. **Mule Ear Peaks,** southwest of the South Rim, draws both hikers and photo buffs to its twin angular rock fragments and remains of volcanic rock flow. This is a 4-mile hike that takes three or four hours to complete.

Southeast of the Basin is ◆**Mariscal Canyon,** where the Rio Grande's southernmost dip cuts through 1,600-foot limestone walls of the Mariscal Mountains. You can explore this canyon, which is littered with abandoned quicksilver mining structures, if you're a very serious, experienced hiker. This, along with other canyons pushing against the park from Mexico, is discovered most often on rafting trips. Among the nearby rafting outfitters offering trips lasting from a half day to several days—with hiking, lunch, and camping options—are Outback Expeditions in Study Butte (915–371–2490); Far Flung Adventures in

Terlingua (915–371–2489); and Big Bend River Tours in Lajitas (915–424–3219). Guides are not only adept at the rowing and navigation of white water, but also are trained to give you all the information you want regarding history, geology, plant and animal life, photography, and folklore. Exquisite riverside meals and entertainment can be arranged through these rafting companies, too.

In the park's southwestern section, the village of **Castolon** is reached on a 22-mile paved road branching off from the main park road. Old cavalry barracks sit deserted where a U.S. Army garrison and trading post was active from 1914 until 1916. A little store sells a few basics, such as T-shirts, snacks, books, souvenir coffee cups, and paper products. Grab some sandwich meat, cheese, and a loaf of bread for a picnic at Cottonwood Campground, adjacent to Castolon. There's superb scenery, too, down the 14-mile Maverick Road, but you need to ask a ranger if it's passable.

Morning is ideal for exploring **Santa Elena Canyon,** when the sunlight exposes walls of rose and rust. On the Texas side, the wall you can ascend of steep cement steps is called Mesa de Áquila, and the sheer cliff on the Mexican side is called Sierra Ponce. Santa Elena Canyon is the one most often seen on the shorter raft trips.

This is but a scant overview of a tremendously complex park. If you're itching to explore the lesser-known places bearing names like Devil's Den, Telephone Trail, and Grapevine Hills, ask at the headquarters for appropriate maps and information. The rangers can also provide you with names and phone numbers of personable, knowledgable guides for hire.

Barely 2 miles west of the western park boundary on Ranch Road 170 at Texas Highway 118, ◆**Study Butte** is a 24-mile drive from the park headquarters and has lodging and food. Pronounced STEW-dee B'yewt, this is where travelers relax at the Big Bend Motor Inn and Mission Lodge (both 915–371–2218), offering clean rooms, gift shop, swimming pool, TV, gas, and convenience store. **Roadrunner Deli,** next to the store, sells gourmet coffees, bagels, and elaborate or simple picnic lunches. Other nearby lodging choices are the Chisos Mining Company Motel (915–371–2430), not quite a mile away; Terlingua Ranch Motel (915–371–2416), 30 miles north and east of Study Butte;

and the Longhorn Ranch Motel (915–371–2541), 12 miles north of Study Butte. These are good to know about, since the park's lodging tends to be full.

Just 4 miles west on Ranch Road 170 from Study Butte, ◆ **Terlingua** (pronounced Tur-LING-gwuh) is often called a ghost town—although it isn't anymore. This is a celebrated chili cook-off site where things are really wild in November, and a place to find photo ops in ruined houses, a jail, and a rocky cemetery bearing aged wooden crosses. Next to Far Flung Adventures's office and the Terlingua Trading Post is the **Desert Deli and Diner** (915–371–3205), offering breakfast, lunch, and dinner. Nearby, the **Starlight Theatre Restaurant** (915–371–2326) is an old movie house made over into a snazzy, adobe-sided eatery and bar.

Between Terlingua and Study Butte there's the dependable **La Kiva** (915–371–2250), a very cool and funky rock cave sort of establishment, entered underground and built into the side of Terlingua Creek. The bar is inside and an amazing patio is outdoors—you have to see it to understand it. Barbecue and steaks are the fare; open for dinner only.

Another 13 miles west on Ranch Road 170, you'll come to ◆ **Lajitas on the Rio Grande,** a re-created western town that's really a resort created by a Houston developer. Lajitas is first and foremost a varied lodging center for the area, with overnight choices including a motel, bunkhouse, hotel, and condos, outfitted with period reproduction furniture and all the modern amenities. It's a one-stop shopping outfit, reached by calling (915) 424–3471. Along with that, Lajitas has a nine-hole golf course, stables, tennis courts, two restaurants, a bar, drugstore and soda fountain, liquor store, art gallery, and gift shop. This is where to rent mountain bikes and book tours with **Desert Sports** (915–424–3366), an outfitter leading half-day, full-day, overnight, and multi-day trips in the region.

Lajitas is also the home base for ventures into the state's largest park, the new **Big Bend Ranch State Park,** a 265,000-acre spread adjacent to Lajitas. Here you'll find abundant fascination in the form of wildlife, mountains, a herd of Texas longhorns, geological formations, and exotic plants and animals. There are three primitive camping areas and three hiking trails; admission is $3.00

per vehicle. The park is open daily from 8:00 A.M. until 5:00 P.M. Call (915) 358–4444 for information. There are monthly bus tours with a chuckwagon lunch, too; call (915) 424–3327 well in advance to reserve. Of special interest is the **Barton Warnock Environmental Education Center** (915–424–3327) at the entrance, a wonderful museum with old photographs, fossils, and an arboretum. It's open from 8:00 A.M. until 5:00 P.M., and admission is free.

As Ranch Road 170 continues to unwind west from Lajitas, the road is called ✦**El Camino del Rio,** Spanish for "the river road." It's been widely called one of the most scenic drives in the nation, while technically it's known as the 55 miles of Ranch Road 170 between Study Butte and Presidio. El Camino del Rio traces the Rio Grande in a series of dips, climbs, and twists, marked most dramatically by **The Hill,** a mile-high climb with an average grade of 14 percent. That's steep, and there are extraordinary photography spots. Adobe homes dot the hilltops, peering out over the river, and intriguing little metal teepees are part of a highway department roadside park. Drive slowly to savor the scenery and to avoid the horses and cows usually wandering in the road.

Just shy of **Presidio,** 50 miles west of Lajitas, ✦**Fort Leaton State Historic Site** is on Ranch Road 170 (915–229–3613). The private fort and trading post was originally a Spanish mission founded in 1759 but was taken over in 1848 by frontiersman Ben Leaton, who monopolized profitable trade with the Native Americans in the area. The adobe fortress now holds a museum covering Leaton's controversial personal and business ethics, along with the area's Mexican, Indian, and pioneer heritage. Exhibits offer bilingual signage and include natural history, along with chronology of commerce, settlement, and cattle and silver industries. A slide show covers the desert ecology. Open daily from 8:00 A.M. until 5:00 P.M. Admission is $2.00.

Presidio sits in some of the most rugged land Texas can offer, an isolated Rio Grande settlement that's often mentioned in the news as having the hottest temperature in the country. Besides that, it's the self-proclaimed Onion Capital of the World and a good jumping-off place for travelers wishing to journey southwest into Mexico to tour the magnificent Copper Canyon; for information on such trips, call (915) 229-3221. Presidio's sister city across the Rio Grande is the Mexican village of **Ojinaga,** good for a beer and a spot to eat at La Fogata or Los Comales. Also look for clay crafts at Casa de Artesanias and bakery delights from Panaderia Ideal.

From Presidio, follow U.S. Highway 67 north 61 miles, looking first to the west along the drive at the slumping Chinati Mountains, followed by the Cuesta del Burro Mountains. Watch carefully and you'll spot some pronghorn antelope hopping and bounding along in the tall grasses to the east. You'll wind up in the ultra-western town of **Marfa,** seat of Presidio County and home to 2,400. The town is becoming well known for a mysterious phenomenon called the ♦**Marfa Ghost Lights,** seen after dark, of course, by driving west on U.S. Highway 90/67 8 miles—there will be a sign on the south side of the highway to indicate the official viewing area. Look southwest toward the Chinati Mountains and just wait. Soon, poof!—there's the first one, a tiny ball of white light, not quite standing still. Then, poof!—it splits into two slightly wavering, shimmering spheres. In another moment or so, another and another appear to the right of the first two, and so on. This is just one variation of how an evening's viewing may go, but count on bobbing balls of light to mystify you.

Several stories and theories circulate about what the Marfa Lights are all about, but no one is sure—not even scientists who've made quite a study of them. Choose which tale you wish to believe: The lights may be those of an Indian chief's spirit lighting signal fires to help lead his lost tribe home; a pioneer could be lost in a blizzard and the lights are trying to lead him to safe shelter; perhaps headlights are being reflected off layers of the atmosphere; or it could be that bats' wings are carrying radioactive dust. Or ask around, as the locals have many more possibilities to offer. If you're around for Labor Day, you'll get to help celebrate the **Marfa Lights Festival,** which includes a fun run, street dance, food and arts booths, parade, evening concert, Mexican folkloric dancers, and Mariachi musicians. For details, call the chamber of commerce, (915) 729-4942.

By daylight, Marfa shows off its beautiful **Presidio County Courthouse,** at the north end of Highland Street, a stone-and-brick creation in the Second Empire design, built in 1886. The view of the surrounding land is stunning from the dome up top, which is open Monday through Friday from 8:30 A.M. until 4:30 P.M. Admission is free.

A few yards away, the ❖ **El Paisano Hotel,** North Highland Street at West Texas Street (915–579–3145), is a lovely, 1927 hotel that hosted Franklin D. Roosevelt, Harry S Truman, and John F. Kennedy, among other dignitaries. Bearing state and national historical markers, the hotel is beloved by movie buffs for having been the home of Elizabeth Taylor, Rock Hudson, James Dean, and Dennis Hopper, plus all the other actors who appeared in the epic film *Giant,* filmed close by. Past the fountained courtyard, inside the Spanish-detailed hotel lobby, there are glass-fronted cases of *Giant* memorabilia, including signed photos of the cast, clippings from *Life* magazine, and numerous news clippings regarding the shoot.

If you get high on golf, head 2 miles east on Oak Street, and you'll find the **Marfa Municipal Golf Course** (915–729–4942), the highest golf course in Texas, sitting almost a mile in elevation above sea level. There are nine holes open to the public, and green fees are $6.00. Open daily from 8:00 A.M. until 5:00 P.M.

For a more in-depth look at the region, head west on U.S. Highway 90/67 for 26 miles to Alpine, seat of Brewster County and home to 5,600 West Texans and Sul Ross State University, right on U.S. Highway 90. On the campus you'll find the ❖ **Museum of the Big Bend** (915–837–8143), which contains a small but impressive collection of artifacts from the Spanish explorers, Native Americans, ranchers, and cavalry soldiers who figured into the history of the region and national park. A reconstructed frontier general store, stagecoach, and blacksmith shop are exhibited, as well as traveling art exhibits. Open Tuesday through Saturday from 9:00 A.M. until 5:00 P.M. and Sunday from 1:00 P.M. until 5:00 P.M. Admission is free, but donations are accepted.

Two miles west of town on U.S. Highway 90, **Apache Trading Post** (915–837–5149) is located in a log cabin and is a treasure chest of sorts, stocked with genuine Native American–crafted jewelry in silver and turquoise; pottery; rugs; agate necklaces; belt buckles and bolo ties; postcards, posters, and calendars; cactus jams and jellies; Mexican pottery and moccasins; arrowheads and geodes; and books on geology, natural history, Big Bend history, and folklore. Open Monday through Saturday from 9:00 A.M. until 6:00 P.M. and Sunday from 1:00 P.M. until 6:00 P.M.

Rock hounds will enjoy a trip to **Woodward Agate Ranch,** south of Alpine 16 miles on Texas Highway 118 (915–364–2271). More than seventy varieties of cutting stones on this 4,000-acre ranch include gemstones such as red plume, pom pom agates, amethysts, and opals. Ranch managers will tell you where to find the best stones, which cost 35 cents per gram. Open dawn till dusk.

Stick around a while and maybe rest up at **The Sunday House,** a two-story inn in town on U.S. Highway 90 (915–837–3363) with reasonable rates, swimming pool, cable TV, and free coffee in the morning. Across the street, the **Holland Hotel** (915–837–3455) is a historic, three-floor hotel with twelve restored rooms and two suites. A restaurant and bar are on site.

If you're ready for more adventure, head out for Jeff Davis County and its county seat, **Fort Davis,** north 26 miles via Texas Highway 118. A cavalry post was established in 1855, the town later became a haven for sufferers of respiratory problems, and commercially grown Delicious apples eventually became a primary industry. The highest town in Texas at just over 5,000 feet, Fort Davis is cool enough to warrant wearing at least a sweater eleven months out of the year.

A good home base in town is ◆ **The Limpia Hotel,** on the square in the middle of the tiny town (915–426–3237). The hotel was built in 1912 by the Union Trading Company, was remodeled in 1978, and is a member of the Texas Historical Hotel Association. There's an upstairs balcony and an enclosed veranda full of rocking chairs, potted flowers, and oak tables—plus a lovely view of the sunset. The front desk's stained-glass detail and an old ranch house door add to the period mood. High-ceilinged rooms and suites are filled with antique oak furnishings, and the big main lounge has a native-stone fireplace. Next door is the Union Trading Company, a vintage hardware store. Across the square, there's a book store and post office.

The best orientation to the area's wonders is found by driving the **74-Mile Scenic Loop Road,** beginning and ending in Fort Davis. An array of mountain vistas, Madera Canyon, and roadside parks bounded by ancient boulders are the rewards for following Texas Highway 17 south of town just 2 miles to Texas Highway 166 west to Texas Highway 118, then southeast back to Texas Highway 17 and Fort Davis.

Then it's time to see the reason Fort Davis came into being: As Indian raids increased with the numbers of settlers arriving or traveling through this part of the state, usually en route from San Antonio to El Paso, a cavalry post was built in 1855. ♠ **Fort Davis National Historic Site** is the restored site, named for U.S. Secretary of War Jefferson Davis, who ordered the army's posting here. Active from 1854 until 1891, with lapses during the Civil War, when fire destroyed the fort, it was home to twelve cavalry and infantry companies—numbering up to 800 men—stationed here in fifty buildings. The renovated stone-and-adobe remains sit in a scenic box canyon, sheltered on the west by towering cliffs, and are as complete and impressive as any in the Southwest. This indoor-outdoor museum was also the post for black troops from the Ninth, Tenth, Twentieth, and Twenty-fourth U.S. Cavalries. As was the case at Fort Concho, the enemy Comanche and Apache soldiers named these men the Buffalo Soldiers, which has been interpreted as a term of respect.

During the summer, a living history program demonstrates pioneer and fort life with costumed participants; the fort's Labor Day celebration draws as many as 2,000 spectators, and a special Black History event is a February highlight. Otherwise, the place is easily seen on self-guided tours with a slide-show introduction. A bugle sounds twice daily, starting the audio of a formal ceremony on the parade yard. Images of hundreds of mounted and marching soldiers in full dress are easy to see in the mind's eye. The commander's house was occupied the longest by Colonel Benjamin H. Grierson, and his original furnishings show luxury's spotty hand in a usually mundane frontier post life. Antiques, silver, and linens decorate the parlor and dining areas; giant beds and ornate wardrobes are characteristic in the over-sized bedrooms. A museum in the main building contains a display illustrating Trans-Pecos frontier days, the overland gold rush, stagecoach and Indian raiding routes, plus artifacts such as an officer's scabbard, pistol, and musket. A gift shop sells books and more books, including Old West cookbooks, art books, and children's coloring books. Open daily in summer from 8:00 A.M. until 6:00 P.M. and the rest of year 8:00 A.M. until 5:00 P.M. Admission is $1.00 for adults and free for those under seventeen and over sixty-two. Situated immediately north of town on Texas Highway 118, (915) 426–3224.

You can be enveloped in the area's solitude and natural beauty by a stay in **Davis Mountains State Park,** 4 miles north of town on Texas Highway 118 (915–426–3337). Sandwiched ideally between the grassy desert plains and the fragrant, woodsy mountains, this 2,700-acre park offers numerous hikes, from easy to challenging, as well as a rewarding Skyline Drive. Camp if you like, or call ahead for a room at the very cozy **Indian Lodge,** a pueblo-style motel with plenty of amenities, plus the hand-carved cedar furniture fashioned by Civilian Conservation Corps workers, who also built the lodge in the 1930s. The park is open daily for day use from 8:00 A.M. until 10:00 P.M. and at all hours for campers. Admission is $5.00 per vehicle.

Or hang your hat at the **Prude Ranch,** also just north of town on Texas Highway 118 (915–426–3202). A working ranch run by the same friendly West Texas family since the 1930s, it offers bunkhouse and motel-style lodging, horseback riding, tennis, Jacuzzi, and plenty of ranch-hand chow.

Another site worth a look is the **Neill Doll Museum,** on Court Avenue at Seventh Street (915–426–3969), doubling as a bed-and-breakfast home. Inside the restored, 1898 home built as a summer retreat for a Galveston family, there are more than 300 cataloged antique dolls dating from the mid-1800s, including Victorian clown dolls, German bisque dolls (1890–1910), and an 1835 lady doll in white dress with red velvet sash, Marie Antoinette hair, and pearl choker. The young Princess Elizabeth and Prince Phillip dolls are striking likenesses. Open in summer Tuesday through Saturday from 10:00 A.M. until 5:00 P.M. and Sunday from 1:30 P.M. until 5:00 P.M. The rest of the year it's open by appointment. Admission is $3.00.

Star-gazing travelers won't waste time driving up to the ❖ **McDonald Observatory,** a University of Texas operation reached by driving from Fort Davis 17 miles northwest on Texas Highway 118, then 2 miles southeast on Spur 78. Sitting atop 6,800-foot Mount Locke, the observatory features a 107-inch telescope, plus tours for visitors to see its 160 tons of moving parts. Programs at the visitor center include solar viewings, and star parties are staged Tuesday and Saturday evenings for looking at celestial objects through small telescopes. Even if you're not in time for a viewing, pay a visit anyway to see the fascinating, thirty-minute video on the universe, produced by NASA. A great gift shop with unusual goods is on site. The visitor center is open daily from 9:00 A.M. until 5:00 P.M. Tours are conducted daily in summer at 9:30 A.M. and 2:00 P.M., and at 2:00 P.M. only for the balance of the year. Admission is free; call (915) 426–3640 for details.

If you're hungry, looking for a comfortable place to sleep, or in search of good postcards or a western belt, head to **The Drugstore,** right on the town square (915–426–3118). Inside there's an honest-to-goodness soda fountain, making great breakfasts, lunches, and dinneres—the old-fashioned burgers, malts, and ice-cream floats are hard to beat. The gift shop sells souvenirs, and the upstairs is the **Old Texas Inn,** reached at the same phone. Six rooms are available, each with a private bath. Stop in or call daily from 7:30 A.M. until 5:00 P.M., or until 9:00 P.M. in summer.

TRANS-PECOS COUNTRY

From Fort Davis, the next stop is ✦**Balmorhea State Park,** north on Texas Highway 17 39 miles. Truly unusual in this modern day is a pool like the one here: Said to be the world's largest spring-fed swimming pool, Balmorhea's measures nearly two acres, is thirty feet deep, and contains three and a half million gallons of water. Talk about cool—the water is between 72 and 76 degrees year round, so your only swimming opportunities fall between the end of May and Labor Day. In addition to a vintage bathhouse and concession stand, you'll find tent and RV campsites and a small hotel on site. The grounds are green and roomy, so even if you miss the pool season, this is a delightful place to kick back and plot your next move down the road. Call (915) 375–2370 for reservations. Open daily from dawn till dusk. Admission to the park is $5.00 per vehicle; to the pool, $2.00 for adults and $1.00 for children.

If you've come at the right time, this is the point at which to make a detour 33 miles north on Texas Highway 17 to Pecos, home on July 4th to the world-famous ✦**West of the Pecos Rodeo.** The massive affair has been held annually since June 1883, when cowhands from the Hashknife, W, Lazy Z, and NA ranches argued in Red Newell's saloon over which had the best ropers and riders among its brethren. Ever since, the summer holiday has been set aside for competitors in saddle-bronc riding, steer roping, bulldogging, and plenty of other tough events.

Things have progressed considerably since that first rodeo, when a thousand spectators showed up to watch the cowhands compete for a $40 prize—the numbers have increased by the thousands. Pecos, known far and wide also for its cantaloupes, hosts its Cantaloupe Festival the first weekend in August, as well as a World Championship Bar-B-Q Contest the first weekend in October. For tickets and information, call the tourism office at (915) 445-2406.

Whatever the season, your path from Balmorhea is northwest to ◆ **Guadalupe Mountains National Park.** You can reach it by driving west for 71 miles, through parts of Reeves, Jeff Davis, and Culberson counties to the town of Van Horn. Here, you'll turn north on Texas Highway 54 and go 55 miles to the park. Note that once inside the park, you've entered Mountain Daylight Time. This former ranchland is blessed with 80 miles of hiking trails, assorted mountains (some up to 8,700 feet high), breathtaking overlooks, ancient canyons colored in ridges of brilliant oranges and reds, abandoned ranches, springs, and spectacular foliage in autumn—all of it a photographer's delight. Because of its remote position, this isn't ever a crowded park; those mountaintop pine-and-fir forests are usually just yours to relish. The only company you might have is that of mountain lions, elk, wild turkeys, and black bears. More tame in the way of wildlife are cacti blooming with purple, pink, and ruby flowers. Stop at the visitor center first and inquire about ranger-guided hikes, programs in the amphitheater, and the best places to view or photograph McKittrick Canyon, El Capitan, and Guadalupe Peak. Camping is available at Pine Springs and Upper Dog Canyon campgrounds in the park. The headquarters visitor center is open daily from 7:00 A.M. until 6:00 P.M. in summer, and 8:00 A.M. until 4:30 P.M. the balance of the year. Admission is free; call (915) 828-3251.

If you head west on U.S. Highway 62/180 70 miles to Farm Road 2775, then make a turn north and follow it 8 miles to ◆ **Hueco Tanks State Park,** you'll find odd, blobbish rock formations with caves and cliffs containing some 2,000 ancient Indian pictographs, some from the Apaches, as well as ruins of an old Butterfield stage station. The park's name comes from the vast, natural rainwater basins, or *huecos* (WHAY-coes) in Spanish, making this spread a giant oasis for dwellers and travelers for as long, some studies reveal, as 10,000 years. Camping, picnicking, nature study, and rock art tours are offered. Open daily in day-light hours and at all times for campers. Admission is $5.00 per vehicle. Call (915) 857–1135 for information.

Your final area for West Texas exploration is **El Paso,** 30 miles west of the Hueco Tanks turnoff, via U.S. Highway 62/180. Jammed into a pass of the mile-high Franklin Mountains, the ancient city clings to and curves around the mountains' base. Inspirations all around are as Indian and pioneer as they are Mexican and Spanish. Combined with Juarez, El Paso's twin across the Rio Grande, the population pushes one and a half million—and some days there's the smog to prove it. In spite of all those people, El Paso feels wide open and very much a part of the Wild West. The purple-and-orange-layered sunsets soften the craggy mountains, giving them a blue cast and the city a somber back-drop. Annual visitors number around fifteen million, due in part to the sunshine, which brightens at least 300 days each year. The story goes that World War II servicemen stationed at massive Fort Bliss discovered the margarita, but they were preceded in discoveries by the sixteenth-century Spanish conquistadors who found this pass of the north from Mexico, and so named the place for its use.

Older even than California's, ✦ **El Paso's historic missions** occupy a lower valley along El Camino Real, or the Royal High-way used by the missionaries and conquistadors and the longest historic road in the United States. The first to explore is the **Ysleta Mission,** situated at Zaragosa and Alameda, next to the Tigua Indian Reservation, which we'll cover soon. Founded by Franciscan padres in 1680, this one has been rebuilt several times and is thought to be the nation's oldest mission and possibly the oldest continuously used parish in the nation. Don't be confused, but the church's official name is Our Lady of Mount Carmel, yet there's a St. Anthony statue on the outside, as he is the patron saint of the Tigua Indians, who fled New Mexico during the Pueblo Revolt in the seventeenth century. All missions are open daily from 8:00 A.M. until 5:00 P.M.; admission is free.

Socorro Mission, 3 miles southeast of Ysleta Mission on Farm Road 258, was also founded in 1680. This one is of the classic, stark adobe design, and its ornate, hand-hewn roof beams are the oldest in Texas. Travel 5 miles southeast next to **San Elizario Presidio Church,** also on Farm Road 258, to see the

1770s architecture in a lovely courtyard. This is still an active Catholic church. Note that drives to the missions are prettiest in autumn, when cottonfields are overrun with white bolls, pecan groves stretch without end, and row upon row of chiles and onions burst in reds and greens. Farmers are usually found on roadsides tending their stands, selling roasted chiles or big, fat *ristras*, those hanging bunches of chiles that are very fashionable in southwestern decor.

For a deeper look into history surviving to the modern day, visit the ◆**Tigua Indian Reservation,** at 119 South Old Pueblo Road (915–859–3916). This is the home of descendants of those Tiguas who fled during the Pueblo Revolt in New Mexico over 300 years ago. There's a living history pueblo, with demonstrations of pottery, jewelry, and weaving crafts, plus bread baking in dome-shaped ovens. Tribal dances are performed during special events, while the twentieth century threatens to impose itself, as the Tiguas prepare to bring high-stakes gambling to the reservation to increase tourism income. In the Arts and Crafts Center, a cafe serves fajitas, puffy Indian tacos, and the hottest bowls of green and red chile (much like stew on fire) on earth. You can find fairly good deals on pottery and silver jewelry here, too. Open daily from 8:00 A.M. until 5:00 P.M.; admission is free, but donations are accepted.

Of two scenic drives, the **Scenic Road** is shorter and easier to access. Drive behind the Sun Bowl and wind between formidable walls of rock for 2 miles west to east, from Rim Road to Richmond Avenue. From Murchison Park at the road's apex 4,200 feet high, your vista includes two cities, three states, and two countries. You can see a stone peg that marks the end of the Rocky Mountains, a giant Christ statue on Sierra del Cristo Rey, and several war memorials. Sadly, you may also see a fair amount of graffiti and trash.

The other route is the more lengthy **Transmountain Drive,** a highway cutting through Smugglers Gap in the North Franklin Mountains. The summit is almost a mile above sea level, and the Wilderness Park is up there with great Chihuahuan Desert hiking trails. A nature trail passes replicas of a Pueblo ruin, kiva, and pithouse. The view of mountains reveals geologic history—gray shades indicate where ancient inland sea waters lapped, and reds are the leavings of volcanic lava flows.

Take off for an Old West retreat by visiting ◆**Indian Cliffs Ranch,** 30 miles east of town on Interstate 10 and 5 miles north on Farm Road 793 (915–544–3200). The multilevel complex is part sprawling ranch, part adobe, part movie set, and all romance. Cattle graze here, but primarily it's a place of entertainment and social interest. There's a restaurant with huge steaks and Mexican dishes, a gift shop with plenty of jewelry, and a terrace from which to watch achingly beautiful sunsets over a spread of cactus and corrals. A ride aboard a wagon pulled by huge Belgian horses takes you to Fort Misery, an 1860s fort replica for overnight guests and campfire dinners. Call ahead for activities schedules and reservations.

Among the favorite restaurants in town, **Avila's,** at 10600 Montana Street (915–598–3333), gets very high marks. You'll find hearty Mexican eats and precious little for the dieter. The service is faithfully pleasant, and the interior is exactly what a great Mexican cafe's should be—cheery and colorful. Open for lunch and early dinner (till 8:30 P.M.) daily.

El Paso is packed with museums and fine arts performances, but the most culturally rewarding ventures are found at the other end of any of three international bridges. No visit to the Texas border is complete without a tour on the friendly, infinitely relaxed Mexican side. Unfortunately, this part of the Rio Grande isn't scenic—just a concrete ravine crossed by three bridges. But cross it you must if you are to explore all of El Paso, which includes ◆**Juarez,** both physically and spiritually. Without the international border, it would be impossible to tell where one city ends and the other begins, they are such mirror images of each other. Spanish and English are spoken interchangeably, American dollars and Mexican pesos are spent indifferently. Locals from both sides make business-lunch and shopping trips back and forth, often several times daily. You can walk across, take a taxi, or board the El Paso–Juarez Trolley, which leaves the Civic Center Plaza on Santa Fe Street hourly. Tickets are $7.50, or free for children three and under.

Juarez is quite the shopping and dining mecca, ideal for morning, afternoon, or all-day excursions. The city market, on Avenida 16 de Septiembre, is a huge spread, with baskets, pottery, jewelry, clothing, blankets, and snacks. It's important to go to Juarez with a big appetite, as the food is good and plentiful. Among many,

many excellent and often upscale restaurants is **Sanborn's,** at Paseo Triunfo de la República 3809 (011–521–616–9105). You simply can't find a better plate of *enchiladas suizas,* a smooth and flavorful dish of tortillas rolled and stuffed with shredded chicken, white cheeses, a perky tomatillo sauce, and cream. It's a lovely way to sample the Tex-Mex border, and there's a very nice retail store on the premises. Open daily from 7:30 A.M. until 1:00 A.M.

INDEX

About the Author

A native of Fort Worth, Texas, and a sixth-generation Texan, June Naylor Rodriguez spent nine years as a travel writer and assistant travel editor for the *Fort Worth Star-Telegram,* where she is currently a features writer covering entertainment and points of interest in the Dallas–Fort Worth area, as well as dining, food, and fitness. June's travel and features stories are carried nationwide on the *New York Times* wire service, and she contributes travel stories to magazines such as *Texas Highways, Vacations, Travel 50 & Beyond,* and *Honeymoon.* She has received several photography and writing awards from the Society of American Travel Writers and is a founding member of the Association for Women Journalists.

Acknowledgments

To properly thank everyone who supported me in this endeavor seems overwhelming, but I'll try. Many thanks to Laura, for her faith, unlimited patience, and kind guidance, and to Jill, for her vast knowledge and keen eye. More thanks still go to Mike G., who calmly wrought miracles at all hours. Much appreciation is due to O.C., Richard, and Mike M., who first guided my travels throughout Texas as a writer. My thanks extend also to Michael and Micki, in today's state tourism office, for their expedient help. Some of the warm souls across Texas who generously shared their wonderful corners of the state include John Robert in Fort Davis, Ruthmary in Jefferson, Doris in Blanco, Sharon in San Antonio, Gail in Marshall, Bob in Corpus Christi, Clay in Bandera, and Charles and Ann in Nacogdoches. My gratitude and love are for John, Sr., June I, Corinne, Nell, and Jennifer, for spurring me on; to Barbara, for being my inspiration; and to Jemmer, for the enthusiasm, wit, and companionship that made a treasure of every Texas journey.

Also of Interest from The Globe Pequot Press

Journey to the High Southwest, 4th Edition $19.95
". . . Best Guide to this part of the world I've ever seen . . ."
                                                    Tony Hillerman

Daytrips From Houston,   5th Edition $ 9.95
An enticing choice of 22 day trips

Recommended Country Inns: The Southwest,
                              4th Edition $12.95
". . . One of the most reliable resources . . . " The Inn Times

Outlet Guide to the Southwest $ 9.95
Guide to great discount opportunities in the Southwest

Other Titles in this Series:

Hawaii: Off the Beaten Path, 2nd Edition $10.95

Colorado: Off the Beaten Path, 3rd Edition $ 9.95

Oregon: Off the Beaten Path, 2nd Edition $ 9.95

New Mexico: Off the Beaten Path, 2nd Edition $ 9.95

Arkansas: Off the Beaten Path $ 9.95

And additional Off the Beaten Path™ guides to more than 30 other states!!

Available from your bookstore or directly from the publisher. For a free catalogue or to place an order, call toll-free 24 hours a day 1-800-243-0495 (in Connecticut, call 1-800-962-0973) or write to The Globe Pequot Press, P.O. Box 833, Old Saybrook, Connecticut 06475-0833.